The Courageous Gospel

The Courageous Gospel

Resources for Teachers, Students, and Preachers of the Fourth Gospel

ROBERT A. HILL

WIPF & STOCK · Eugene, Oregon

THE COURAGEOUS GOSPEL
Resources for Teachers, Students, and Preachers of the Fourth Gospel

Copyright © 2013 Robert A. Hill. All rights reserved. Except for brief quotations in critical publications or reviews, no part of this book may be reproduced in any manner without prior written permission from the publisher. Write: Permissions. Wipf and Stock Publishers, 199 W. 8th Ave., Suite 3, Eugene, OR 97401.

Wipf & Stock
An Imprint of Wipf and Stock Publishers
199 W. 8th Ave., Suite 3
Eugene, OR 97401

www.wipfandstock.com

ISBN 13: 978-1-61097-374-8

Cataloguing-in-Publication Data

Hill, Robert Allan 1954–

    The courageous gospel : resources for teachers, students, and preachers of the fourth gospel / Robert A. Hill

    x + 250 p. ; 23 cm. Includes bibliographical references.

    ISBN 13: 978-1-61097-374-8

    1. Bible. John—Textbooks. 2. Bible. John—Study and teaching. 3. Bible. John—Sermons. I. Title

BS2616 H5 2013

Manufactured in the U.S.A.

Contents

Frontispiece / vii

Part One
1. Abstract / 3
2. Introduction *by Cathryn Turrentine* / 6
3. Summary of Courages in John / 17

Part Two
4. Two Battles—John 1:1–18 / 21
5. Two Brides—John 2:1–11 / 29
6. Two Births—John 3:1–16 / 36
7. Two Biographies—John 4 / 43
8. Two Blessings—John 6 / 51
9. Two Beggars—John 9 / 58
10. Two Beliefs—John 11 / 65
11. The Spirit of Truth: Communion—John 13 / 71
12. The Spirit of Truth: Conversation—John 14 / 75
13. The Spirit of Truth: Commandment—John 15 / 83
14. The Spirit of Truth: Catechesis—John 16 / 89

Part Three
15. An Embraceable Variant—John 17:1–11 / 95
16. An Introduction to Gnosticism for Students of John *by Jason Ford* / 102
17. Book Review: *Understanding the Fourth Gospel* / 116
18. Teaching through John Ashton / 119
19. Summary—Raymond E Brown / 128

20 "The Word Being Made Flesh, and the Priesthood of All Believers" *by Ray L. Hart* / 131
21 The Community of the Beloved Disciple—Raymond E Brown / 138
22 The Gnostic Worldview: Frederik Wisse Lectures / 142
23 The Jewish Background to the New Testament / 153
24 The Two Level Drama / 160
25 The Insights of George MacRae *by Jason Ford* / 165
26 Gnosticism—Gnosis, The New Testament, and the Gospel of John / 175
27 Toward a New View of Eschatology in Gnosticism / 187
28 Hill's Thesis / 194
29 An Overview of Hill's Thesis / 195
30 The Treatise on the Resurrection / 201

Part Four

31 A Brief History of Christian Theology / 225
32 The Gospel of John—Final Examination / 227
33 The Gospel of John—Midterm Examination / 228
34 The Gospel of John—Quiz #0 / 231
35 The Gospel of John—Quiz #1 / 233
36 The Gospel of John—Quiz #2 / 234
37 The Gospel of John—Ashton Content: Quiz #3 / 236
38 The Gospel of John—Ashton Content: Quiz #4 / 238
39 The Gospel of John—Quiz #5 / 240
40 The Gospel of John—Quiz #6 / 241
41 Finale: The Gospel of John for Today / 243

Frontispiece

The Courageous Gospel

John in Sermon, Lecture, Essay and Discussion

I. This book is intended to provide interpretative aids for the teaching of the Gospel of John. Its first part provides materials of introduction. The Gospel of John continues to receive much attention, whether through monographs or commentaries, journal articles or conference papers, or courses on the New Testament and early Christianity. With voluminous material available on the Gospel of John students often find it difficult to move beyond an introduction to the Gospel of John. Such difficulty may result from a lack of certainty about navigating the well-tread path of Johannine studies or from simply trying to make sense of the rich, deep, polyphonic voice of the Fourth Evangelist, or a host of other reasons. The author first studied John in New York City, during the late 1970s, with Dr. J. Louis Martyn and Dr. Raymond Brown. Their excellent teaching, their emphasis on the 'two level drama', and their emphasis on the Jewish background to the Fourth Gospel continue to be compelling, convincing interpretative perspectives. The author then studied John in Montreal, in the 1980s, with Dr. Frederik Wisse (along with Dr. George Johnston and Dr. N.T. Wright). Wisse's expertise and emphasis upon the Hellenistic background to the New Testament, and his work on the Nag Hammadi Library, continue to be equally compelling and convincing interpretive perspectives. A stereoptic vision of a different sort, one eye in New York and one in Montreal, provides the angle of vision for this book. At some point, Johannine scholarship will find a way to synthesize these two great and lasting visions of and versions of John. Almost forty years of work on John, both in the pulpit and in the classroom, thus stand behind this collection. *Coda: The Courages in John* encapsulates the introductory work of part one.

II. The second part of the book offers a series of sermons on John, written and delivered in 2004, alongside class notes from much earlier. Professors, pastors, and Johannine scholars recognize the need to assist students as they proceed with their study and use of the Gospel of John, in relationship to interpretation in general and preaching in particular. Divinity schools and schools of theology want to encourage students to develop the necessary tools for integrating their learning in areas of theology and biblical studies with their teaching and preaching. Homiletics, in divinity and theological schools, is a necessary component of Master of Divinity degrees. But, too often, students are left on their own to try to synthesize the material from their numerous years of study. It is for this first reason that the book provides students with a series of sermons on John. These sermons provide a resource that helps students see what a "final product" looks like when based on certain Johannine texts. The sermons are connected to original notes on lectures by Raymond Brown, which he delivered and I noted, in the 1970's. *Two Battles*, an opening sermon on John 1, exemplifies this emphasis on interpretation.

III. The third part of *The Courageous Gospel* assembles a collection of lectures and lecture materials on John, which are largely provided in an attempt to rebalance or reset the current emphasis in Johannine studies on the Gospel's Jewish background. That is, the focus of this third section is a somewhat neglected area of study in recent research on the Fourth Gospel, the relationship between Gnostic thought and the Gospel of John. The Martyn-Brown hypothesis of the "levels" of the Johannine community continues to provide the necessary foundation for any historical study of this Gospel. Brown, in particular, helped us realize the deeply Jewish nature of the Fourth Gospel. Though Brown and Martyn have deeply assisted our understanding of Johannine thought, their hypothesis and Jewish background alone do not fully explain the Johannine thought world in its entirety. The religious world of the Mediterranean in the late-first century and second-centuries is diverse and varied. Scholars tend to demarcate "Hellenistic" or "Jewish" thought but such clear boundaries are scholarly constructions. However, that does not mean there is no advantage to identifying material in this way or from searching the plurality of sources available to ancient writers and thinkers. An aspect that deserves more scholarly attention is this relationship between Gnostic and Johannine thought. The author's own earlier book and annual lectures in this regard provide a portion of the collection here. Mentors and friends—T. J. Weeden, R. L. Hart, F. Wisse, J. Ford, R. Walton, J Ashton—provide the rest.

The third part of this volume attempts to be a catalyst for future work on John's Gospel in this important area. Included in this section are comments on gnostic thought and its relationship to New Testament studies and, specifically, Johannine studies. I make use here of the work of George MacRae—a gifted scholar who passed away too soon. MacRae was on the front lines of gnostic studies and his lucid presentation of gnostic and early Christian materials continues to provide a path for further study. Though his work is somewhat dated, MacRae's assessment of the Gospel of John continues to offer much material worthy of attention. Aspects of the Fourth Gospel—especially, but not limited to, the Farewell discourse—demonstrate thoughts quite parallel to gnostic thought. Part II of this volume, then, will highlight the areas of convergence between gnostic and Johannine thought. Gnosticism, a broad lecture on the topic, epitomizes the direction of this section.

IV. The fourth part of the volume is meant to assist students and ministers in their further endeavors. Included here are certain materials helpful for one preparing sermons, classes, or essays on John. The chapters here include: various teaching tools, summary outlines, and sample quizzes and tests.

PART ONE

1

Abstract

—Robert Allan Hill
BOSTON UNIVERSITY 2011

SOME WHO HAVE TAUGHT the Gospel of John over the last generation have recognized a need for a second book, for class use, beyond the commentary (Ashton, Brown, Bultmann, Barrett, et al.). The second book is needed to engage the commentaries with the hermeneutical, exegetical, homiletical, and pastoral implications of the study. *The Courageous Gospel* intends to meet this need. (In fact, at Boston University, 2007–2013, in offprint form, and with annual redaction, it has done so).

The book has four parts. The first is a succinct summary of the key matters of introduction, taken from the author's lectures, and summarized by a graduate student. The second is a collection of sermons on the Gospel's key chapters, with reflective reminiscence and remembrance of what Raymond Brown said in lecture about the sermons 30 years ago (to my knowledge no one has yet offered anything like this). The third is a series of lectures which attempt on the one hand to honor the key insights of the current opinion communis (Jewish apocalyptic background explains John) and on the other hand to open the door to key insights from an older perspective (now new again) needed for us fully to interpret John (Hellenistic Gnostic background explains John). In this section I refer not primarily to my first teachers (Martyn and Brown) but to my dissertation advisor and mentor

(F. Wisse). The fourth is a set of pedagogical appendices, employable in the classroom. Together, the four parts attempt to provide the necessary second book for an Introduction to the Fourth Gospel.

All of the material for the book has been written in connection with teaching at Lemoyne College, Colgate Rochester Crozier Divinity School, and Boston University, and has already been repeatedly used—field tested in various settings.

Here is the argument of section two, in sermonic form:

The two basic historical problems of the New Testament are ancient cousins, first cousins to our two fundamental issues, the two existential battles in your salvation today.

The first historical problem behind our 27 books, and pre- eminently embedded in John, is the movement away from Judaism. How did a religious movement founded by a Jew, born in Judea, embraced by 12 and 500 within Judaism, expanded by a Jewish Christian missionary, become--within 100 years--entirely Greek? The books of the New Testament record in excruciating detail the development of this second identity, this coming of age, that came with the separation from mother religion.

The second historical problem underneath the Newer Testament is disappointment, the despair that gradually accompanied the delay, finally the cancellation, of Christ's return, the delay of the parousia. Jesus was an apocalyptic prophet. Paul expected to be alive to see the advent of Christ. Gradually, though, the church confessed disappointment in its greatest immediate hope, the sudden cataclysm of the end.

These two problems, historical and fascinating, create our New Testament: the separation from Judaism and the delay of the parousia. In the fourth Gospel the two come together with great ferocity. What makes this matter so urgent for us is that these very two existential dilemmas—one of identity and one of imagination—are before every generation, including and especially our own.

Here is the argument for part three, in lecture form:

We come now to the strange, mysterious figure of the Paraclete (actually the second Paraclete, for Jesus himself is the first comforter). The Paraclete functions as Jesus' eternal presence in the world, Jesus on earth. In this way, the Paraclete himself creates the two level drama. Where the world is mono focal, and can see only the historical level of Jesus in history or only the theological level of Jesus in the witness of the Christian community, the Paraclete binds the two together. The Word dwelling among us, and our beholding his glory are not past events only. They transpire in a two level drama. They transpire both on the historical and contemporary levels, *or not at all*. Their transpiration on both levels is itself the good news.

Abstract

Martyn's hypothesis has won the day and has been able to stand the test of time. While several points of criticism have arisen, still, the key turns very well in the lock. Interpretation of the fourth Gospel not only deserves but requires acknowledgement of the two-level drama, acknowledgement of the historical movement from Christian Judaism to Jewish Christianity, and acknowledgement of their homiletical embedding in John.

What Martyn describes is the way the community was 'pushed out.' He depends on the Jewish background to the NT, and to the sources for John in his reading, his constructive and imaginative reengagement with the text. Apocalypticism, broadly construed, provides the language and imagery for his interpretation. What Martyn's thesis does not address is the foreground not the background of the Gospel. John was not only pushed, he also was pulled. The two go well, and surprisingly well together. The expulsion from the synagogue pushed John forward. But what pulled him? From the outside, from the Gnostic foreground of the NT, John was pulled forward. Gnosticism, broadly construed, provides the language and imagery for this further interpretation. Gnosticism provided the speculative intrigue which equipped the community in its primitive Christological imagination. Gnosticism provided the communicative connection with the new wilderness, the non-Jewish world and thought world for life outside the synagogue. Gnosticism provided the audacity of hope in a new language, not that parousia but that of paraclete, not that of the end of the age, but that of the realm of light. Gnosticism especially provided the language and imagery of new identity, the confidence of identity in the face of alienation, which pulled the community along in its growth and change, even as they were pushed out of the synagogue. Hence, the fourth Gospel is not only a two *level* drama, it is also a two *stage* drama. In its first stage, that robed in Apocalypticism, the community is expulsed from Judaism. In its second stage, that robed in Gnosticism, the community is drawn to Hellenism. To understand both its history and its theology, both its origin and its meaning, the Johannine interpreter will need both Apocalypticism and Gnosticism. You cannot understand John 9:1 without the former. You cannot understand John 1:9 without the latter. To date, from Bultmann to Brown, we have had one or the other. We need both in order to do justice to the interpretation of what Clement rightly called "The Spiritual Gospel."

2

Introduction
—Cathryn Turrentine

People are passionate about the Gospel of John, in both directions. They may simultaneously love its soaring spiritual language, abhor its representation of "the Jews," and find some of its discourses maddeningly obscure. This book is intended to lead students into a passionate interaction with the Fourth Gospel. It is written for students who have already had an introduction to the New Testament and are ready now for a closer look at the Fourth Gospel. This introduction briefly summarizes some background information that students will need in this quest.

AUTHORSHIP, DATE, AND LOCATION

The author of the Fourth Gospel is not identified anywhere within the text itself. The inclusion of many favorable references to the "Beloved Disciple"—who is not named in this Gospel nor mentioned at all in the Synoptics—led to the assumption that this Gospel was written by him. It has been traditional, beginning with Irenaeus, to associate the Beloved Disciple with

John, son of Zebedee, and so authorship of the Fourth Gospel has long been ascribed to him,[1] and all of the Johannine corpus has taken his name. Modern scholars differ as to whether the Beloved Disciple was, in fact, John, son of Zebedee,[2] but they are in accord in asserting that it was not the Beloved Disciple himself but one of his own disciples, a later member of the Johannine community, who was the Fourth Evangelist.[3]

The version of the Fourth Gospel that we read today is not exactly as the Evangelist created it. Sometime after it was first recorded, a redactor added materials and likely changed the order of some sections. The opening hymn and the final chapter of the Gospel are examples of likely additions by this editor.[4] Scholars disagree, however, about the purpose of these emendations. Bultmann asserts that the redactor had an ecclesiastical focus, and wanted to make this text less Gnostic and more acceptable to the wider church, outside the Johannine community.[5] Raymond Brown argues that the redactor's principal interest was to preserve Johannine materials that had not been included in the original text.[6]

The Fourth Gospel was the last gospel to be recorded[7] (possibly 90–110 CE).[8] The author's location is disputed, however. Tradition, beginning with Irenaeus in the second century argues for Ephesus,[9] and most scholars now accept this view.[10] Bultmann objects, however, noting that "nothing in the Gospel points to its origin in . . . Asia Minor." He suggests Syria as a more likely location.[11]

---

1. Irenaeus, *Against Heresies*, 3.1.1; available from http://www.ccel.org/fathers2/ANF-01/anf01-60.htm#P7304_1933972.

2. So L. Michael White, *From Jesus to Christianity* (New York Harper, 2004) 306; contra Rudolf Bultmann, *The Gospel of John: A Commentary*, trans. G. R. Beasley-Murray, R. W. N. Hoate, and J. K. Riches (Philadelphia Westminster, 1971) 11; and Raymond E. Brown, *An Introduction to the New Testament* (New York: Doubleday, 1977) 369.

3. White, 307.

4. Francis J. Moloney, *The Gospel of John: Text and Context* (Boston: Brill, 2005) 117.

5. Bultmann, *Gospel*.

6. Raymond E. Brown, *The Gospel According to John*, Anchor Bible 29–29A (New York: Doubleday, 1966–1970) xxxviii.

7. Brown, *Gospel*, 215.

8. Raymond E. Brown, *The Community of the Beloved Disciple: The Life, Loves, and Hates of an Individual Church in New Testament Times* (New York: Paulist, 1979) 23.

9. Irenaeus, *Against Heresies*, 3.1.1.

10. Brown, *Introduction to the NT,* 368.

11. Bultmann, *Gospel*, 12.

THE COURAGEOUS GOSPEL

STRUCTURE

The Gospel is comprised of two main sections. The first is widely referred to as the Book of Signs, roughly chapters 1–12. This section describes Jesus' public ministry. It is named for the seven signs that Jesus performs, pointing to himself as the One who came down from heaven to reveal the glory of God. These are the signs:

1. Changing water into wine at the Cana wedding (chapter 2)
2. Healing the official's son (chapter 4)
3. Healing of the man who had been sick for thirty-eight years (chapter 5)
4. Multiplication of loaves and fish (chapter 6)
5. Walking on the sea (chapter 6)
6. Healing of the man born blind (chapter 9)
7. Raising of Lazarus (chapter 11)

In this section of the Gospel, signs are followed by discourses in which Jesus explains the meaning of the signs. For example, chapter 6 contains both the multiplication of loaves and fish and also the Bread of Life discourses.

The last sign, the raising of Lazarus from the dead, is the proximate cause of Jesus' arrest, trial, and crucifixion, according to the Fourth Gospel. This sign creates a bridge from the Book of Signs to the second major section of the Gospel, which may be called the Book of Glory. In this section of the Gospel, Jesus turns away from public ministry toward his own disciples and his passion. This section contains the lengthy final discourses, with their promise of the Paraclete to sustain the disciples in Jesus' absence, and it tells the story of Jesus' passion and resurrection.

INTENDED AUDIENCE

All of the canonical gospels were stories of the life, death, and resurrection of Jesus Christ, written for an audience that already knew about and believed in the resurrection. As time passed, the early Christians' practical circumstances diverged significantly from those of the original disciples, and they needed more and more assistance understanding and interpreting the gospel story in the context of new events. Each of the gospels was written for a different community in a different time, responding to a different set of circumstances, and these differences (as much as any variation in sources) help to explain the different approaches that the Evangelists take to the same basic story. In the words of Raymond Brown, "The deeds and words of Jesus are included in the Gospels because the Evangelist sees that they are (or have been) useful to the members of his community."[12] So to understand any of the gospels, one must understand something of the community and circumstances into which it was written. This is especially true of the Fourth Gospel and its relationship to the Johannine community.

This faith community, like the Fourth Gospel, shared an emphasis on realized eschatology; a high, pre-existence Christology; and a belief in the indwelling of the Holy Spirit, or Paraclete, in each member of the community, from whom each Christ-believer individually received divine truth. Each of these characteristics of the Johannine community is described below.

THE PASSAGE OF TIME AND REALIZED ESCHATOLOGY

Eschatology is the "doctrine about 'last things' (final judgment and the afterlife)."[13] Around 225 BCE, an apocalyptic eschatology developed in Jewish thought and continued through at least the first century CE. This apocalyptic world view provides a main backdrop for understanding the New Testament In apocalyptic eschatology, the idea of end times did not originally refer to the end of the world but to the end of the present evil age, in which God's people would at last be vindicated against their oppressors by an in-breaking of God to set things right. This Day of the Lord would be inaugurated by a final battle between the forces of God and the forces of evil. Apocalyptic literature classically includes vivid images of "battles, angels, demons, dramatic appearance on clouds, [and] wrathful judgment on God's enemies."[14]

The synoptic gospels and the Pauline letters adopted and adapted this apocalyptic world view by associating the eschaton with the second coming of Christ (parousia). Then the dead would be resurrected and all would be judged, receiving either eternal life or damnation on that day. In the early letters of Paul, it is clear that this return is expected soon—within the lifetime of most early Christians.[15] For Mark, the fall of the Temple in 70 CE was "the birth pangs for the eschaton."[16] This expectation of a near and coming eschatological fulfillment is seen in Matthew, as well, in the pas-

---

12. Brown, *Community*, 18.

13. Geddes MacGregor, *Dictionary of Religion and Philosophy* (New York: Paragon, 1992) 224.

14. Raymond E. Brown, *An Introduction to the Gospel of John*, edited, updated, and concluded by Francis J. Moloney (New York: Doubleday, 2003) 238.

15. 1 Thessalonians 4:16–17.

16. White, *From Jesus to Christianity*, 228; see Mark 8:38—9:1 and 13:30–32.

sages where Jesus says that the Kingdom of God is at hand.[17] The problem for Luke-Acts was that the Temple had fallen and Christ had still not yet returned. Luke solved this eschatological dilemma by associating the eschaton with Pentecost, while still anticipating a second coming of Christ in the indefinite future, a "present and future eschatology."[18]

By the time that the Gospel of John was written, at the end of the first century or early in the second, Christians had begun to realize that the second coming was not coming soon, and might not be coming at all. This great disappointment created a crisis of faith. On what could believers rely, if not on this? The Fourth Gospel responds to this great disappointment with a new eschatology—an affirmation that the Kingdom of God has already come in Jesus Christ. This characteristically Johannine view is called realized eschatology (or inaugurated, proleptic, or fulfilled eschatology) and Raymond Brown argues that the Gospel of John is the best example of it in the New Testament.[19] He writes,

> For John the presence of Jesus in the world as the light separates men into those who are sons of darkness, hating the light, and those who come to the light All through the gospel Jesus provokes self-judgment as men line up for or against him. . . Those who refuse to believe are already condemned [3:18], while those who have faith do not come under condemnation. . . For the Synoptics "eternal life" is something that one receives at the final judgment or in a future age [Mark 10:30; Matt 18:8–9], but for John it is a present possibility for men; "The man who hears my words and has faith in Him who sent me possesses eternal life. . . he has passed from death to life" [3:24]. For Luke [6:35, 10:36] divine sonship is a reward of the future life; for John [1:12] it is a gift granted here on earth.[20]

HIGH CHRISTOLOGY AND EXPULSION FROM THE SYNAGOGUE

The Fourth Gospel presents a layered picture of Jesus that reflects the development over time of the Johannine community's uniquely high, pre-existent Christology. One can perhaps see this development most clearly in the titles

---

17. Matthew 10:22–23, for example.
18. Acts 2:17; White, *From Jesus to Christianity*, 258.
19. Brown, *Introduction to the NT*, 238.
20. Brown, *Gospel*, cxvii–cxviii.

that refer to Jesus.[21] Although the various titles are scattered throughout the gospel, in general one can say that the lowest view of Jesus is found in the Book of Signs. This earliest stage is characterized by references to Jesus as the Messiah (a term that is clearly not divine). There is a middle stage with a somewhat higher Christology, which may be associated with the title Son of God (a higher, but still not necessarily divine, title). The highest title associated with Jesus, according to Ashton, is Son of Man, a truly divine figure.

Although there are traces of the whole upward development of the community's Christology in the Fourth Gospel, the final, received text overall gives us the highest Christology that is found anywhere in the Bible. The gospel begins with the beautiful Christological hymn, "In the beginning was the Word, and the Word was with God, and the Word was God." The original ending of the gospel text was Thomas's confession of Jesus as "my Lord and my God." Between these two affirmations, the divine name formula—I AM—recurs as a leitmotiv throughout the gospel. Over and over again, Jesus claims the name of God that was revealed to Moses at the burning bush. He uses it dozens of times in this text, for example in the walk on the sea and in his trial before Pilate. The evangelist clearly intends that the reader and believer understand that Jesus is divine, representative of the Father, one with the Father, revealer of the Father's glory, himself truly God.

The development of this high Christology over time created serious social and political problems for the Johannine Christians. Like other Christian groups, the Johannine Christians were originally part of the local synagogue. They were Christian Jews, believing in Christ, but continuing to worship as Jews. Somewhere toward the end of the first century, these Christians were kicked out of the synagogue altogether, and evidence from the Gospel text indicates that this expulsion occurred because the Johannine Christians' Christology was so high that it became unacceptable to Jewish monotheism. Johannine Christians were persecuted and beaten by the Jewish leaders, and the fact that they were no longer counted religiously as Jews made them vulnerable to persecution by the Romans. The decision by the Jewish leaders to evict these Christians from the synagogue placed them in mortal danger, and it cut them off from all the social networks that had sustained their lives. They were politically, socially, emotionally, and theologically dislocated. Martyn has demonstrated that the whole Gospel can be read as a two-level drama.[22] One level tells the story of the life, death, and resurrection of Jesus Christ. On the other level one can discern

---

21. This description follows John Ashton, *Understanding the Fourth Gospel* (Oxford: Oxford University Press, 2007).

22. J. Louis Martyn, *History and Theology in the Fourth Gospel*, 3rd ed. (Louisville, KY: Westminster John Knox, 2003).

the story of the Johannine community itself, struggling to make theological sense of their life cut off from the synagogue.

The Johannine community did not begin with such a high Christology, and it cost them quite a lot to retain it as they were expelled from the synagogue, so the question arises, how did this higher Christology develop? Bultmann proposed that the evangelist was a converted Gnostic.[23] For decades scholars rejected this view, defending the orthodoxy of the Johannine text by distinguishing between the Gnostic and apocalyptic world views, asserting that since the Fourth Gospel contains at least some elements of apocalyptic eschatology, it would not have been compatible with Gnostic influences. Hill has shown that there was more variety in both Gnostic and apocalyptic literature than had previously been acknowledged, so that their world views overlapped and the possibility of Gnostic influences in the Fourth Gospel can be supported.[24]

Raymond Brown suggests that it was the incorporation of converted Samaritans into the Johannine community that pressed the group toward a higher Christology.[25] Ashton rejects this view, arguing that Samaritan beliefs would not have militated in this direction. Ashton himself argues that Judaism was not monolithic in the first century, and that there were many existing Jewish motifs that were incorporated more or less organically into the Johannine faith, pressing it toward a higher Christology. As some were expelled from the synagogue for affirming the divinity of Christ, their commitment to this belief was strengthened.[26]

Another possible source of the higher Johannine Christology is the Paraclete. In the final discourses of the Fourth Gospel, Jesus tells the disciples that he cannot explain everything to them, but he promises that the Paraclete, the Spirit of Truth, will come later to teach the disciples all they need to know. Like all the early Christian communities, the Johannine Christians looked back on Jesus' life through the lens of the Resurrection, reinterpreting the pre-Easter events in light of Easter Day. Claiming the authority of the Paraclete as the source of revelation, each member of the Johannine community was free to reinterpret Jesus' life in light of the Resurrection in almost any way he or she chose. At least some Johannine Christians may have read the Resurrection a lot more broadly than others, resulting in a more divine understanding of Christ. They were probably encouraged to do

---

23. Bultmann, *Gospel*.

24. Robert Allan Hill, *An Examination and Critique of the Understanding of the Relationship between Apocalypticism and Gnosticism in Johannine Studies* (Lewiston, NY: Mellen, 1997).

25. Brown, *Community*.

26. Ashton, *Understanding*.

this by the presence in the culture of Gnostic and Essene views as well as the various Jewish images that Ashton cites.

JOHANNINE ANTI-SEMITISM

The Fourth Gospel is well known for its negative portrayal of people the Evangelist refers to as "the Jews." This enmity has been used by some Christians for centuries as an excuse for violent anti-Semitism, and it is today a source of great concern for students who want to feel free to love the soaring beauty of the Gospel but who must reject its anti-Semitic character. How can one make sense of this?

To understand the characterization of Jews in this Gospel, he first question one needs to answer is, Who are "the Jews"? Many people have asked why Jesus and the disciples, who were Jews themselves, would refer to "the Jews" as though they were the "other" group in this gospel. This term probably does not refer to all Jews, but primarily to the Pharisees and other Jewish leaders who took control of the synagogues in the chaotic period after the fall of Jerusalem and the destruction of the Temple by the Romans in 70 CE.[27] Under their leadership, this group began to enforce a uniformity of belief and practice that had not been emphasized so much in the decades around Jesus' lifetime. This group of Jewish leaders made decisions that seriously affected the Christian community for whom the Gospel of John was written, including their eventual expulsion from the synagogue. Since the gospel writer was writing for a community that was trying to make sense of this period of stern religious enforcement, he retrojected the actions and attitudes of this group of Jewish leaders back into the story of Jesus' life and his interactions with the Jewish leaders of his own day.

The decision by the Jewish leaders to evict the Johannine community from the synagogue placed them in mortal danger, and it cut them off from all the social networks that had sustained their lives. At the same time that this eviction solidified these Christians' belief in the divinity of Christ, it made them angry and fearful of the Jewish leaders who had put them in this position.

One can see this fear and anger most frequently in the little asides that the gospel writer provides to guide his readers in interpreting his story. For example, in Chapter 20, which describes Jesus' resurrection appearances, the gospel writer tells us that the disciples were hiding in a room that was locked "for fear of the Jews." It is impossible to know if the first disciples were feeling this fearful on that first Easter Day, but it is certain that the Johannine

27. Ashton, *Understanding*.

Christians were hiding behind locked doors to protect themselves from the Jewish leaders who wanted to persecute them.

One can also see this negative attitude toward Jews in Jesus' own conversations (as reported by this gospel writer). For example, in the eighth chapter, Jesus calls the Jews liars and sons of the devil. It is unlikely that Jesus himself had quite such an antagonistic relationship with Pharisees as this story describes,[28] so this part of the gospel suggests instead the kind of interactions that the Johannine Christians were having with the Jewish authorities around 100 CE.

Finally, and most famously, the negative portrayal of the Jews appears in the Passion story. The Jewish leaders are painted as sinister and cowardly, wanting to kill Jesus, but conniving to get the Romans to do it for them; and the crowd chooses Barabbas to be saved rather than Jesus, shouting "Crucify him!" In this gospel, Pilate is portrayed as the one official who finds Jesus to be innocent, but who yields to pressure to crucify him nevertheless. It is impossible to know, two thousand years later, exactly what the role of the Jewish authorities or the Jewish populace was in the crucifixion of Jesus, but it is clear that this gospel writer portrays them in the worst possible light, because he wanted to use the gospel story to help his community make sense of their own lives, which were endangered and cut off from social support by the Jewish leaders.

This story was written to provide spiritual and emotional support for an early second century community that was under persecution. It is the responsibility of modern readers to keep those defensive messages from being turned in persecution against Jews today. This does not mean that one must reject the whole gospel, however. Having understood and rejected the text's hateful messages about Jews, it is also the privilege of Christians today to glean from the rest of the gospel the beautiful and lofty affirmations that led to the persecution in the Johannine community in the first place—that Jesus was in the beginning, and all things were created through him; that he is the Light that has come into the world and the darkness did not overcome it; that Jesus and the Father are one. These remain the foundation of the Christian faith, and the Gospel of John contains the most beautiful statements of them that are found anywhere in Scripture.

---

28. Ashton, *Understanding*.

Introduction

THE PARACLETE

Clement of Alexandria famously called the Gospel of John the "spiritual gospel."[29] Indeed, spirit is a major theme throughout the Gospel, beginning in Chapter 1: "John testified, 'I saw the spirit descending from heaven like a dove, and it remained on him'" (1:32). The final appearance of the Spirit in the Fourth Gospel is in the insufflation—the scene in Chapter 20 in which the risen Christ breathes on the disciples and says, "Receive the Holy Spirit."

Throughout the Gospel, Spirit is associated with images of breath and water. The linking of Spirit and breath is consistent with the Hebrew scripture's use of *ruah YHWH* to indicate the powerful spirit (breath) of God that authorized and informed prophets. The linking of Spirit and water suggests baptism, and in fact the first chapter of the gospel contrasts John's baptism with water to the baptism of the spirit that Christ will provide.

Unique to the Fourth Gospel is the description of Spirit as Paraclete in the Final Discourses. This appearance of the Paraclete in the second half of the Gospel of John, and nowhere else in the whole Bible, has raises interesting and important questions. For example, is this Paraclete the same as the Holy Spirit described elsewhere in the Fourth Gospel? Many scholars believe that the Paraclete references may be later additions that have no clear connection to the use of Spirit in the rest of the Gospel. They point out that the functions of the Paraclete appear to be more closely associated with Christ than with a separate Spirit figure. Tricia Gates Brown disagrees with this view, arguing that "the interrelationship of Jesus and the Paraclete . . . does not require pneumatology to become subsumed in Christology."[30]

A second important question is the source of the Spirit. In chapter 14, Jesus says, "But the Advocate, the Holy Spirit, whom the Father will send in my name, will teach you everything, and remind you of all that I have said to you" (14:26). But in chapter 20 Jesus breathes on the disciples himself and says, "Receive the Holy Spirit." The first passage states that the Spirit is a gift of the Father, while the second demonstrates that it is a gift of the Son. This issue has occupied theologians for centuries, arising most famously in the question of the appropriateness of the *filioque* in the Nicene Creed. These differences are not irreconcilable, however. Bultmann is among those who argue that the insufflation in Chapter 20 is, in fact, the authoritative

---

29. Eusebius of Caesarea, *Ecclesiastical History*, Book VI, Chapter XIV. http://www.ucalgary.ca/~vandersp/Courses/texs/eusebius/eusehe6.html#XIV.

30. Tricia Gates Brown, *Spirit in the Writings of John: Johannine Pneumatology in Social-Scientific Perspective* (New York: T. & T. Clark, 2003) 13.

fulfillment of the promises throughout the Final Discourses of the gift of the Paraclete.[31]

However these and other pneumatological questions about the Paraclete are resolved, it is clear that the presentation of the Paraclete in the Fourth Gospel is a very particular view of the Spirit. The Final Discourses describe the Paraclete as Spirit of Truth, Advocate, Teacher, Comforter.

The Paraclete gave the Johannine Christians (and only them) personal and individual access to divine truth. In the context of the Fourth Gospel, Jesus' promise of the Paraclete lent support to any theological claims that the Fourth Evangelist might make that went beyond the written and oral records of the original ministry of Jesus Christ himself, since the insight he recorded had come from Jesus via the Paraclete.[32] The Paraclete is the irrefutable source of authority for this Gospel.

ORGANIZATION OF THIS TEXT

This is not a comprehensive commentary. Readers will see from a glance at the table of contents that this book does not address every chapter of the Fourth Gospel. Some readers may be surprised, for example, to notice that the passion story is not included here. Rather, the chapters 2–8 revolve around two major issues discussed above: the disappointment that the Johannine Christians faced in the delay of the second coming, and their dislocation after being expelled from the synagogue. Then chapters 9–12 examine the gifts of the Paraclete, Spirit of Truth.

Each of the following chapters selects a key passage from the Gospel and wrestles with it in different ways. Each begins with a sermon. Most also include some class notes from a course taught by Raymond Brown at Union Theological Seminary in 1978. The chapters close with other related materials.

Readers become lovers of this Gospel by wrestling with it. This book is intended to lead students into a just such a passionate interaction.

---

31. Bultmann, *Gospel*, 692.
32. Brown, *Community*, 28–29.

3

Summary of the Courages in John

THE COURAGE TO:
- Raise Christology
- Employ Gnosticism
- Discard Apocalyptic
- Dismiss Parables
- Leave Home
- Leave Momma, Papa, and Abba
- Revise Eschatology
- Call for Decision
- Set Sail
- Re-imagine the Gospel
- Use Gnosticism against Gnosis
- Diminish the Baptist
- Displace Peter
- Eliminate the Sacraments
- Trust the Truth

THE COURAGEOUS GOSPEL

- Offer Jesus Only
- Dare to be Different
- Risk Di-Theism
- Probe Divine Relationships
- Declare Words more durable than deeds
- Use Legal Language
- Enter Night Talks
- Jazz the Gospel
- Discard the simple direct faith of signs
- Write Theology
- Rewrite the Gospel
- Make a Meta-Gospel
- Enlarge Christianity
- Name a culpable blindness
- Include many formal contradictions
- Not only leave the synagogue but also take up gnosis

PART TWO

4

Two Battles
John 1:1–18

"These things are written that you may believe that Jesus is the Christ, the Son of God, and that believing you may have life in his name" (John 20:31).

This year we will scale a great promontory, the highest peak in the Bible, which is the Gospel of John. John is Slide Mountain in the Catskills, Mt. Marcy in the Adirondacks, Pikes Peak in the Rockies, Mt. Everest in the Himalayas, the Matterhorn in the Alps, Mt. Fuji in Japan. John is the bride, the Synoptics are the bridesmaids; John the groom, the others the ushers. John is the gospel for which the others were made. Before John, the rest is prelude.

The Gospel of John is a story of dislocation and disappointment. Your life is such a story, too. In fact, these are the two battles of salvation, the two great battles of the salvation we work out daily in fear and trembling, are battles with dislocation and disappointment. The Gospel of John brings grace for dislocation and freedom in disappointment, and hence is great and good news!

THE BATTLE FOR IDENTITY

A freshwoman sat last week between her mom and dad, having a sandwich at the Colgate Inn. They were tightly seated, mom and dad and daughter, although the room was not full. They huddled together, like geese heading for the water. Mom and Dad drank coke and spooned soup, wordless, mute, silent. They never dared to catch each others' eyes, so filled were each others' eyes. They spooned and listened, and waited, for that last trip to the room, coming (you could tell) after dinner, and that last hug and that last gift and that last goodbye. There are no atheists in foxholes, and all parents pray when they leave the freshman dorm.

She roamed the world by cell phone while her parents spooned soup. A friend in Milwaukee, was it? Can you hear me now? High school sweetheart in Boston. Can you hear me now? Sister in San Diego. Can you hear me now? I could not hear her then, but I can hear her now. She was not about to let her geographical dislocation become a matter of relational disorientation. By Glory, she was carving out her own virtual dorm, her own telephonic suite, her own cyber city. What *they* faced in despair, *she* addressed in anxiety. The dislocation would come soon enough.

The great and surprising good news of Jesus Christ, in this Gospel, is that grace may be found, may *especially* be found, in the upheaval of dislocation. Students or parents, hear it well; future students or grandparents, hear it well: "All things were made through him and without him was not anything made that was made."

You can do it. You will get through it.

Oh, prayer will help, and reading of the scripture and a church family and the habits of generosity and service. All will help. But it is largely and lastly Grace that will see you through.

Out they walked, the dislocated trio, arm in arm, into a dark and unforeseeable future. Is that not grace, the faith to walk into the dark?

Today's text is from the first chapter of John, and there is bitter hurt in this sublime chapter, caused by a break with the first identity, a cutting of the umbilical cord, a leaving home, a separation from the family, a dismissal from the synagogue.

The religion of origin said, "In the beginning, God. . ." Replies John, "In the beginning was the Word."

Inherited religion said, "In the beginning God created. . ." Rejoins John, "All things came into being through *Him*."

Old time religion said, "God created the heavens and the earth." Retorts John, "In *Him* was life."

Inheritance said, "God said, 'Let their be light.'" Rebuts John, "In *Him* was life, and that life was the light of all peoples, which shines in the dark."

Two Battles

Old time religion said, "We are his people, the sheep of his pasture." John retorts, "He came to his *own people* and his own people did not accept him."

This Gospel is born in dislocation. The Gospel of John is written in the pain of dislocation. In John we overhear the bitter pain of the church being thrown out of the synagogue.

The community that formed this Gospel has been given the heave-ho, shown the door, given the bum's rush, given the wet mitten by their former community. You are listening to a family feud, nineteen centuries old.

I return from summer vacation to find a thriving church community, and growth, and dislocation. A growing service to the hungry—and some dislocation. A new ministry to the homeless—with a little dislocation. A new baroque organ—did some of you sense dislocation? A completely re-colored Sunday School—laborious dislocation.

Dislocation visits every age and place. The past decade of dislocation in Rochester has yet to find full expression. Corporate dislocation: I thought this job was for life! Medical dislocation: Were we not the pride of the country in health care? Economic dislocation: Someone threw a recovery party and forgot our upstate invitation! Geographical dislocation: I left two generations to the west or east to come here; now what? No wonder we think of Ma Joad now and then.

The Gospel of John is not focused on ethics. There is only minimal ethical teaching here. One looks in vain for a sermon on the mount or plain. One searches without result for a parable with a point. One hungers without satisfaction for a wisdom saying, an epigram, a teaching on virtue. In John we have the teleological suspension of the ethical. Only the command to love remains.

Instead, the Fourth Gospel focuses on your need to become who you are.

THE BATTLE FOR IMAGINATION

I believe it is very difficult for us to appreciate the courage in John, the theological courage of this writing. One of the most precious beliefs of the earliest Christians resided in the confidence that very soon the world would come to an end and the Lord would return for his people. This expectation of the end governs the letters of Paul and the first three Gospels. It was, if you will, the bedrock belief of the primitive church. Had not Jesus preached, "There are some standing here who will not taste death until they see the Son of Man coming on the clouds of heaven"? Yes he had. And he was wrong. Had not Peter left nets, family, homeland, and life itself on the expectation of the apocalypse? Yes he had. And he was wrong. Had not Paul predicted, "We the living, the remaining, will be caught up together with him in the clouds"? Yes he had. And he was wrong.

Only John faces this grave disappointment with utter honesty. The others hold onto the old religion, the expected return. John admits delay. John has the guts to say to his people: "What we once believed is clearly not true. Let us look about us and see what this means." And behold! In place of parousia, we find paraclete. In place of cataclysm, we find church. In place of speculation, we find spirit. In place of Armageddon we find artistry and imagination! When finally we stop chasing what is not to be, and wake up to what is, we may be utterly amazed.

Seasoned Religion said that the end was near. John says the beginning is here.

Old Time Religion saw the end of the world. John preached the light of the world.

Inherited spirituality waited for the coming of the Lord. John celebrated the Word among us, full of grace and truth.

Old Time Religion feared death, judgment, heaven, and hell. John faced them all every day.

Traditional Religion clung fiercely to an ancient untruth. John let go, and accepted a modern new truth, and hugged grace and freedom.

Our inheritance, and Matthew and Mark and Luke and Paul all looked toward the End, soon to come. John looked up at the beginning, already here. They said with Shakespeare, "All's well that ends well." John replied, "*Gut begonnen, halb gewonnen!*" (Well begun is half done.)

John alone had the full courage to face spiritual disappointment and move ahead. So we memorize John 8:32: "You shall know the truth and the truth shall set you free!" Copernicus knew that truth. Galileo knew that truth. Darwin knew that truth. And Robert Lee caught that truth on the lips of Clarence Darrow: "The Bible is a book. It is a good book. It is not the only book." All faced the need to change from inherited untruth to new insight and imagination.

Perhaps our greatest present disappointment is 9/11. We face new truth: The world is smaller and starker than we wanted to believe. We have not yet found our way out of the psychic rubble of that dreadful day. We are trying, and we are moving, but the almost unspeakable disappointment of that moment remains. Here is why: We have to change our understanding, our philosophy, our theology even. We have to face the hard fact, that the future is open, freely open, both to terror and to tenderness. And here is John. He who wrote in the ancient rubble of dislocation and disappointment, telling us something wonderful and good: The Word became flesh and dwelt among us. It is in the spirit of the Fourth Gospel that we affirmed three years ago on this Sunday: "Terror may topple the World Trade Center, but no terror can topple the World Truth Center, Jesus the Christ."

The World Trade Center, hub of global economies may fall, the economy of grace still stands in the World Truth Center, Jesus the Christ.

The World Trade Center, communications nexus for many may fall, but the communication of the gospel stands, the World Truth Center, Jesus Christ.

The World Trade Center, symbol of national pride may fall, but divine humility stands, through the World Truth Center, Jesus the Christ.

The World Trade Center, legal library for the country may fall, but grace and truth stand, through the World Truth Center, Jesus the Christ.

These things are spoken that you may believe that Jesus is the Christ, the Son of God, and that believing you may have life in his name.

Faith is personal commitment to an unverifiable truth. It involves a leap.

Faith is an objective uncertainty, grasped with subjective certainty. It involves a leap.

Faith is the way to salvation, a real identity and a rich imagination. But it does involve a leap.

Tomorrow morning, which will it be? "In the beginning. . ." What? Creation or Grace? Covenant or Freedom? Law or Love? An eye for an eye or the second mile, the coat and cloak, the turned cheek? "In the beginning. . . was the Word."

All of us are better when we are loved.

Now is the time to jump.

NOTES FROM RAYMOND BROWN'S LECTURES ON JOHN
Union Theological Seminary
Spring 1978

April 27, 1978: John 1

The prologue was a hymn of the Johannine community. There are similar hymns to be found in Philippians, Colossians, and Ephesians. All of these hymns were highly Christological, and carried a high Christology. They typically begin with something prior to the material world, and they tend to move from creation to redemption. 1 Timothy 3:16 is one other example.

The prologue came from the life of the community. Perhaps it was written by the evangelist, and perhaps it was not. It certainly came from Johannine circles.

RB thinks that the gospel originally opened with John the Baptist, and with those materials. The term *Word* presents a realization of a problem. If one wants to present a pre-history of the earthly Jesus, one faces difficulties, trying to speak of the human Jesus before time. How do you do it? *Christ Jesus* is one way. *Son* of God is one way. *Word* is used in John. In the fourth century, the councils of the church decide that the *Son* existed from all eternity (but Jesus did not). Early on, as here, there was no such sophistication.

The *Word* is of course a direct connection to Genesis, though of course in a different sense. This beginning is an earlier beginning. The verb is "to be," not "to become." The reference is to the great IAM, which is translated "o ov"—"the existent." The word *Word* has a two-fold directionality—to God, from God. The *Word* thus has community with both God and Man. There is a staircase parallelism here.

The last "God" in the opening has no article. Why? Because you still cannot say that the *Word* is the Father. This same struggle was to continue for centuries later. And there is even some struggle along the way here. This may also be simply a predicative use. (In the later New Testament books, God is predicated of Jesus Christ, but the usage is not common). There are growing Christological tendencies as the New Testament develops.

This *Word* must tell us about God. The *Word* that was God is spoken—to you. This reflection is not strange to Judaism. What is strange is the personification. Isaiah 55: God's *Word* has its own reality. Both word and thing are expressed in *dabar* (Hebrew). The *Word* spoken is eternally existent. "My *Word* shall not return to me empty" (Habbakuk 3:5). *Dabar* can also be pestilence. Some read: *before him went his word*. This is tied into divine wisdom, a *female* figure. This figure is personified with God from the moment of creation. Both Proverbs and the Book of Wisdom give evidence of this. The *Word* is an emanation of God through which God creates. Wisdom creates things by God's wisdom.

There is an increasing resistance to the use of the divine name. The Aramaic translation spoke of God's "memra." It became eventually a technical term (like Logos for us). To what degree did people sense this play on words?

Word is a term understood both in Greek and Judaic communities. The *Word* creates. The *Word* is the coming into being of life. Life here (verse 4) must be a reference to Genesis—God sharing his life with his creatures.

And this life is the light of human beings. Verse 5 carries a question: Should it read "receive" or "overcome"? Or does the verse mean both?

Where does incarnation occur in this hymn? Not until after John the Baptist's entrance. In verse 9 we hear of the coming of Jesus. With this comes a kind of pessimism of judgment. When John speaks of world, he speaks of those who do not receive Jesus. But those who accept him became God's children. Light vs. Darkness. From then on he is speaking to his own.

Introductory Material: February 15, 1978

The author's hope is to lead people to the light by bringing his own community to the truth. "And believing you may have life." He has an almost unique purpose for writing: Is its thrust "come to faith" or "continue in faith"? It is probably the latter. John's purpose is Christological. He is exploring the identity of Jesus Christ. This has come in part out of the community history. The real problem is the claim to divinity, which is rejected by the synagogue. John's community is caused to suffer for its Christology.

Hence the Gospel becomes quite different. Jesus comes to tell of God and of God's demands. There is no mention of the kingdom of God. In John, Jesus is the kingdom of God realized. Jesus is the mirror of God. So, we see the logic of the early church: Kingdom of God talk gives way quite early to Jesus talk. The act of faith centers on Jesus, not on the kingdom. This probably reflects outside interests, but also inner Christian questions as well. John is not satisfied to identify Jesus as the foundation of the community. Rather, Jesus is the vital principle of the community. Here the church is taking over the role of salvation. Jesus is the principle of life, the vine and the branches. If you are not a branch, you do not have life. Thus John has thrown out foundational language, in order to connect things to Jesus' life rather than to his directives. John wants to mold, of words and deeds, the living truth for community life.

This must be a voice of warning, and complaint, as the institution grows. The Spirit is the presence of Jesus. Thus an abiding presence through spirit is affirmed, unperturbed by time and space. In his teaching, Jesus speaks of the most simple, temporal ideas for eternity.

Life is the term John gives to Jesus' gift of God's own life, and this life is the nature of the Christian message. For him, the natural life is not as real as the life Jesus gives. Real love is God's, as with life. John talks quite realistically about eternal things. We receive God's eternal life and nourish it with water and with food. This is not abstraction. It is concrete language about Jesus and as such it is a somewhat dangerous message.

THE COURAGEOUS GOSPEL

John's Christology brings him into conflict with other Christians. His pre-existent Logos is tough for people to swallow. Jesus' followers never really understood Jesus fully. There is no mention of pre-existence in other books. Here there is a different sonship. Christology is not a matter of conception, but a matter of incarnation, based on the pre-existent principle.

5

Two Brides
John 2:1–11

"THESE THINGS ARE WRITTEN that you may believe that Jesus is the Christ, the Son of God, and that believing you may have life in his name" (John 20:31).

I look out at the back hill which rises out from our summer home. The hillside once offered pasture to Holsteins and Guernseys, but now simply watches over valley and lake. To climb it, though, low as it is, does require energy and strength.

This year we will scale a far greater promontory, the highest peak in the Bible, which is the Gospel of John. With every cut-back trail, at every rest point, atop every lookout, with every majestic view, this spiritual gospel will address you with the choice of freedom, with the ongoing need to choose, and—in choosing—to find the life of belonging and meaning, personal identity and global imagination. More personally, this Gospel helps those who struggle with dislocation and disappointment. The Bride in Cana experienced dislocation, and so have you. The Bride of Christ experiences disappointment, and so have you.

The two basic historical problems of the New Testament are ancient cousins, first cousins to our two fundamental issues, the two existential battles in your salvation today.

The first historical problem behind our 27 books, and pre- eminently embedded in John, is the movement away from Judaism. How did a religious movement founded by a Jew, born in Judea, embraced by 12 and

500 within Judaism, expanded by a Jewish Christian missionary, become--within 100 years--entirely Greek? The books of the New Testament record in excruciating detail the development of this second identity, this coming of age, that came with the separation from mother religion.

The second historical problem underneath the Newer Testament is disappointment, the despair that gradually accompanied the delay, finally the cancellation, of Christ's return, the delay of the parousia. Jesus was an apocalyptic prophet. Paul expected to be alive to see the advent of Christ. Gradually, though, the church confessed disappointment in its greatest immediate hope, the sudden cataclysm of the end.

These two problems, historical and fascinating, create our New Testament: the separation from Judaism and the delay of the parousia. In the fourth Gospel the two come together with great ferocity. What makes this matter so urgent for us is that these very two existential dilemmas—one of identity and one of imagination—are before every generation, including and especially our own.

How do I become a real person? How do we weather lasting disappointment? How do I grow up? How do we become mature? What insight do I need, amid the truly harrowing struggles over identity, to become the woman or man I was meant to become? What imagination—what hope molded by courage—do we need to face down the profound despair of nuclear twilight and break free into a loving global future?

Dislocation and disappointment. More than any other document in ancient Christianity, John explored the first of these great dilemmas. More than any other document in Christianity, John faced the second.

THE BRIDE IN CANA: THE BATTLE WITH DISLOCATION

Some years ago after a particularly warm July wedding, we had the opportunity to join newlyweds, families, and friends at an evening reception. A wedding folds two worlds into one new creation, and does so with alarming speed. It is quite amazing what can happen in forty minutes. During dinner a round, large man accosted me to say, "Nice service Reverend. But I have two words for you: 'air conditioning.'" We then enjoyed the round of food and drink, of dance and music, none of which really has changed very much since Jesus went up to Cana in the north country of Galilee. Roles have changed. Power shifts have occurred. The age of betrothal, the economics of the household, the rhythms of procreation, the status of women, the frequency of divorce—all these have changed. The wedding banquet is about the same. It was in this sort of universal spirit that my new, large and round friend offered his second wisdom saying. Like most epigrams, its context has long been forgotten. In fact I may not have been listening closely enough, given band and dance and cake and all, to have grasped the context in its origin. I just remember my head snapping back when he stated, in the flat, easy sense in which someone remarks about a universally held belief: "Of course, all men hate all weddings."

I took some offense to this, as a man who has spent a good percentage of summer weekend life at weddings, and not hated, at least not all of them. Whatever was he thinking? What did the wedding represent for him that was so recognizably hateful?

Perhaps it is the inherent element of falsehood as several people publicly put forward their best feet. Perhaps it is the flummery. Perhaps the very time, tedious and full, that such an event requires. Perhaps the recognition of mortality, the sense of ending. And the ending (or at least the limits) of personal freedoms.

The first great battle of salvation is with dislocation, and dislocation is the stuff of every wedding. Dislocation is the fact of life that every bride-- and every groom and both their families—must face.

THE BRIDE OF CHRIST: THE BATTLE WITH DISAPPOINTMENT

The second great battle of salvation is with disappointment, and every wedding has its share of that as well. This is what makes weddings, in Cana and elsewhere, so interesting. Things are just not ever simple.

I do not believe that there is much of anything that might happen in the course of a wedding that would at all surprise me. Not any more. I have had bomb threats, no shows, late shows, sickness, faintings, forgotten rings, electrical problems, plumbing problems, family fights, and neglected fees. Once a groom paid me four dollars for a wedding Jan and I hosted in our living room. My own daughter's wedding, according to a close friend, hit several records: longest, hottest, most music, most attendees, most faintings, and most memories. It is hard to imagine a setting more apt to disappoint the hope of simplicity with the reality of life. Maybe that is why the first recorded sign in John occurs at a wedding. One in which the simple task of buying the right amount of wine apparently was too much for somebody to do right.

1 Corinthians 13, so often read at weddings, should give us a clue. I expect many of you could recite portions of this chapter. Speak with

tongues...men and angels...noisy gong....bears, believes, hopes, endures....faith, hope, and love abide...the greatest of these is love..... But as a speaker at Riverside Church said in late August, we may too often miss the most important verses in the whole chapter, the next to last. Faith, hope and love abide...yes, wonderful. But do you remember what comes before them? Words to live by in the complexity of life. Words to live by in the confusion of marriage. Words to live by in the strange, twilight condition that is ours. Now we see in a glass darkly, then face to face. Now I know in part, then I shall know in full. Along with the tide of fear that we spoke of last week, there is an undertow of simplicity around us. We want things simple. They are not. We are disappointed.

In 1989, three days before Christmas, our son Ben suddenly proclaimed a hankering for a train set. We had already bartered for the season's gifts, and Christmas being what Christmas is in a parsonage, we made a mental note for next year. Next year, a train, for Ben.

I remember that at our staff Christmas party on December 23 I had mentioned this desire of Ben's, as some sort of illustration of some now fully forgotten interpretation of the Incarnation. So it goes.

At 1 am on Christmas Eve, or rather morning, we return down the slope of Acorn Path and entered our garage, walking toward the backdoor. There on the steps we found a big box, wrapped in a red bow, "for Ben, from Santa." Ben loved his simple, new train. In January I spent many hours coaxing, cajoling, thanking, pressing my staff about who had given Ben the train. Our organist, former supervisor of music in Onondaga County, G. Frank Lapham—he loved kids, surely he had brought the train. My friend and student minister, now Bruce Lee-Clark, whose own train set covered his basement in full—he loved trains, surely he was the one. My dearest colleague, Al Childs, now 85 and four years from death—he was just the kind of guy to do such a thing. My sweet secretary Jo Stewart, then 80 and looking 55—she loved Ben liked the son she always wanted; it was she.

But they all denied it. To a man. Vociferously, they denied it. They seemed puzzled that I was sure it was they. I hate secrets and surprises, so I would not let it go. I was still at it the next Christmas. Finally, Al took me out to lunch and said, "Bob, drop it." So I did.

Until this summer. At a June graduation party in the old neighborhood, something marvelous happened. Marvelous like Spirit, full of surprise. Marvelous like real church, beyond any naming or denomination. Marvelous like life, true and good and present. Marvelous like love. I ran into Sue, who asked about Ben, and then said that Stan, her husband, a lawyer, a sometime Catholic, a quiet, quizzical guy, the last person on earth you would call religious, she said that Stan would like to know about Ben for a host of reasons, and, as she ended, "Well, all the way back, you know, to the train that Christmas. . . ." Stan was really angry with Sue for spilling the beans. I, though, was grateful.

This is what we are hoping for, what we imagine at our best: an experience of being alive, an experience of love, an experience of God.

The Gospel of John is not focused on ethics. There is only minimal ethical teaching here. One looks in vain for a Sermon on the Mount or Plain. One searches without result for a parable with a point. One hungers without satisfaction for a wisdom saying, an epigram, a teaching on virtue. In John we have the teleological suspension of the ethical. In John, only the command to love remains.

These things are spoken that you may believe that Jesus in the Christ, the Son of God, and that believing you may have life in his name.

This week you can choose to grow in faith, and so find a fuller part of your second identity. This week you can choose to grow in love, and so open a fuller part of the world's imagination. This week you can fight through dislocation, like that known by the Bride of Cana, and discover your own courage to be. This week you can fight through disappointment that things aren't simpler, like that known by the Bride of Christ, and learn to simply live.

Faith is personal commitment to an unverifiable truth. It involves a leap.

Faith is an objective uncertainty grasped with subjective certainty. It involves a leap.

Faith is the way to salvation, a real identity and a rich imagination. But it does involve a leap.

Now is the time to jump.

And all of us are better when we are loved.

NOTES FROM RAYMOND BROWN'S LECTURES ON JOHN
Union Theological Seminary
Spring 1978

March 9, 1978: The Wedding in Cana of Galilee

The Cana miracle could have been an earlier narrative. In the final form of the narrative, Mary takes on another significance. John brings Mary back at the end of the gospel. This is not a complete rejection of Mary (as in

Mark). There is no attempt at all to reclaim the physical mother in Mark. John brings her back at the end. The beloved disciple takes her under his wing. Then the mother of Jesus and the brothers depart. The brothers return in chapter 7. "His brothers did not believe in him."

James became a great figure for Jewish Christians. John was not in that group. There is a great deal of apocryphal material about James. Paul mentions James in 1 Cor 15. The voice here is hostile to Jewish Christianity. Ignatius of Antioch has very bitter relations with Jewish Christians. This hostility is expressed toward Jesus' brothers. But Jesus' mother is connected to the beloved disciple, and at the very least is put into another category. This is interesting: in Luke and John, Mary becomes a part of the Christian community. We do not know that from Mark. So there is reflection about Mary going on in the early Christian tradition.

Who were Jesus' brothers? They are mentioned in all the gospels. Mark and Matthew also mention sisters. And what about Joseph? Some explain Jesus' brothers as step-brothers. Tertullian vs. Jerome. Jerome says Jesus could not have had siblings. Jerome's position prevailed past the Reformation. This, says RB, was not a very good argument, not an authentic NT argument. James, Simon, Jude, Jospephus: the first three are supposed to have been early church heads. John is polemicizing here. Luke has no hostility to brothers. What view would readers have had of the brothers? And why would he call Mary "woman"? Jesus addresses all women as woman. Does this refer to the book of revelation? Is Mary here in the Eve mode? Jesus "resists using his power in a merely practical way."

Are there seven days in the first two chapters? For instance, the author of the Revelation is honest about his sevens. Is this a retelling of the Genesis story in which Adam chooses the will of the father? RB thinks not.

There is very little about Capernaum in this gospel, as opposed to the Synoptic tradition. The Cana scene ends with the disciple and his inaugural glory. But they will not understand everything. Understanding and belief "take a long time." God puts them on the road to faith and belief, but not full belief for the disciples (except for the beloved disciple).

At the end of chapter 2, scripture and the word of Jesus are put side by side. 2 Peter (~130 AD) contains the first mention of Christian scripture.

Now the Passover of the Jews was near. There are three Passovers in John. This is where the notion of Jesus' three-year ministry comes from. These feasts may be more symbolic than chronological. Also, the ministry itself may have lasted 10 years. Jesus must go to Jerusalem and to the feast. Paul celebrates Passover, but not John. The cleansing of the temple and the destruction of the temple have no connection in the Synoptics. Here, they do. Who is right? This is far from a minor issue. According to the Synoptics, this is the issue which brought Jesus' death. The temple is an identity point, and so is a very sensitive point. The teacher of righteousness at Qumran is dumped on for the temple attack.

But in John, Caiaphas kills Jesus over the raising of Lazarus. Here Jesus starts his ministry where he ends it in other books. The real goal is the replacement of the temple with Jesus' body. There is a different cast to Jesus' direction. The changing of water into wine is meant to symbolize that the old is over, and something completely new has come. God is present in the temple, the space for God's name and glory. So it is with Jesus.

In each of the four gospels there seems to be some sense of replacement. Mark has the temple of hands contrasted with the temple not built with hands. The physical vs. the spiritual. The others struggle to interpret this. To get his own interpretation in, John has to play with the base saying. The Body of Christ becomes the Temple of God. In John's mind, the Jews brought the temple destruction upon themselves.

6

Two Births
John 3:1–16

"These things are written that you may believe that Jesus is the Christ, the Son of God, and that believing you may have life in his name" (John 20:31).

This year we are scaling a great promontory, the highest peak in the Bible, which is the Gospel of John. With every cut-back trail, at every rest point, atop every lookout, with every majestic view, this spiritual gospel will address you with the choice of freedom, with the ongoing need to choose, and in—choosing—to find the life of belonging and meaning, personal identity and global imagination.

The interpretation of the Gospel of John is a dangerous job. Luther recalled most carefully what the church has realized most generally, which is that for the Bible to be rightly heard, for the preacher to handle the word of truth, one first needs some understanding of what the passage meant in its first hearing. What did its writer mean to say, and what did its hearers or readers first hear or read? To the extent that we have some handle on this first incarnation of truth, we may be able to apply the meaning of the Bible to our own time and place.

It helps us to understand the prophets of Israel to learn the history through which they lived. We can appreciate the wisdom books when we know a little about their background. The first three gospels become meaningful to us, as we come to grips with their historical struggles. The letters

Two Births

of Paul take existential shape for us when we know something about his life, his missionary journeys, his relationships with others.

John's history is in many ways the toughest for us to understand. Two primary theories have been advanced in the last hundred years, and I am an interpretative child of both. One emphasizes Judaism, one Hellenism. One emphasizes Gnosticism, one apocalypticism. One emphasizes space, one time. How are we to judge? This year I propose we use them both and hope for the best.

GRACE DURING DISLOCATION

Nicodemus is a ruler of Israel. He is a teacher and a religious leader. He has stayed by the mother tongue, the mother tradition, the mother religion. He has stayed in the womb. He has never left home. But you cannot become yourself if you never leave home. To become who you are you have to go somewhere else. Not always geographically. Jesus never traveled more than fifty miles from Bethlehem.

John is concerned with Spirit, not speculation; with the artistry of the everyday, not with Armageddon; with the church, not with calamity.

You have already learned the heart of this text: that Nicodemus and Jesus are representative types of religion—past and future, law and liberty; that the word for Spirit and wind is the same word and that John can and does mean both; that the command to be born from above is plural, you all, or as they say in the South, "all y'all."

John turns his gaze now away from inherited religion to focus on culture, away from Judaism to address the Gnostics, who wanted fervently to be saved by knowing "whence we come and whither we are going." Says Jesus, "The Spirit blows where it wills."

Cultural religion says, "You know whence you came." Spirit says, "You do not."

A pre-Christian culture says, "You know where you are going." John says, "Not so: Those who are born of the spirit, of them you do not know whence or whither."

John's neighbors affirm: we know whence and whither. John replies: not so of those born of the spirit. You are left with confusing liberty, the assorted decisions of a complex life. You are free. In Christ, you are set free. In Spirit, you do not know, you believe.

Here stands Nicodemus, a man in full. A religious leader, really a representative of the best in spiritual inheritance. He ventures out at night, choking from the challenge of truth, new truth, full truth. Where he has been will not take him where he needs to go. He is a person on the edge of a great dislocation: he is about to make up his mind to change his mind about something that really matters.

Some years ago the Christian Century ran a series of articles by nominally great religious leaders, titled "How My Mind Has Changed." A disappointing series. One found really little significant change of mind in any of them. Typical of preachers—stubborn, self-assured; it takes one to know one.

But here stands Nicodemus, a courageous soul. He is facing the great heartache of maturity. You face it too. He is facing out over a great ravine, a great gorge, a great precipice. On a matter of mortal meaning, he is making up his mind whether to change his mind. That takes real courage.

Benjamin Franklin found this courage when he left behind his beloved Europe and his confidence in diplomacy to take up arms with his fellow colonists. Abraham Lincoln found this courage when he finally moved to side fully with the abolitionists. Robert F. Kennedy, then the junior Senator from the Empire State, found this same courage when he left the Cold War mind of his own past and of his dear brother to oppose the war in Vietnam. Sometimes you get to a point where you have to make up your mind whether to change your mind. To face facts, as Nicodemus courageously faced the works, signs, deeds of Jesus the Christ. It takes great courage to change your mind about something of mortal significance. In fact, it may not even be humanly possible, apart from grace.

It means admitting error. We would sooner be proven sinful than stupid. John takes us to higher ground. We have an easier time receiving forgiveness for sin than we do receiving grace for change.

Yet did not Samson finally see the error of his ways with Delilah? Did not David finally see his mistake with Bathsheba? Did not Peter break down and weep on understanding his betrayal? Did not Paul find the courage, in earshot of unmistakable evidence, to cease persecution, and in fact, to suffer it for Christ's sake? The Gospel of Jesus Christ is one of persistent failure, of persistence through failure, and of the grace to make up one's mind to change one's mind.

It takes more courage to lay down the broadsword of misjudgment than to cling to the spear of stubborn willfulness.

Two Births

FREEDOM FOLLOWING DISAPPOINTMENT

The author of John had to drink the cup of disappointment in its most bitter form. His dream died. It is hard to have a dream die. A dream deferred is like a raisin in the sun.

While every life carries secret sorrows, there are serious and lasting disappointments that can shake the foundations of life, heart, and soul. It is one thing to have your favorite team lose in the World Series, or to have your chosen candidate lose at the polls. It is another to face the lasting hurt of a dream deferred. What has happened has happened. And the way out of this disappointment is the way through marked by the road signs of freedom. Man is born to disappointment as the sparks fly upward.

Faced with hard news, individuals and groups may respond in one of three ways: blame, deny, ignore. Who is at fault? It cannot be true. True it is, but it does not matter. "This is her fault." "Things are fine, you are mistaken." "Oh, that doesn't matter."

Yet this Gospel offers freedom following disappointment. Freedom in emotion and confidence and vision.

Have you looked recently at your emotional life? Spelunking in among the damp stalactites and dank stalagmites of the visceral cave of emotion can bring exhilarating freedom. Have you shown a flashlight on anger, fear, sorrow, or joy lately? Emotion fires freedom.

So does confidence. What you lose in Christ in certainty, you more than recover in confidence. Confidence is born of obedience, the obedience of faith.

One of our greatest lasting disappointments is the hard truth that the past is immutable. What is done is done.

My cyclist friend went over his handlebars head first at twenty miles an hour. As he tumbled forward into bone breaking pain he thought, "This cannot be happening. Where is the rewind button on this tape?" But facts are stubborn things, as John Adams said.

One man begins his group meeting by bowing his head and saying softly, "I always wanted a better past." After a moment, he raises his head and affirms, "Now I have a better past, one day at a time."

You cannot change the past and all its disappointment. But you can live in freedom from the past, by honestly facing it, and moving on.

Here is good news! John faced disappointment and so can we. John admitted disappointment and so can we. John replaced disappointment over the past with the freedom to decide for a new future. John had the courage fully to face the delay in Christ's return, the disappointment of the earliest church's highest hope. That same courage became the heart of his gospel: the courage to be, in freedom. This same courage can become yours as well.

A global village needs this for salvation: a global village green, full of grace and freedom.

Here is the point of John's plundering of the Gnostics: the Gnostic dualism of fate has become a dualism of decision.

Faith's freedom from the world is the decision, the choice, the selection, the predilection, the preferential option to love.

These things are spoken that you may believe that Jesus is the Christ, the Son of God, and that believing you may have life in his name.

This week you can choose to grow in faith, and so find a fuller part of your second identity. This week you can choose to grow in love, and so open a fuller part of the world's imagination.

Faith is personal commitment to an unverifiable truth. It involves a leap.

Faith is an objective uncertainty grasped with subjective certainty. It involves a leap.

Faith is the way to salvation, a real identity and a rich imagination. But it does involve a leap. Now is the time to jump.

Love is faith's freedom in the world.

Love is faith's freedom from the world.

Love is faith's freedom to transform the world

All of us are better when we are loved.

NOTES FROM RAYMOND BROWN'S LECTURES ON JOHN
Union Theological Seminary
Spring 1978

March 14, 1978: Nicodemus

This brings us to the problem of inadequate Christians, or "crypto-Christians." These are probably also baptized, confessing Christians whose faith John still does not trust. In the midst of this question of adequate faith, Nicodemus will arrive on the scene. For John, Nicodemus' faith is not wrong, it is just not adequate. In John's mind, Jesus is the only one ever to have come from God. The Nicodemus dialogue may be a description of the form of Christianity which John opposes.

Jesus was certainly a teacher, but that is just not enough. These titles are wrong if you stop there. Jesus was more than a teacher. Ignatius always

Two Births

worries about those within Jewish Christianity who think of Jesus as a great teacher, but not as the Word spoken from God's Silence. But there is hope left for Nicodemus, who is "coming out of the night and into the light."

How do we enter the Kingdom of Heaven? You must become like a little child? Those who are more dependent are more open. Those who are independent are less open. Utter dependence: you must be begotten by God. Here baptism, as with Paul, is an imitation of Christ. To born again or to be born from above is radical! But our questions were not in the author's mind. The sacraments are visible things which serve to represent invisible things. Eternal life is God's own life given to human beings, and you cannot be a "child" without that gift. It is a divine begetting. For Augustine "unless" meant there was no exception. His logical conclusion was therefore that "all must be baptized" and therefore little children unbaptized are in "limbo." Now, did John ever think of such a problem? Probably not. One principle involves human life from a human parent. God's life comes from God. But this is not universal. American Protestant individualism therefore reads this individualistically, "God is my personal savior." But a first century Jewish author would never have thought in any other way than thinking about the "salvation of a whole people." The real issue is: how do you become a part of a saved people? Answer: by being born from above.

There is a parallel in Luke 18:18. A member of the Sanhedrin asks about eternal life. Matthew 25 is another example. *Born Again*: this refers to a divine engendering. Male or female? Nicodemus however misunderstands both words. The Greek word *anothen*: from above or again? Nicodemus thinks "again" but John means "from above" (though early Christians did themselves speak so). One enters by divine action. This is the main point. Why God's people? Because God has chosen his people. The sense and meaning of grace has changed. The divine begetting creates people of God and children of God.

Here the Gnostic background is possible. True life in John's sense does go in a Gnostic direction. "By nature divine"—this is Gnostic. But is John saying that? No. Rather, we become children of God through God's graciousness. Now the immortal soul was later deemed naturally immortal. This is immortality from creation. Not in John. Natural birth is "of the flesh." This is not pejorative, but in itself it cannot reach to God.

1. Begetting. 2. Breathing upon. Spirit. Breath. Wind. God is breathing again. The ancients would have been likely to take this far more literally than do we. John has no such sense of a giant sacramental system working through the chapters of the Gospel. Baptism is your eternal birth. Water from within is what brings the baptism, making present a particular action of God. You feed things through the Eucharist. How does this fit into John's

conception of Jesus? Jesus is the source of God's life. The life giver, in and through all the sacraments, is Jesus. In the Nicodemus story, John is talking to both insiders and outsiders.

The play on words, spirit and wind is central. There is different lighting at different points in this scene. "We testify to what we know." John 3:13: Elijah and Elisha are being attacked (along with Enoch and Moses) here. Or are they? Elijah went up to heaven. What about the horses and chariots? Can anyone go into God's presence? Some say yes, some say no. Proverbs 30:3 comes to mind. Only Jesus has seen God. Jesus came from God in the first place. (The order of this works against a later Gnostic tradition.) We have to recognize the unpredictability of Johannine symbols. The serpent images may be from the Old Testament or from Targums (Aramaic translations). Hebrew is to Aramaic as Spanish is to Italian.

The transcendence of God is very important for John. *Memra*: Word. The word of God is present. A bronze serpent was kept in the temple in Jerusalem. Such a symbol leaves itself open to folk lore. John uses that symbol for Jesus on the cross. There is the presence of God in both. The "lifting up of the Son of Man" is a central image for John. There are three forms of "lifting up" passages in John, and another in Mark 8 and 9. Is there not then some relation between these two?

Community and Spirit are both given at the foot of the cross. Jesus brings eternal life.

3:17 Realized eschatology. Three messiahs? As in Trinitarian discussion? Judgment in John is not a matter of sheep and goats. Rather Jesus' very presence brings judgment. The coming of the Son of Man brings a crisis. People judge themselves.

7

Two Biographies
John 4

"THESE THINGS ARE WRITTEN that you may believe that Jesus is the Christ, the Son of God, and that believing you may have life in his name" (John 20: 31).

In old Castile, northwest of Madrid, out on the arid, brown central Spanish highland, you may look toward the mountain range once toured by Robert Jordan and his muñequita, before his fictitious but nonetheless atoning, salvific, Christlike death, at the hands of Franco's soldiers. The mountain range, high and in its own way majestic, looks very much like a woman asleep, so the Segovianos call her or it or the mountain *"la mujer muerta."* As I and Robert Jordan and perhaps you also have found, it is a day's long hard hike up into the Castillian mountains.

The Gospel of John is such a mountain range, high and lifted up. It challenges our endurance. It tests our orienteering. It measures our preparation and execution. There is an exacting and perfecting quality to this Gospel, similar to the exacting and perfecting character of fellowship at this church. With every cut-back trail, at every rest point, atop every lookout, with every majestic view, this spiritual gospel will address you in the midst of two crucial battles, those of dislocation and disappointment, with the good news of grace and freedom, with the ongoing need to choose, and—in choosing—to find the life of belonging and meaning, personal identity and global imagination.

THE COURAGEOUS GOSPEL

I realize belatedly that the most lastingly formative aspect of my theological education, at Union Seminary in the City of New York, in the years of the Carter administration, was the preaching of William Sloane Coffin. In his recent collection of wisdom sayings, Coffin has a typically urbane, piercing word to say about hypocrisy. It is as close to the mind of Jesus in John 4 as I think you can come: "Generally we try to pass ourselves off as something that is special in our hearts and minds, something we yearn for, something beyond us. That's rather touching."

We all have at least two life stories, the one we publicize and the one we privatize. They both have meaning. Nor should one be eliminated or the other. In this chapter, following on the opening given in our lesson today, Jesus addresses the two biographies of a woman from Samaria. . . Go call your husband. . . I have no husband. . . You are right in saying you have no husband for you have had five husbands and he whom you now have is not your husband. . . As people and as a culture, we have more than one story to tell, more than one biography. Two biographies, like the woman at the well. Our best foot and then the other foot. The gospel this morning, a saving and healing truth for you, is that Jesus the Christ knows both biographies, all our stories, and loves us still.

"We put our best foot forward, but it is the other one that needs the attention."

The Jesus of the Fourth Gospel is not easily blended with his counterparts in Matthew, Mark and Luke. Rather than projecting our own needs for uniformity out onto these ancient, holy, mysterious, puzzling and powerful writings, we first to listen to them. Listen. We need to let the Bible speak to us, as Robert McAffee Brown used to say. The Jesus of John 4 sees into others' minds. He knows things without being told. He divines the secrets hidden in the heart. He stands alone and in public view with a woman, a Samaritan woman, a troubled Samaritan woman. This Jesus is guided along in a lengthy mystagogical conversation, full of riddles, double entendres, hidden meanings, mysterious silences. He offers living water. In none of this does one find a single correspondence with the earlier three quests for Jesus in Matthew, Mark, and Luke. John's is an entirely different Jesus. So, asked a bright teenager in September, which is true?

And here is my answer. They all are. They all truly represent the actual historical experience of Jesus Christ, crucified and risen, which various little communities in his fledging church did have of him. All four are historically accurate. With accuracy they describe the Jesus known in the actual lives of the communities of Mark, forty years after Calvary; Matthew, fifty-five years after Calvary; Luke, sixty years after Calvary; and John ninety years after

Calvary. They give us grace and freedom to sense Jesus, as they did, present among us, as He was among them. He is risen. He is not here. See the place where they laid him.

The account of the woman at the well provides one of two eyes needed to see. The other is the experience of Jesus, crucified and risen, which John knew and felt and preached. This Jesus, in 120 AD, knew his people. They felt his knowing presence. They felt his probing spirit. So do we. They faced his clairvoyant candor. So do we. They acknowledged his healing voice. So do we. A voice like no other—equanimous and serene. They sensed his love. They preached his love. They shared his love. Even across ranges of personal, intimate, generic confusion. And so do we. It is not the water of the well that slakes our thirst for salvation, but the water of eternal life. This water bathes both of our feet, both of our biographies, both the one we put forward and the one we hold back.

GRACE DURING DISLOCATION

Young soldiers in their first year of service, at home or abroad, know about the dislocation that comes with growing up. So do their parents and aunts and uncles. Young women and men settling in at college for the first year know about the dislocation that comes with developing that second identity, that real self, yourself. At mid-life a man finds that he is ready to make up his mind to change his mind. Dislocation is mainly, but not only, the work of salvation for youth. Ask the eighty-year-old who sells her house. Or the ninety-year-old who keeps his. Salvation is not a matter of chronology, only, but of ontology and theology and psychology.

Our lasting health will rely in part on grace uncovered during dislocation. That John's Gospel emerges out of the tide, the great sea change, of dislocation is itself a profound affirmation of grace. If this community, disoriented and discarded and dismembered amid Jews and Gnostics in 120 AD, could receive courage in change, then so can we. We need not fear change. You need not fear change. For down in the depths of dislocation, John discovered grace.

The most pervasive social change of the last thirty years, across our culture, lies in the rearrangements related to gender and to sexuality. The social distance between me and my grandfather is dwarfed by that between my grandmother and my daughter. My grandmother learned to drive using a buggy whip and sitting behind a team of horses. My daughter flies across the continent week by week. Elsie was born thirty years before she gained the right to vote. Emily rocks the vote. Gramma was one of a very small percentage of women to graduate from college. Emily runs the place. Elsie raised children, cooked meals, supported the church, and listened. My daughter works, leads, earns, and speaks. Women are still undergoing the tears and strains of pervasive social dislocation. Nor is feminism finished. Nor is equality achieved. Nor does freedom fully ring, not for women in America nor certainly for women around the globe.

Yet with this righteous dislocation, every bit as necessary as that which liberated John, has come an undertow of anxiety, much of it related to our understanding of sexuality. Sex, physical genital intimacy, is not what it used to be. And women are still largely paying the bill. In the great sea of sexual dislocation, certainly alive in the text of John 4, is there any grace to be found?

What are we teaching our children about sex? Do we happily and strongly affirm the covenant of marriage? Do our sentiments and advisements short of marriage lead, for the most part, to preparation for healthy marriage? Across the gender divides, can we still be responsible not only *to* but also *for* one another, without yet patronizing or prevaricating? Why are young men so largely absent from our churches?

I have no word of the Lord on this, but what insight I have I share.

You are a grandfather or grandmother. With rosy cheeks and a smile, before dinner, you may recall a harvest moon, an evening of affection, with gentle hints at what chivalry can mean, did mean, will mean.

You are a mom or dad. Books with information can be bought and shared. But priceless and purchasing power is what comes next. Your sense of gratitude for life. Your honest joy, happiness, and pleasure in intimacy. Your witness to the vulnerabilities of such closeness. Your conviction that God made humans as sexual beings and means to help us as sexual beings to become as humane as possible. Then stop. Look. Listen. Listen. Listen.

You are an aunt, uncle, teacher, neighbor, youth counselor. Bless you. Do you realize that you are, in trust, safe space and trusted freedom for younger person who may need to rely on you?

You are such a youth. Remember these five things: You are made in the image and likeness of God. You are precious. You know the difference between loving someone and using someone. You need not be afraid to stand apart from the crowd. You have right to sense how you are feeling, what you are thinking. Does this seem right to me? Does this feel right for me? If you make a mistake, well, remember forgiveness, consider what you have learned, shake the dust from your feet and move ahead. And you can also, if the moment is right, quote Anne Lamotte: "No is a complete sentence."

You are a church on East Avenue. Say this: "Jesus is among us, speaking and healing. His grace tells us that the Word became flesh, that we are

Two Biographies

made in God's image, that physical pleasure and sexual intimacy are God's good gifts, that we can live with integrity, that we can become self-aware, that we can learn from but not be defined by our mistakes, that the covenant of marriage provides the best and surest and healthiest and safest location for sex amid the great dislocations of our time."

Life is good. The Word became flesh and dwelt among us. This is the ringing affirmation of the Fourth Gospel. Physical life, in all its panoply of intimacy and estrangement, is good.

FREEDOM FOLLOWING DISAPPOINTMENT

Now that we have come to chapter 4, we need to name and regret a biblical disappointment. If we are going to read John at all, and hear the gospel of John together, then we need to be honest about a scriptural disappointment. As with all of our lives, the Bible itself, the very Word of God, does nonetheless harbor disappointments. Hear the good news: there is even freedom following religious disappointment.

Sometimes our great strengths occasion our most glaring weaknesses. If John is the Bible's great strength, it would then be possible that here too we might find great weakness. And we do.

Oh, I give no ground with regard to the truth of Scripture. The Bible is freedom's book, the pulpit is freedom's voice, the church is freedom's defense. It is also occasionally true that the Bible is a holy disappointment. Nowhere in Scripture is the height of Christian freedom more powerfully depicted than in John, and yet, at the same time, nowhere is the Bible more of a disappointment.

This gospel is anti-Semitic, at least to our ears after 1940. It was composed in the white heat of one small group leaving a synagogue in order freely to worship what the synagogue could only understand as a second God. It was the charge of ditheism, though denied and controverted, which moved John's little church out into a free and frightening future. So the Gospel of John speaks roughly of its Semitic mother religion, of its own tradition. The living water is meant to surpass the dead water of Jacob, of Jacob's well. Notice the way the writer refers with oral scare quotes to "the Jews," like Robert E. Lee calling Yankees "those people." Notice the dismissive explication, here and elsewhere, of Jewish rites. Notice that even though salvation is from the Jews, his own people "received him not." Notice Jesus saying, "All who came before me are thieves and robbers." We have an obligation to notice. And to regret, to express contrition and compunction. These words from this gospel have done immeasurable harm, from Augustine to

THE COURAGEOUS GOSPEL

Luther to the Third Reich to today, and that is a spiritual disappointment. As Christianity puts its best foot forward, it is really the other one that needs attention. We have two biographies ourselves. That of persecuted, and that of persecutor. Of all religious bodies, we have the most work to do with regard to anti-Semitism.

How are we to find freedom following such spiritual disappointment? By facing facts, by learning from our experience of success and failure, by moving ahead: The fact is that Christianity has been pervasively guilty of latent and patent anti-Semitism and the Gospel of John has been one of its sources. We have and can learn from this failure, by carefully monitoring our use of religious language. And we can move ahead. John is guiding us toward a global vision, an ecumenical spirituality, a universal Truth, a global village green, space for grace and time for freedom. And our Jewish brothers and sisters can teach us to continue, with Jacob, to wrestle with God.

In 1978 Jan and I had dinner with Elie Wiesel in the home of Robert Mcafee Brown. Wiesel survived the death camps and spent 10 silent years in Paris before writing *Night*. Its pathos, its witness, its question, its challenge need to stay before this generation as well:

> Where is God? Where is He? The third rope was still moving, the child was still alive . . . For more than half and hour he stayed there, struggling between life and death, dying in slow agony under our eyes. And we had to look him full in the face. He was still alive when I passed in front of him. His tongue was still red, his eyes not yet glazed . . . Behind me I heard the same man asking: Where is God now? . . . and I heard a voice within me answer Him. . . . Where is He? Here he is—He is hanging here on this gallows.[1]

These things are spoken that you may believe that Jesus is the Christ, the Son of God, and that believing you may have life in his name.

This week you can choose to grow in faith, and so find a fuller part of your second identity. This week you can choose to grow in love, and so open a fuller part of the world's imagination.

Faith is personal commitment to an unverifiable truth. It involves a leap.

Faith is an objective uncertainty grasped with subjective certainty. It involves a leap.

Faith is the way to salvation, a real identity and a rich imagination. But it does involve a leap.

Now is the time to jump.

All of us are better when we are loved.

1. Elie Wiesel, *Night* (New York: Hill & Wang, 1960) 62.

NOTES FROM RAYMOND BROWN'S LECTURES ON JOHN
Union Theological Seminary
Spring 1978

March 30, 1978: The Samaritan Woman

We turn now to the longer narratives. Here John is at his best. Against the many theories of multiple sources, we also must mention the remarkable, flowing nature of the longer narratives. Until now, John has dealt with disciples, Jewish believers, and Nicodemus. Now the disciples are spectators.

Samaritan interlude: there is a possible historical basis for this material. The story may be a parable for the story of the conversion of Samaria. There is nothing in the other gospels about Samaria. Therefore, this story is probably an integral part of the self-understanding of the Johannine community.

Question: *Was this Samaritan influx the straw that broke the camel's back of relations with Judaism?* Ditheism? Further, in chapter 8, Jesus is called a Samaritan. So, this may be autobiographical. 4:4 by the way is not meant to be geographical. Sychar: Mount Gerizim was the central place for northern worship. Jacob's well was given to Joseph, the Samaritan hero. (In Steven's Acts speech they are buried in Gerizim.) This recalls the meeting of Isaac and Rebecca. The question, then, is a very natural one. Where is the true God worshipped?

How far should one press this symbolism? The sixth hour would have been about noon. (RB doesn't think much of this). The conflict between Jews and Samaritans is also recorded in Sirach (a great rabbinic text). Again: RB thinks that there were Samaritans in the community of the fourth gospel. The dialogue is very carefully built up. Here as elsewhere in John's writing there is the enactment of the challenge to believe: you must be open to the gift that only he can give.

"Living waters" refers to flowing waters (7:38–39). But all of this terminology also refers to the Law in Jewish and Samaritan thought, and in Wisdom. Jesus is also speaking of himself as the living water (as in Chapter 6). Food and bread are also wisdom symbols. Jesus is all that the Old Testament says about God. Wisdom, Law, and Word are all found together in the intertestamental works. All this is still true, the gospel argues, but now it is tied to Jesus. Both sides use the same language, except one embodies it in a person, and the other in the law.

At a second level, the symbolism of the Old Testament here also interprets the sacraments of the community, baptism in particular. He uses the same language to refer to two different things. John may here be worried about the community having too static a notion of what they do sacramentally. Therefore he ties in community action with things Jesus did in his own life. Jesus' talk with the Samaritan woman is concomitant with his talk with people in John's community.

John never argues purely polemically. He wants in the end to say something meaningful to the community. Purpose and direction are both inward and outward for John. *(A crucial point lightly touched)*. At first he wrote against outsiders, but second he wrote about the nature of their own life. Give me this water..."

4:18—The husbands depict the wife as not only Samaritan, but also one who even for Samaria is below par. Of course Jesus knows exactly what type of woman she is. But this is no problem to grace, if the woman will come to the Son of Man. "I can see you are a prophet."

The heart of this scripture is the question of where God shall be worshipped. This again is reminiscent of Steven in Acts. God is not worshipped in a particular place. This is a break from Jewish Christianity and from Paul. Jerusalem has no longer any importance. There is a replacement theology at work in this gospel. God is Spirit. So we must worship God in spirit and in truth. You cannot worship Him unless you have His spirit. Both Jerusalem and Gerizim are out, not for worship by those "begotten from above." Here again we have the conflict and contrast between the flesh and the spirit. This relativizes all the other questions.

The final author wants people to know that the Samaritans, though accepted, neither provide basis for nor constitute the heart of the group, the community. Their theology—John's theology—is preserved through Judaism, and is a fulfillment of its promises.

This is no crude notion of baptism. Individuals must still confess Jesus as the Christ.

Now the disciples arrive. They have had nothing to do with this. The disciples did not convert the woman. (Perhaps this means that the disciples did not start John's community). There is a remarkable role given to the woman here. Do others resent this? In Asia Minor in the late second century the Montanists do have female spirited prophets, which is opposed to the practice of the rest of the church. Does this have some roots in John's time? The debate over the status and role of woman goes a long way back in time.

Interchangeable symbols: food and water. Here the harvest is already taking place. The harvest follows immediately. Not so much "one sows and another reaps." Maybe so with John the Baptist. But here, the woman sowed but the disciples will reap. Is the Samaritan belief positive? Maybe they are sign types: we know this is the savior.

8

Two Blessings
John 6

"THESE THINGS ARE WRITTEN that you may believe that Jesus is the Christ, the Son of God, and that believing you may have life in his name" (John 20:31).

Our New Testament was formed around questions that needed good answers in the life of the early church. The letters of Paul provide such answers to such questions. Will those who die before Christ returns be saved? Thessalonians. How do we teach those who have faith to live in ways that become faith? Corinthians. Must a Gentile become a Jew in order to become a Christian? Galatians. How are we to think about Jesus Christ? Romans. Is there a joyful way to live through conflict? Philippians. Does faith involve what one owns? Philemon. Paul writes his answers in the years 50–58, and he does so with no reference to Jesus. No parable, no teaching, no life incident, no birth story, no healing, nothing. On what does he rely? On the cross and resurrection, and on the spirit, and on his own experience and reason.

Some decades later the church had more questions. These found responses in the Gospels, narrative responses that used traditions about Jesus to answer questions of the day. How are men and women to relate? What is the place of children? Can we have any guidance about money? How and for what are we to hope? Who shall not have and who shall have authority? Does the Old Testament count at all? In answer to these issues and questions the churches of Mark and Matthew and Luke recalled what they could, many years later, of sayings about and a few sayings of Jesus. The Gospels were formed in the church, for the express purpose of answering saving questions.

John comes along many years later. He plays the old tunes, but in a new way. Did you ever hear Louis Armstrong play some of the patriotic hymns? Or Ray Charles sing the national anthem? It is the same, sort of. It is like Mark Trotter said about his 100 year old axe: "It is still the same axe, my grandfather's axe. It has just had many different handles and many different heads. But it is the same." Sort of.

So here in chapter 6, John plays the same traditional music, to a jazz beat. He relates again the well traveled tales of miraculous feeding and salvation on the sea. A new manna and a new Jonah. But listen to his horn, with a New Orleans kick; to his piano, with a little bit of the blues.

He has something new to emphasize about two fish and five barley loaves. He has something new to report about a boat and a storm and a dark night. He has two blessings to deliver! The Fourth Gospel is really a stitched-together series of sermons which emerged in a church that found freedom following disappointment and grace amid dislocation. He himself is gracious and free. If the earliest Christians could be free savingly to apply their tradition to new times, we can too! Two blessings are ours today, as well.

FREEDOM FOLLOWING DISAPPOINTMENT

Sometimes churches, groups, even families need the discipline of serious editing. Here is a young man's confession: "In pain and with great disappointment I finally let go of my family. Everything among and between us had become toxic. Everything I tasted and touched had become a kind of poison. It was all unhealthy. I tried for years to help but my help was not helpful. There are just so many times you can cringe and cry when those you love make terrible, costly, irreparable mistakes, after you have warned and cautioned and cajoled. So the best, the very best thing I could do for all was to leave. And I did."

And in that disappointment is when and where he found freedom.

GRACE DURING DISLOCATION

In John 6, food carries memory. The feast of Sukkoth, in Judaism, an autumn meal consumed under a partial roof, symbolizes a meal with memory. Surely the feast of Passover, with its herbs and vegetables and spices and questions conveys memory in a meal. One of three great meanings of Holy Communion is remembrance. Holiday meals, Thanksgiving and Christmas, are meals laden with memory, more laden with memory even than with calories, if that be possible.

I turn again to Marcel Proust, whose thousands of print pages burst forth from the memory of a long lost moment of tea and Madeleine cakes, the cakes swirling dreamily in the tea. Meal and memory.

The other day, because I had some coupons, I stopped at the Subway to by sandwiches for my class lunch. Fewer came to lunch than I had thought, so, later in the afternoon, the extra tuna sub did beckon sufficiently to be consumed. Somewhere in the late afternoon of a non-descript autumn Monday, I found myself slowly and a little guiltily enjoying an extra sandwich.

Did you ever find yourself just sort of in a strange reverie, carried along by an avalanche of physical memory, occasioned in a simple meal?

When I was sixteen, in the middle of the autumn we were dislocated or relocated to a new home by the remarkable ministrations of the Methodist church. It was November, and we all suddenly had a new house, a new neighborhood, a new room, a new city, a new school, a new church, and not a single friend. The school was a large urban school that was in the throes of serious unrest, some chaos and violence, and yet still with a fine building, faculty, and program. I have not thought, or felt, clearly about those November days of 1970 in a long, long, time. Maybe I have never done so.

For some reason the humble tuna-fish and bread carried me fully back. . .

There is a teenager alone in the cafeteria. For some days he goes alone to lunch, after trigonometry and before chemistry. He is not very artfully dressed. Some of that is the culture of the day and some is just who he is. He knows really no one. He is white in largely black school, overtall and awkward, hoping in vain against hope to make the basketball team, bright but not too eager to show it, curiously glad for a new and strange city environment and deeply lonely at the dislocation of the move. You can see him on these many days at the first lunch period. He sits with his back to the wall, close enough to some others not to appear solo. The school—and by extension the world around—run quite well without any recognition of his being there. He feels something that is hard and throat-lodged and aching and chilling and strange. He is homesick for a home that no longer exists. He hurts too much to laugh and he is too tall and adult–looking to cry.

In a month or so a group of other young men, Chris Bennett and Joel Burdick and Chris Heimbach, will somehow oddly include him in lunch, as if he had been there for the previous ten years, which he had not. But right now he is out on the boat, and shore is a long way off. And a shared meal seems like it will never come and if it did it might just be too awesome and too wonderful to receive. So he leans the chair against the wall. He watches the racial tensions and hatreds. He memorizes the periodic table. He tries not to look conspicuous in any single way. He looks at the girls and wonders what he could possibly say to any of them. He looks forward to basketball. He feels what it takes a young heart really to feel.

Every day he carries to his back table a brown sack. This is a full meal, fairly hastily but utterly lovingly prepared in the earlier morning before the two mile walk to school. It is the same lunch every day. Bread and fish. Two full sandwiches. Some chips. Carrots. Cookies, sometimes made at home. And it will take another thirty-five years for him to fully appreciate—to taste—what he could already feel against the cafeteria wall. At least here, in this meal, for all the depressing dislocation and frightening foreignness and leavened loneliness all around, here was something to eat. Prepared with love. As reliable as the sunrise and the seasons. Grace, in the midst of dislocation. The sandwiches come slowly out of their tight wrap. They taste the same, reassuringly the same. Maybe, day by day, this is really all we get, a taste.

Simple bread and fish. The five barley loaves and two fish of this complex Gospel passage clearly continued to carry for John such a memory. John is looking back many years, through the lens of a tradition of a feeding and a boat ride. He makes his changes in the way the story goes. More than at first you might think. But it is the memory of the meal that carries him here. Two fish, five loaves, lots of people, all satisfied, baskets to spare. Grace. And the meal is the ticket.

What John is able to see, so many years later, is more than those five thousand could ever see. He could see the stature of a Christ whose grace lived in dislocation and whose freedom survived disappointment. He could begin to sense the marvelous self-gift of the God-beyond-God who was made known in Christ. He could ponder, generations later, the enduring influence and power of the Bread of Life, for whom even the cross—no *especially* the cross—is a moment of glory. He could accumulate the other stories of meal and memory, the other experiences of the earliest church, both the heart of Peter and the mind of Paul, and begin to piece together the puzzle of providence. John could look back and see that through it Love did abide. This love. . .freedom in the world, freedom from the world, freedom to make the world a better place.

And so, too, the teenager, now fifty, can look back and see that through it Love did abide. He did not know it then. He could not. How could he? Look at him in those dungarees and long hair and faded shirt. How could that awkward teenager ever possibly have known, feasting on bread and fish, that the very pain of dislocation would give him his whole life: a real home, a girl to marry, a sense of purpose, a community of faith, a voice to lift, seven beautiful pulpits, three children, and a darn good jump shot. He could not possibly know that then.

Nor can you know now what grace will emerge in the heart of your current dislocation.

This is why John says something very odd, but very true. Your work is not your work. Work is not the real work. To believe. To have faith. To carry yourself and your inner being, and your soul, and your chin in a way that show you and the world around you that you may be the loneliest teenager in the world, but somebody packed you an awesome lunch, and don't you forget it.

These things are spoken that you may believe that Jesus is the Christ, the Son of God, and that believing you may have life in his name.

This week you can choose to grow in faith, and so find a fuller part of your second identity. This week you can choose to grow in love, and so open a fuller part of the world's imagination.

Faith is personal commitment to an unverifiable truth. It involves a leap.

Faith is an objective uncertainty grasped with subjective certainty. It involves a leap.

Faith is the way to salvation, a real identity and a rich imagination. But it does involve a leap.

Now is the time to jump.

All of us are better when we are loved.

NOTES FROM RAYMOND BROWN'S LECTURES ON JOHN

Union Theological Seminary
Spring 1978

March 30–April 4, 1978: John 6

John 6 reflects both inner and outer misunderstandings. There is a shift from water to food. Chapters 4 and 5 are about water.

The importance of this story is part of the Elijah\Elisha parallelism. 6:14 ("This is indeed the prophet. . .") is a remnant. John may have older echoes than the others! There were probably three or four different accounts of the feeding of the five thousand in early tradition. In theology, the so-called nature miracles are often too quickly shoved aside. Yet this feeding is by far the best attested miracle: two in Mark; two in Matthew; one in Luke; one in John. John's source seems to be a third, independent source. (Of course, no one in the first century would have made the nature\healing distinction.) Twenty Loaves of Barley are connected to Elisha (2 Kings 4:22).

In all the narratives, there is some liturgizing done. There is anticipation of the Eucharist. Does John emphasize this more than the others? In the Didache, chapters 9 and 10 are very similar (except the cup comes first). The gathering of the crumbs may be Eucharistic too.

Bread is scattered upon the mountain. Also, the fish image is often used in early explanations of the Eucharist. Now this also may reflect Moses feeding the people in the desert. There is a great deal of symbolism in and behind all of this. Also, the walking on water may be tied loosely to the parting of the Red Sea. Is the great "I Am" a return to the Pentateuch? Or to Isaiah 51?

John 6: 22–24 is probably a polyglot of verses. John 6:25 is probably a two level question. "The Son of Man" will give you another type of food. Have faith in him whom he has sent. Most important: believe in Jesus Christ as the one sent by/from God, *because* he has eternal life to give. He can give God's own life.

John 3: 30–33. Peter Borgen, *Bread from Heaven*. He uses a homiletic technique.

A recent study by Eileen Guilden analyzes worship in the Fourth Gospel. Her argument is that the gospels were designed according to a Jewish lectionary. Dubious, says RB (but he mentions it!) Guilden agrees with the above, and adds a three year cycle of the text. So, in her view, the author of John is playing on the synagogue lectionary. The law is most sacred, with the prophetic commentary second. The problem is that we do not have enough hard evidence to support her theory.

There was lots of eschatological hope around a second manna deposit. Like Moses, like manna. Where are the signs of the Messiah? Here we enter into an exegetical thicket. He is not Moses but God. The Hebrew *ntn* "give" (Nathan), give in text. Jesus says "he gives." Wrong He, Wrong Tense, Wrong Bread. My Real Father Really Gives The Real Bread. The People who ate manna died: those who come to me will never die. Jesus gives life to the world.

This chapter sets the model for Christian liturgy. Wisdom feeding (readings) plus sacramental feeding. Luther and Calvin emphasized the Eucharist. Their followers did not. Likewise, the Roman Catholics lost sight of

Two Blessings

the sermon. The two traditions here are dividing unnecessarily. (RB thinks the split was unnecessary).

Even some of the disciples object. Ignatius says Jewish Christians did not believe in the Eucharist! For some it is more about fellowship than about power. There are clearly some tensions, conflicts, and problems in John's community. John has a very exalted view of the Eucharist. The Eucharist was a point of contention in the early church.

9

Two Beggars
John 9

"These things are written that you may believe that Jesus is the Christ, the Son of God, and that believing you may have life in his name" (John 20:31).

This year we are scaling a great promontory, the highest peak in the Bible, which is the Gospel of John. With every cut-back trail, at every rest point, atop every lookout, with every majestic view, this spiritual gospel will address you with the choice of freedom, with the ongoing need to choose, and—in choosing—to find the life of belonging and meaning, personal identity and global imagination.

In John 9 we reach the summit. Here this morning is the crucial chapter within the Fourth Gospel. In it we see clearly the two level drama of faith that John acclaims.

Today we meet two beggars. One is a man lost in the mist of memory, who somehow recovered his sight at the pool of Siloam. The other is the church, John's church, and by extension this church, existentially lost, who somehow recover sight at the hand of Jesus the Christ. John has two eyes at work. One is trained on the distant memory of a powerful Jesus. The other is trained on the experience of the Risen Lord in the life of the church. Both see again, by the healing action of the divine.

This blind beggar and his healing, and all the trouble that such a good deed occasions is important to John because in him John sees clearly what is going on in his own church. At Siloam, there was a lonely beggar. We are beggars, too. In Jerusalem, one was powerfully healed. We have been healed, too. With Jesus, a man's sight, his most prized faculty, was restored. So, too, our spirit. So long ago, Jesus was heard to say, "I am the light of the world." He is the light of our world, too. Did Jesus of old bring healing to the needy? By grace he does so every week in our midst still! What the earthly Jesus did for the blind beggar, the Risen Lord does for the beloved church.

At Siloam, Jesus heals on the Sabbath. We, too, have learned that the Sabbath was made for man and not the other way around. In Jerusalem, there is immediate conflict over what this new power means for old traditions. We, too, know the conflict between gospel and tradition. With Jesus' healing there comes a division between generations. Such contention and difference is ours as well.

Our Gospel shows us two beggars, one in Jerusalem a long time ago. And one which is the church itself, to whom Jesus speaks, the Risen Lord speaking in the spirit through the very human voice of John.

Of the first beggar, blind in Jerusalem, we may say: He was visited by Jesus; he was exonerated by Jesus; he was touched by Jesus; he was sent by Jesus; he was commanded by Jesus; he trusted in Jesus; he was healed by Jesus; he was questioned about Jesus; he witnessed to Jesus; he told the truth for Jesus; and for this, and for his Lord, he paid a price. He was shunned. He was thrown out of the synagogue.

Of the second beggar, the community for whom the Gospel is written, blinded by dislocation and disappointment, we may say: They were visited by Jesus; they were exonerated by Jesus; they were touched by Jesus; they were healed by Jesus; they were commanded by Jesus; they trusted in Jesus; they were healed by Jesus; they were questioned about Jesus; they witnessed to Jesus; they told the truth for Jesus; and for this, and for their Lord, they paid a price. They were shunned. They were thrown out of the synagogue.

Two blind beggars, one a man and one a church. Expulsed, thrown out, shunned, set apart.

Most especially, in this crafted memory, the blind man given sight is then thrown out of the synagogue for consorting with Jesus. And this is the central communal dislocation of John's church. The beggar was thrown out of the synagogue, and John's church too, is like a beggar, wandering outside of inherited tradition. And we are, too.

The expulsion from the religious family of origin has two dimensions, one of sight and one of sound, one sociological and one theological. First, in actual experience, the little and poor community has lost its roots and its support. It is dislocated. Second, in the nature of hope, the community has now to find new resources, new ways of thinking about hope. It is disappointed.

(Why the separation? For the Jewish community, John's high claims about Christ amounted to a breach of monotheism, a kind of ditheism, two gods. "Hear O Israel, the Lord our God is one. . ." And the charge had merit. Now we can say so many years later, "Why, this is minimal! Look, by the fourth century the church acclaimed not one, nor even two, but three persons in the Godhead!)

Now we may ask, is there any application we may make of this text to our life today? Two applications quickly appear, one of grace in dislocation and one of freedom following disappointment, one sociological and one theological, one of faith and one of hope, one for the church and one for the world.

DISLOCATION

For nine years we have moved heaven and earth to reconnect our congregation to the connection of the United Methodist Church. In our church life, at the same time, the Risen Christ is healing our blindness in stewardship and evangelism. We are learning to share our money and we are learning to share our faith, and the mud and spittle of the Savior's hand are bathing our spiritual eyes in sight. Our new sight is somehow a troubling condition to our mother religion. We have paid massive apportionments, and yet relationally we are shunned in our conference. We have instituted a connectional Sunday, sponsored a pulpit exchange, participated in youth ministries, and yet our voice is not heard for the future of the denomination. We have sent our clergy now every year to conference, and have taken our places, hours on end, in the Visioning Committee, on the Board of Ministry, on the Finance Committee, in teaching and preaching across the area, yet we are "put out of the synagogue" when the voting occurs. We have hosted the meeting of the conference, even, and yet in the gathering we are distant cousins. Why is it that this moment for us, this epoch of new sight, of beggars finding sight and bread, of health and growth, in spite of all our effort, becomes an occasion for emotional and relational contention with our beloved denomination, our community of origin?

John's gospel can really help us, here and now. We are not the first to know the endless contention and intractable difference that is a part of all institutional life. There will be grace enough and to spare in this period of turbulence. We can be kind without being dishonest. We can be honest without being unkind. And we can say to the mother religion, our inherited tradition, "Let me find a way to help you get down off my back without hurting yourself."

Two Beggars

Here, just here, right here in our communal need stands the Gospel of John, a moment in the Day of God and the Gospel of Christ: you will find grace for every time of need. In the supreme dislocation, the movement from dysfunction to well-being, from addiction to sobriety, you will sense and you will know real grace.

That is one possible application of this gospel, John 9, to our church life. Here is another.

DISAPPOINTMENT

On Friday I was brought to heel sitting at the red light on Goodman and East. At the corner a man was being tutored in the use of a seeing-eye dog. The old black lab, harnessed and steady, was ready to guide him across the street, and his care-giver, a strong woman, held in at the shoulder from the back. Green came for him and the dog pulled forward. But the noise was great, and the wind was blowing, and the traffic was heavy, very heavy, and drivers were zinging left and right, all in the shadow of the Lutheran Church. And this dear young man held fast in fright. He could not move. The dog pulled and the woman pushed and he froze. At last, she saw that he was not ready. And her arms went around him to a great hug from the back, and she pulled him back toward the safety of the sidewalk. I had no right to see the utter disappointment on his face and covering hers too. Yet I see there an autumnal holiness, a real freedom, a love. Her hands moving from his shoulders to his cover his chest and enfold him told me, somehow, that one day, one day, one fine day, he would muster the courage to shake free of disappointment. I cannot even begin to imagine what it must take to trust a mute animal, a dog, amid the cacophony of urban traffic. But I know he will find it. Why, I bet by today he has done so. Sometimes you just have to jump, you know: when you learn to swim, and let the water hold you. When you take a leap and take a new job. When you ask someone to marry you. When you decide to leave a relationship or a friendship. When you retire. When you join or leave a church.

Looking out over sixty years of theological imagination in this country and abroad, speaking now both of, and to, the liberal Protestant communities, it will have been in retrospect rather a disappointment to see that we have not moved beyond Genesis 9, and in particular that we have not made our way out six more chapters to Genesis 15, in these sixty years. It is Noah who receives the rainbow, the covenant of color; but it is Abraham who receives the firmament, the covenant of light!

Jesus says, I am the light of the world.

I love the rainbow too. I love what Bishop Roy Nichols used to preach, that the world needs a spiritual rainbow. We can sing a rainbow. And we have. But Jesus here does not say I am the color of the world. He says light. John reminds us of the light from which all colors are refracted. And for the twenty-first century, we will need more light than color. W.E.B. Dubois was right that the issue of the twentieth century would be the color line. The issue of the twenty-first century is light.

I like color. Indigo and yellow, great colors. Orange, a personal favorite. You like blue, he likes red. Good for you. It is not easy being green, I know. Color is great, as long as color remembers the light from which it is refracted. We are all far more human and far more alike than we have recently envisioned. It is John who fills our existential disappointment with a great, universal hope! That this world can work! That in Christ there is no east or west! That God is at work in the world to make and keep human life human!

It can be dangerous to focus too much on difference. Friends, we are all more human and more alike than we regularly affirm, all of us on this great globe.

We all survive the birth canal, and so have a native survivors' guilt. All six billion.

We all need daily two things, bread and a name. (One does not live by bread alone.) All six billion.

We all grow to a point of separation, a leaving home, a second identity. All six billion.

We all love our families, love our children, love our homes, love our grandchildren. All six billion.

We all age, and after forty, it's maintenance, maintenance, maintenance. All six billion.

We all shuffle off this mortal coil en route to that undiscovered country from whose bourn no traveler returns. All six billion.

And in the light of the light of the world, what of all our colorful difference? It is the covenant of the rainbow that fascinates us still. We have not yet opened our eyes, or had our eyes opened, to the awesome bounty and beauty of the covenant of Abraham, the promise of firmament. We need to leave the rainbow and gaze at the firmament, to leave the fretting about color coordination for the joy, the expansive great joy of welcoming the fifty percent of this county that has had no first helping of faith, no first exposure to the light. That is where the fun is.

Here is one great, freeing hope for the twenty-first century, that we will move from Noah to Abraham, from rainbow to firmament, from difference to grace.

"These things are written that you may believe that Jesus is the Christ, the Son of God, and that believing you may have life in his name."

Good news: in dislocation, hold onto grace, the grace to be co-dependent no more; in disappointment, hold onto freedom, the freedom to walk in the light as he is in the light.

This week you can choose to grow in faith, and so find a fuller part of your second identity. This week you can choose to grow in love, and so open a fuller part of the world's imagination.

Faith is personal commitment to an unverifiable truth. It involves a leap.

Faith is an objective uncertainty grasped with subjective certainty. It involves a leap.

Faith is the way to salvation, a real identity and a rich imagination. But it does involve a leap.

Now is the time to jump.

All of us are better when we are loved.

NOTES FROM RAYMOND BROWN'S LECTURES ON JOHN
Union Theological Seminary
Spring 1978

April 12, 1978: John 9

The blind man is obviously a hero in the Johannine Community. In antiquity, blindness and sin were connected. Is he sinful? The sin is being spiritually and physically blind. Light and Dark. Here the signs or miracles, though not alone, play a part in this blind one's conversion. (It is not the initial conversion, but in how you live after the initial conversion that counts). Spittle only appears in John and Mark. The others leave it out. This is probably a very old story. Siloam: *slh*: *sylh*: *sybh*: Isaiah 8:6. Genesis 49:10. Shiloh. Is this a personal name? What is it? Is John playing "the one sent means Jesus"? By this stage, baptism may already have been connected with anointing or spiritual sight. Then each set of questions brings out a little more, but ironically makes the interrogators blind. The level of blindness in one decreases, while the level of blindness in the others increases. Question: Do you really believe in the things which you were taught? Question: do you judge the new by the old, or do you judge the old by the new. What do you do with something that both seems good and violates your tradition? We have here a vision of the group that is hardening.

The blind man is a hero because he is willing to declare for Jesus. He is willing to bear witness to and for Jesus. *We know* (9:24) and other verses represent an unfavorable report on the Jewish enemies. The disciples of Moses are set against the disciples of Jesus. This is pretty well the whole of the self-understanding of the Johannine community.

Here is the Johannine faith. If you know that Jesus comes from God, that he is the Son of Man, come for judgment, then you have faith. The point of the whole chapter is found in John 9:37. "Do you believe in the Son of Man? You have seen him and it is he who speaks to you." The man is moved from physical to spiritual sight. There may be a kind of liturgy behind this. You do not see Jesus until you have got to make a real tough decision about it, a real tough decision for him. Not until the tough choice comes is the real choice made. This group must have pushed the issue and earned themselves a lot of hatred. People who bring things to decision often provoke others to be more hostile than normal.

10

Two Beliefs

John 11

"These things are written that you may believe that Jesus is the Christ, the Son of God, and that believing you may have life in his name" (John 20:31).

This year we have scaled a great promontory, the highest peak in the Bible, which is the Gospel of John. With every cut-back trail, at every rest point, atop every lookout, with every majestic view, this spiritual gospel will address you with the choice of freedom, with the ongoing need to choose, and—in choosing—to find the life of belonging and meaning, personal identity and global imagination.

In the Gospel of John we have found grace amid dislocation and freedom following disappointment. These are the twin gifts of this twilight gospel, grace and freedom, John Wesley's two favorite words. In dislocation we meet grace: going off to college or military service; on the cusp of the courage to change our mind; in the matters, intimate and crucial of human sexuality; in the course of finding a new home; in the throes of struggles with our denomination. Yet all these foreground dislocations, and many others, really are meant to prepare us for the one great dislocation, death. What grace does the gospel give in this dislocation of death?

Our text today does not cast aside the primitive Christian hope, even in its most primitive garb. Mary says that she knows her brother will be raised, at the resurrection of the last day. John lets this hope stand, as does our traditional liturgy of committal at the grave. That is, whether we trust that in the hour of death we are translated to God's presence, or whether in this apocalyptic hope we trust that at the end of time, with all the children of God, still, in both cases, grace is found amid the dislocation of death. This is our belief, our first belief. And whether the hope is traditional or contemporary in its expression, the courage of this belief is what gives us the capacity to be truly human.

We lived for some years right across from a large cemetery that also hides a back entrance to the Carrier Dome. I used to keep count of how many friends, real friends, I had, and how many were on one side of Comstock and how many were on the other.

One late autumn Saturday, a football game day, our kids parked cars for five dollars a piece in the backyard. Then all became quiet in the neighborhood, except for the strong wind of the day and an occasional muffled shout, like heaven's trumpet, from the dome behind the cemetery.

I had determined, wind or no, to rake, and so with my ears muffled, I set out to rake the front lawn. So quiet, so empty, that street, during a football game. Back to the cemetery I raked and raked, wind rearranging all my art and labor. Back again, and raking again. I was lost in worries about Sunday to come, or some other bother. I raked and mused.

Suddenly, I turned for once to face the graves across the street. There, standing shoulder to shoulder was an army of men and women, a great sea of orange, now in the wind ready to cross at me, hundreds, more, coming, streaming out of the graveyard, walking at me with no more warning than Lazarus gave his sisters. Lost as I was in reverie, I really did not know for sure, whether the resurrection of the dead was upon us, or more simply whether the game had ended early. The resurrection at the last day.

In less mythological terms, and more general biblical phrases, we express something of this same, first, belief, in future hope, in grace at the dislocation of death. As we said last week, during the memorial for one of our greatest saints:

> If we believe that life has meaning and purpose.
> If we believe that the Giver of Life loves us.
> If we believe that divine love lasts.
> If we believe that justice, mercy, and humility endure.
> If we believe that God so loved the world to give God's only Son.
> If we believe that Jesus is the transcript in time of God in eternity.
> If we believe that all God's children are precious in God's sight.
> If we believe grace and forgiveness are the heart of the universe.
> If we believe that God has loved us personally.
> If we believe in God.

Two Beliefs

. . . And we do
Then we shall trust God over the valley of the shadow of death.
Then we shall trust that love is stronger than death.
Then we shall trust the mysterious promise of resurrection.
Then we shall trust the faith of Christ, relying on faith alone.
Then we shall trust the enduring worth of personality.
Then we shall trust that just deeds, merciful words are never vain.
Then we shall trust the Giver of Life to give eternal life.
Then we shall trust the source of love to love eternally.
Then we shall trust that at death we rest protected in God's embrace.
Then we shall trust in God.
. . . And we do.

Grace amid the dislocation of death. Freedom following disappointment. We have known disappointment. Following disappointment we find freedom: following the terror of 9/11; after trials with the complexities of life; in the hard discovery that the past is immutable; through the shameful admission that Christianity, and the Fourth Gospel, have harbored anti-Semitism; subsequent to a Presidential election in which we knew half the country would be chagrined; facing the stunted theological imagination of the last half century. Yet all these foreground disappointments, and many others like them, are merely preparations for our encounter with the one great existential disappointment, which is our enduring condition, what the Scripture names as sin. Our distance from God, from depth, from meaning, from purpose, from love.

Advent for centuries has been the time, the four Sundays, on which the last things, the Christian hope, has been propounded. Often a sermon each on death, judgment, heaven and hell.

Our time, our culture, our world do not readily prepare us for this season. This season of surprise, of hope hidden in the unexpected, this season in particular has a frightful time in a post-Christian world. We just do not handle the unexpected very well. This has been true for two generations, but clearly it has 9/11 overtones as well. We live in a preventive age, a pre-emptive age, an abortive age, a prophylactic age. We prefer what we can control to what we cannot control.

The Greek word for guard is *fulakh*. Hence pro—before, phylactic—guard. This same Greek word, rendered guard, can also mean prison. That which we count on to protect us, also imprisons us. That behind which we hide, also hides us. We need to be careful about what guards, that is what prisons, we permit. It is like Aesop's fable of the horse and stag. To defeat the stag, the horse asks the man to ride him. The man agrees, as long as the horse will accept a bit and bridle. He does, and he is protected—and imprisoned. Here is advent hope: that we may see clearly those things that protect us to the extent that they imprison us.

Snow swirled that day, as the Nursing Home hove into view. Gladys deserved a call, on the line between life and death, and the preacher came prepared, or so he thought.

Would you like me to pray with you? Oh, it is not necessary. Of course I love all the prayers of the great church, particularly, now that I see little, those I carry in memory from our old liturgy. But I am fine.

Perhaps you would like to hear the Psalms? My grandmother appreciated them read as she, uh... You mean as she lay dying?... Yes. Oh, it is not necessary. I mean I do love the Psalms, and was lucky to have them taught rote to me at church camp so that they rest on my memory, like goodness and mercy, all the days of my life. But I am fine.

I know that you sang in our choir. Would you like some of the hymns recited for you? Oh, that is not necessary. I do so love music! I can sing the hymns from memory to myself at night! I found my faith singing, you know. It just seemed so real when we would sing, when we were younger, around the piano, around the campfire, around the church. I knew in my heart, I knew Whom I could trust. But I am fine.

I brought communion for you in this old traveling kit. Oh, that is not necessary. We can have communion if you like. It is so meaningful to me. I can feel my husband right at my side, knee to knee. After he died, I could not hear anything that was said in your fine sermons for so long, my heart hurt so loudly. But I still could get grace in communion. But I am fine.

Gladys, is there anything that I could bring you today? As a matter of fact, there is... Tell me about our church... I have been out of worship for so long... How is the church doing this Christmas?... Are the children coming and being taught to give their money to others? And what of the youth? Are they in church and skating and sledding and hay-riding and falling in love? Tell me about the UMW and their mission goal. Did they make it? A dollar means so little to us and so much in Honduras and China. And tell me about the building... Are the trustees preparing for another generation? It is so easy to defer maintenance... What about the choir—are they singing from faith to faith?... Tell me about your preaching, and the DS, and our bishop... What is going to happen with our little church?... Tell me, please, tell me about our church... It is where I find meaning and depth and love... That is what you can bring me today.

Jesus said, I am the resurrection and the life. She who believes in me, though she die, yet will she live. There are those places where what is beyond us enters among us. Where the line of death is smudged and crossed. Where it is not just so clear what is really death and what is really life. Worship, this hour, is such a moment, too. You can have an experience of God, right in church.

"These things are written that you may believe that Jesus is the Christ, the Son of God, and that believing you may have life in his name."

Good news: in dislocation, hold onto grace; in disappointment, hold onto freedom.

This week you can choose to grow in faith, and so find a fuller part of your second identity. This week you can choose to grow in love, and so open a fuller part of the world's imagination.

Faith is personal commitment to an unverifiable truth. It involves a leap.

Faith is an objective uncertainty grasped with subjective certainty. It involves a leap.

Faith is the way to salvation, a real identity and a rich imagination. But it does involve a leap.

Now is the time to jump.

And all of us are better when we are loved.

NOTES FROM RAYMOND BROWN'S LECTURES ON JOHN
Union Theological Seminary
Spring 1978

April 11–20, 1978: John 11

Instead of the "cleansing the temple" as the immediate cause of Jesus' death and demise, John has put in the scene of Lazarus to function in the same way. It is the life from above that matters. This early resurrection must be seen as a contrast to the eschatological, once and for all claim of Jesus' own resurrection. Why is there such emphasis here on Jesus' own love for Lazarus?

There was a pre-Johannine miracle source or sources. But did they all come from the same hand? Did the two Cana miracles, the healing of man born blind, and the raising of Lazarus all come from the same hand? Lindars objects in this way to Fortna: "Sure, there were pre-Johannine miracle sources. But they were not of the same manuscript." It's not Johannine unless someone has misunderstood?

John 11:5 and 6. This is an odd contrast. Two Eschatologies: 1. The older belief in the resurrection on the last day, in which the dead are called out of the graves, contrasts with another set of beliefs. What happens to believers who die? See Thessalonians and Corinthians. There is no advantage to being alive on the last day, according to Paul. 2. In the light of Jesus' life, death has no force. Do you walk in friendship with God? Do you walk in God's friendship? Thus, *this* life is very important. God's life is already here. This earth, this place, this life is the real place where we encounter God.

John 11:27 seems to combine these two, and we need the two together. John does relativize the body. 1. Death has not absolute power over us. 2. Death is a terrible tragedy, for we have no idea of a life without the body.

John 11:49. Matthew and John know Caiaphas, which points up their historicity at this juncture. The house of Annas also criticized by Jewish sources. Caiaphas has the high priesthood (these were usually Roman pawns) for nearly ten years. That is quite a long time. His is a long term, like that of Pontius Pilate. Pilate gets removed, and then goes quickly to Caiaphas. Perhaps there developed some political agreements between the two. In 11:48 ("If we let him go on thus, every one will believe in him, and the Romans will come and destroy both our holy place and our nation") may have some truth in it, regarding the reactions to Jesus. The Romans will only stand for so much, folks!

John 11:51. Sometimes the High Priest did prophecy. Here his prophecy is an unconscious one. Caiaphas thinks politically. John takes it salvifically. The whole will almost always get rid of the individual to save the group. 11:52: There are gentiles in the community ("to gather into one the children of God who are spread abroad"). Even now. . . being begotten from above is what counts.

11

The Spirit of Truth: Communion
John 13

JESUS MEETS US TODAY in the communion of service, and the service of communion.

The strange world of the Bible includes no more mysterious, different country than these later chapters in John. If Antarctica is our most different continent in all the world, and the desert southwest the most geographically distinct region in our country, then, in like fashion, these chapters full of speech at the end of John are such a tract.

Our passage today makes two affirmations. One is about Jesus. The other is about his disciples.

Our passage reminds us of what we only with great difficulty continue to see: the Christ is incarnate in humility. For some reason, according to my gospel and yours, God has chosen the scandalous way of the cross, the path of humility in which to make God's self known to us—a stumbling block to the religious spirit and sheer folly to the reason. Yet this is the witness of Scripture, tradition, and our own considered experience. It may have been that John, our latest Gospel, could already see the inevitable triumphalism that the sacraments would carry. The pride of place, the less-than-blessed assurance that can come with a signed, sealed, delivered grace, controllable grace, cheap grace. So John, throughout his Gospel, eliminates the sacraments. Almost no reference: to baptism by John the Baptist; to the baptism of Jesus; to the Lord's Supper at the last supper; to the words of institution; to the memory of the upper room; to the revision of the paschal meal. Just here, as closer readers of the Gospel sense, just here, where on the night of betrayal, and in Jerusalem, and in the quiet secrecy of the familiar gathering, just here where we are about to settle into another recollection of the sacrament of the last supper—John turns a corner. Where the holy meal has been, we have the stark, searing, unforgettable humiliation of the footwashing. Jesus Christ is known to us in the scandal of real incarnation, not in the magic of a mystery cult. His presence is found in absence, his power in weakness, his authority in service. The great tradition of growth and strength, found more in the other gospels and notoriously celebrated in Acts, is here rejected. Here, nakedness. Here a towel. Here a basin. Here the humility of a servant's work. Here the grime of feet. This is the word of faith, and for John anything, anything that stands in the way of the Word of faith, including the sacraments themselves, are to be burned. There is no Last Supper in the Gospel of John. There is only Jesus the Christ, incarnate in humility. For some, the greatest dimension of sin is falsehood. For some it is sloth. For John, here, the demon is the sin of pride. Christ, the real Host, is the Servant.

It will take some further chapters for the second aspect of this teaching in John 13 fully to emerge. Here in John 13, there is a service of communion that is the communion of service, not Holy Communion. Then in 14, the spirit of truth is known in conversation. In 15, the same spirit in commandment. In 16, the same spirit of truth in catechesis. In 17, the same truth in consecration. But here, in John 13, there is the divine hand on the human foot. Not only Judas the sword bearer, but also Peter, especially Peter, Peter whom the writer of the fourth Gospel deprecates, Peter, first among the misinformed, expects something else and is horrified. He expects—what? A place? A name? Authority? And he is presented an emblem of humble service. There is to be forever in the community of love, which is the church, a serving humility, a humble service: So the cross. So the bowl and towel on the altar. So the stole, an ox yoke, to mock religious garb, so the collection plate, so the call to prayer, so the serving of meals, so the wiping of children, so the profound service of listening, so the quiet willingness to forgive, so the acknowledgement of ignorance, so the capacity to empathize, so the tithe, so the disciplines of discipleship, so the modest art of politics, so the artless labors of administration, so the season of Lent, so the pathetic simplicity of bread and cup, so the actual, earthly, incarnate, humble replication and resurrection of One, who on the night he was betrayed, took a towel, and when he had blessed it, he took it to his disciples, saying, take, wash, this is my labor given for you, do this as oft as ye shall gather, in remembrance of me. Communion, real communion, is service.

The Spirit of Truth: Communion

A new commandment I give you, that you love one another. Even as I have loved you, so you also ought to love one another. This is my commandment, that you love one another.

One example. Parker Palmer writes movingly of his salvation from depression in *Let Your Life Speak*. I thank my colleagues for identifying this book in connection to the footwashing. Palmer painfully records those many attempts to help that were not helpful. Well meaning but ineffective. Sympathy that only led to greater sadness. Positive advice that made him more depressed. Reminders of his many talents, which left him in greater malaise. Those who said they knew what he was going through, which, of course, no one ever does. He concludes:

> Having not only been "comforted" by friends, but having tried to comfort others in the same way, I think I understand what the syndrome is about: avoidance and denial. One of the hardest things we must do sometimes is to be present to another person's pain without trying to "fix" it, to simply stand respectfully at the edge of that person's mystery and misery.. ... Blessedly there were several people, family and friends, who had the courage to stand with me in a simple and healing way. One of them was a friend named Bill who, having asked my permission to do so, stopped by my home every afternoon, sat me down in a chair, knelt in front of me, removed my shoes and socks, and for half an hour simply massaged my feet. He found the one place in my body where I could still experience feeling—and feel somewhat reconnected with the human race. Bill rarely spoke a word. When he did, he never gave advice but simply mirrored my condition. He would say, "I can sense your struggle today," or, "It feels like you are getting stronger." I could not always respond, but his words were deeply helpful: they reassured me that I could still be seen by someone—life giving knowledge in the midst of an experience that makes one feel annihilated and invisible. It is impossible to put into words what my friend's ministry meant to me. Perhaps it is enough to say that I now have deep appreciation for the biblical story of Jesus and the washing of the feet.[1]

A new commandment I give you, that you love one another. Even as I have loved you, so you also ought to love one another. This is my commandment, that you love one another.

---

1. Parker Palmer, *Let Your Life Speak: Listening for the Voice of Vocation* (San Francisco: Jossey-Bass, 2000), 63.

NOTES FROM RAYMOND BROWN'S LECTURES ON JOHN
Union Theological Seminary
Spring 1978

April 20, 1978: John 13

John 13:1. His own (#1) did not receive him (see prologue). But his own (#2), he loved. Again, John substitutes belief for physical birth. Now we are in the Book of Glory, as Brown calls it. This second section of the Gospel is very different. The gospel and the work are now all inward directed.

This is in the style of the great testaments. From Moses and the Patriarchs we have models of the great dying figure leaving a legacy to his children. Every theme in that literature is soon to be repeated here. We have here a last will and testament. We have here the intention to speak to those outside, *through* the believers. The discourses here refer almost without exception to all Christians. We have here a suspension between earth and heaven, a mélange of images of heaven and earth. *The hour has come...* All of this is one moment in time.

The foot washing is very different. And very difficult. Why is there no Eucharist here? Is the author making a deliberate play on the expectation of the Eucharist? It is fixed in the tradition. Is John resisting ritualization? Is he trying to correct an inner Christian heresy? The Eucharist and the death of Christ are connected. Is it the symbolic death of Jesus? What he has done for us we must do for each other... Demand to do something very lowly... Subsequently this has been used with baptism... This is a challenge to the traditional understanding.

12

The Spirit of Truth: Conversation
John 14

You shall know the truth, and the truth shall set you free. To be set free. By knowing. Truth.

Know the world. Know God. Know others. Know thyself. All these are overshadowed in John by knowing the Spirit of Truth, which liberates, heals, saves, and makes new.

The divine spirit captures our fullest selves, our heads, our hands, our hearts. This is the spirit, the advocate, whom Jesus here introduces, through the preaching of the early church, to the wounded needs of the early church. "I am going away." That, in retrospect, the Johannine Christians could interpret. We get it, too. This is the hour, the moment, the glory, the cross. It is the other phrase that may have puzzled. "And I am coming to you," Jesus said. Here is the hard Scriptural evidence of truth, sent, truth, coming, truth, expanding, truth in the spirit, truth on the move. Jesus makes way for the rest of the truth. The Holy Spirit will (future tense) teach you (plural) everything (boundless expanse). Our imaginations may be kindled today. Our hands may become instruments of love today. Our hearts may be inspired today, all through the same Truth, known in this chapter through ongoing conversation.

John replaces Armageddon with Truth. Here, just where veteran readers of other Gospels would have come to expect apocalypse, after the ministry and before the passion, John affirms the Spirit of Truth. Mark 13 and the wars and rumors of wars are gone. Matthew 25 and the future judgment of sheep and goats are gone. Luke 26 and the children snatched from the rooftops are gone. The earliest hope of the primitive church came a cropper. The apocalypse never lypsed. The end did not come, not after two, three, four generations. And so, dear John.

In place of Armageddon, he puts the artistry of the spirit. In place of eschaton he places the ecclesia. In place of apocalypse, truth. The world is going on for a while, maybe even an eternity. And what we once thought has more depth than once we thought! Heaven is not a matter of the last day but of every day! Hell is not a matter of the last day but of every day! Judgment is not a matter of the last day but of every day! The last day is today—live every one as if it were your last because it is. As Walter Rauschenbusch wrote, "What is more demanding, to believe that on the last day we will stand in the presence of the Lord, or to believe that every day is lived in the presence of the Lord?"

John remembers and rejoices in this truth, in the depths of heartache. The color of these chapters is muted, the tone is mellow, the rhythm is the blues. Grief, profound loss, is the background of John 14. This is loss remembered, the cross of Christ. This is more so loss lived, the loss of community, the loss of home, the loss of inheritance, the loss of relationship, the loss of safety. Your loss finds its depth right here, whatever your loss may be. Jesus teaches in a conversational mode today. Love me. Keep my commandments. This is the Spirit of Truth. He abides with you. Peace I leave with you. Do not let your hearts be troubled. Do not let them be afraid. It is the lasting Spirit of Truth which teaches us today, in the mode of a conversation drenched in grief. If you have come today with the tremendous burden of loss across your heart, hear great good news: there is a self-correcting Spirit of Truth loose in the universe to save and heal and make new!

HEAD: YOU OUGHT TO GIVE IOWA A TRY

Here are some examples of voices that carry truth, to save and heal and make new. They all come from Iowa. You know, there is something windswept and real about Iowa. Not so red nor so blue, just real and true. As a matter of fact, You ought to give Iowa a try. That, as you may know, is not a political reference; it is an old song. "You ought to give Iowa a try."

Of Iowa. . . We remember summer green and rolling hills, beans and corn, trees, and rolling hills. Earth is dark earth, soil is black, roads are straight and gravel, summer humid and hot. Spring comes earlier, daffodils coming soon, May baskets on the doors. In March it is like the wet dirt in the unplanted garden, from tan to black, a sense of fertility. When is the last frost? Who will start first without having to replant? Waking from slumber, silence but you know that something is just about to happen.

When you carry the faithful anxiety of serious love for the church, and you grieve over needless losses and unnecessary hurts, You ought to give Iowa a try. There you will find Marilynne Robinson's precious novel, *Gilead*, with its steady, scriptural, happy-but-not-maudlin reminder that life is good. Morning is good. Prayer is good. Grace is good. Love is good. Family is good. God is good. All the time. She writes:

> I love the prairie! So often I have seen the dawn come and the light flood over the land and everything turn radiant at once, that word "good" so profoundly affirmed in my soul that I am amazed I should be allowed to witness such a thing. There may have been a more wonderful first moment "when the morning stars together and all the sons of God shouted for joy" but for all I know to the contrary, they still do sing and shout, and they certainly might well. Here on the prairie there is nothing to distract attention from the evening and the morning, nothing on the horizon to abbreviate or delay. Mountains would seem an impertinence from that point of view.[1]

When you carry the faithful anxiety of serious parenting, and you grieve over a youth culture that seems heavily material and falsely physical, You ought to give Iowa a try. Listen again to the voice of Mary Pipher, who spoke right in this nave last year. Her *Reviving Ophelia* is still on the money, and on the market, when it comes to reminding us of the challenges of growing up female in America. The Spirit of Truth is alive and well and abides and allows us, however stumblingly, to move forward as a people, to learn, from one generation to another, to grow, to do better. She says:

> I was a teenager in Beaver City, Nebraska, a town of about 400 people. My mom was a doctor in that town. I knew everybody, and I knew the name of every dog in that town. And so when I walked around that world, I was moving among people who I knew well, and who knew me well. Increasingly, that's not the experience of children. They aren't growing up in communities of adults who care about them. They're constantly meeting strangers, and they've been socialized to be frightened of strangers. So they're moving among people they have some reason to fear. They don't get nurtured the way children were nurtured thirty years ago. And they don't get corrected and informed about their behavior the way I did. Now, some of the rules I

---

1. Marilynne Robinson, *Gilead* (New York: Farrar, Straus, and Giroux, 2004).

learned were silly. Some of the rules I learned, I could hardly wait to cast off when I left home. But the fact of the matter is, there were a lot of adults deeply invested in my becoming a well-behaved civic citizen. And that's something children don't experience as much. So loss of community is one thing.[2]

When you carry grief and worry over how best to teach, and you wonder if the classroom will ever be the same, You ought to give Iowa a try. This brings to mind Sarah Hall Maney's "Iowa's Child."

HAND: GIFT AND TASK

This same spirit that illumines our imagination also takes us by the hand and puts our hand to the plow. You have gifts. With your gifts come tasks. The Spirit of Truth is in both gift and task. Be a little careful here, careful of gifts and their stewardship...

You have the gift of a listening heart. You have that rarest ability to listen fully in love until peace comes into another's heart, by grace. What a wonderful gift! Hour after hour. Listening and absorbing. Day after month after year. One in ten returns to say thank you. A wonderful gift. Or is it?

You can speak with the tongues of men and angels. You have that gift of presentation. Good for you. What a wonderful gift! Year after year, learning slowly, that some of that light needs to stay under the bushel lest people say you are "slick." How did Kipling put it? Don't look too good or talk too wise. Yes, speech is wonderful gift. Or is it?

You have the twin gifts of wealth and generosity. Your industry and frugality, or that of your ancestors, has produced the miracle of compound interest. And you enjoy giving, and you have means. Why, someone today could probably write a check for $100,000 to our building campaign and hardly miss it. You have those twin gifts, means and generosity. Great! The whole inhabited world has ideas for you to consider. Every day another request. Every month another balancing decision. Every year end another set of worries. Yes, these are wonderful gifts. Or are they?

You are a denomination, let's say, for instance, Methodist. For two hundred years your strengths have been in addition and multiplication. You have not had the most novel theologies, nor the most cutting-edge (or just plain cutting) theories. You are moderate, mainstream people who love, first, and are happy in God. Only, ours is not an age of addition, nor an age of multiplication, but an age of subtraction and division. And your gift is in

---

2. Mary Pipher, from study guide to *Reviving Ophelia: Saving the Selves of Adolescent Girls* (New York: Ballantine Books, 1995).

The Spirit of Truth: Conversation

addition, and multiplication! Leave the subtraction and division to others who are good at it. You keep on loving and adding and being fruitful to multiply and fill the earth. These are your gifts, and they are wonderful, if not currently fashionable.

Here is the Spirit of Truth in conversation with us today. With every gift there is a task. Gifts, to be good, take care. We are stewards of the mysteries of God, and our hands are meant to take up the excruciating (a good Lenten word) work of the husbandry of gifts.

HEART: STRANGELY WARMED

Truth attends to head and hands, but finally and firstly is a matter of the heart. Perhaps this is why the writer places all these marvelous verses in the context of conversation. A fireside chat. A back porch interview. The dinner table. Time talking and walking.

Faith is a choice you make. Faith is a decision you make. To live a certain life, say a Christian life. Very easy to describe and very hard daily to do. Wonder, love, and praise. That is: prayer, fidelity, and generosity. That is: weekly worship, staying faithful to your spouse, tithing. The truth is that faith is a choice. Faith is first a gift, yes. But faith is a choice to open and keep the gift. Be careful! With every gift there are tasks. Faith is the daring decision to unwrap, use, and take care of God's gift.

How does a moment of faith come? A moment of decision? A moment of heart warmth? It is an Iowa moment, a moment of the Spirit of Truth known in conversation and embracing the head and the hand and the heart. The Spirit of Truth brings to mind Meredith Wilson's *Till There Was You*.

NOTES FROM RAYMOND BROWN'S LECTURES ON JOHN
Union Theological Seminary
Spring 1978

The Paraclete

Another singularly Johannine figure is the *Paraclete*. The Paraclete also appears only in the Last Discourse. For the community, the Paraclete is of the highest importance. *Jesus's final gift is the Paraclete.* Was this originally the Holy Spirit?

This is a very complicated issue. In Trinitarian thought, the two great problems are those of the divinity of Jesus and of the personality of the Holy

79

Spirit. The neuter (*pneuma*) gender originally militated against the personal force of the Spirit. This struggle about the nature of the Spirit existed early in the early Christian community (thinks RB).

John works at the same problem with new names, a new vocabulary. *The Spirit of Truth*. This NT concept is almost equivalent to that found in Qumran. The prince of light, the spirit of truth, Michael. Spirit is also a word for *angel*. Thus Spirit acquires a personality. In Hebrew thought, angels are personal. But this Spirit of Qumran also dwelled in every community member. *And* it was also a spirit of truth. This ambivalence (the spirit in you\the spirit of truth) is precisely the same ambivalence as that found in t he Gospel of John. Angels stand between God and Man. They are intermediaries. They both serve God and cause evil?

With the advent of the Son of God, the transcendent\immanent split in God now is solved differently. Jesus is something like an angel. There were two angelology tendencies. 1. One was to get rid of angels in favor of Jesus. 2. The other was to keep both, side by side. Both Jesus and the Holy Spirit get put above all angels, principalities and powers.

Parakletos is a word used only by John. In the first letter of John the word is used to describe Jesus. The word comes from *kalein*, to call, to call along side of. It is the legal form for advocate, one who has been called along side to help (*ad vocare*). The Holy Spirit will tell you what to say: this is the Synoptic claim. But that is not quite what John says here. Here the Holy Spirit is a prosecuting attorney. He puts the world on trial. There is a legal sense to Paraclete. A lot of this language and imagery ought to be understood in light of the trial of Jesus itself. "The real sin is yours, not that of Jesus." (This gospel is not about sins but about the root of sin: the choice of darkness over light). The Paraclete is Jesus' Spirit. The Spirit is not just a memory but is a living force. The best proof of the vindication is 'we won, we did not lose.'

In Job we hear "I know that my defender lives." The figure here is probably an angelic defender. He will prove to the world Job's innocence. The angelic figure in the Job passage is translated by the rabbi's as "*paraclete.*" "My defense attorney." The angelic spirit is related to the individual. Jesus thinks of people as having angels (?). So that, even if you are defeated, your angel will not be.

However, "the advocate" is not the whole picture. "The Comforter" is also a part of this. The Spirit will comfort, will hold your hand. *Parakletos* has this notion too. Luther's Bible emphasized the notion of the comforter. Thus we have in English the Paraclete as comforter. Furthermore, this figure is a 'he,' though there is no intention to emphasize maleness. This is Jesus'

The Spirit of Truth: Conversation

Paraclete since he is our own defense attorney. And the Paraclete is with us forever.

Even Jesus was confined by time and space. But the Paraclete is not bound by time and space. The Paraclete is given to all who love Jesus and keep his commandments. There is no contract here for John. The Paraclete is not given only to a few. (In Acts, by contrast, the spirit is tied more directly to the twelve). In John, the spirit is the property of all. The spirit is an internal force which the world cannot see. The world cannot see the spirit. And the spirit has no name. His identity comes from Jesus and the Father. The spirit takes on the role of Jesus, and is sent in Jesus' name. He will teach. He will remind. He will tell. Just as Jesus did. This is the *Teacher* for the Johannine community. He will not speak on his own. He will speak only what he hears. He will speak of the things to come. Here is the Christian dilemma: we face new things but without a new revelation. It is from all that he will receive that he will declare to you.

At the end of the century, the apostolic churches had a moment of paralysis. All the leaders were now dead. "How are we going to survive?" *We will hold on. Preserve* what has been given. This is a warning against people with itching ears and novel ideas. One way to cope is to structure, to pass on. This structure is the test of the Spirit. It is a mechanism for preserving the situation. There is a human witness, to be sure. But that witness is only powerful because of the *Paraclete*. Thus the *Beloved Disciple* is so exemplary, because of the Holy Spirit. This is the notion of passing things on, in a viable, adaptable way.

The *Paraclete* teaches.

There are two different visions of Christian mechanisms for dealing with the future. One: Acts, the Pastorals, etc. Preserve and remember. Two: The Spirit. You need both, and you cannot survive with just one (look at 1st John). But the other group has a tendency to freeze up. This is a most interesting tension: spirit guidance plus guidance from structure.

Here the *Paraclete* is also the justification of the community. For your own good, I will go away. The presence of the *Paraclete* in the long run is better.

I have many things to say, but you cannot bear them now. Many of the features of Jesus are shared by the Spirit. He is Jesus' alter ego. The person who possesses the Spirit possesses Jesus. The Holy Spirit is to Jesus as Jesus is to The Father. They are one, but they are not confused. For John, how do you know God when no one has seen God? 1. Moses. 2. the Law. 3. Jesus (through another human life). But then you are faced with the problem of history. 4. Sacraments (John does include this). 5. The living Paraclete. This is the ultimate self-revelation of how the word of God gets translated as

THE COURAGEOUS GOSPEL

God. To a community living in time and space, the Spirit of Jesus in proving the world wrong. People who live by the spirit is the only way others will be convinced of the victory of Jesus.

13

The Spirit of Truth: Commandment
John 15

AT THE VERY END of their years at Colgate, the commencement springtime circle of men would be formed around the swan pond. On a clear, warm spring evening. At dusk, at twilight. As they came to their moment of departure. It was unforgettable to hear those voices, and, even for those of us still on bicycles and in sneakers and blissfully unaware of what they were going through, there was a fine, haunting quality to the amateur three-hundred-voice male chorus. I remember they were dressed in graduation gowns. There was some speaking and some silence. They held torches around the lakeshore, and night fell, the same night regularly depicted in the Gospel of John: In the opening hymn, with Nicodemus, in the passion. Otherwise, too. And spectacularly in these five rare chapters, 13–17. There is nothing like these verses in all of literature, biblical or otherwise. They are dripping with the grief of loss, and teeming with the reception of love during departure. I suppose it might have been appropriate, one year or another, at Colgate, if John 15:12 and following had been read. It may have been read. Now in the full dark the torches burn out bright. You can their warmth even from the hiding place behind the willows. You can smell their birch bark scent. Night falls, and the men sing, "Colgate, alma mater. . ." One by one they depart. One to work. One to marriage. One to teach. One to war. One to study. One to ministry. And all to the open, unforeseen future.

THE COURAGEOUS GOSPEL

Good news meets us today in the Gospel announcement about love and departure. We can discover the meaning and nature of love in times of change—even in the month of change, April. Why should it surprise us that this utterly different Gospel would so accost us? After all, this is John: John whose community found freedom in the aftermath of disappointment, John whose community grasped grace in the aftermath of dislocation.

The greatest hope of the primitive church had been disappointed. Christ had not returned, one, two, three generations later. John alone had the courage to look about and find the freedom to change his thought. Heaven is here and now. Hell and judgment, too. Every day is the last day. As Rauschenbusch said, "Which is more daunting, the thought of meeting Christ on the last day, or the thought that every day is lived in his presence?" Today is the last day, until the next last day, which is tomorrow.

We too need to find our theological voices, after fifty years of wandering in the wilderness. There is hardly any lasting theological writing from the Protestant churches since Tillich. We have been surviving as nomads in a wasteland, now two generations wide. New voices will emerge, voices for a new day. Especially that will help us think again about unity and diversity, and move us from a unified diversity to a diversified unity, which we shall need to survive the challenges of Century Twenty-One, Islamic totalitarianism, and the ventures of the new sciences.

Likewise John and crew had been shown the door of inherited religion, and expulsed from the temple. Yet they found a strange and new grace in this difficult dislocation. In our region and time, too, we are dislocated. Since (taking Vahanian's calendar) the opening of the post-Christian era in 1965, we have been moved from a mode of remembering to one of rebuilding. From Christ in culture to Christ transforming culture. We have one hundred fifty-year-old buildings, one hundred-year-old habits, fifty-year-old preachers, all of which need rebuilding. Rebuilding is harder than building, and more fun. There is more texture, more history, more complexity, more detail—and more fun, for the right temperaments.

And now, in these rare chapters, John concludes his twilight Gospel, by bearing for us the recollection of departure. These five chapters are drenched in sorrow, the sorrow of loss, of grief, of change, of departure. To hear them aright we need to focus on two losses. That of Jesus and that of John. Jesus in 33 CE on the cross. And John, or the beloved disciple, this church's beloved patriarch, who after many himself at last gave up the ghost. These twin shadows, of Jesus and John, lie upon our passage.

This church knows about love shining through loss. You enshrine this love at your altar. The cross of Christ above it, the ashes of Crossland below it. Departure both divine and human. People of God, in your bones, you know about love shining through departure. And April is the month for it, breeding lilacs out of the dead ground. From childhood to adulthood: confirmation. From study to work: commencement. From singleness to covenant: marriage. From home to combat: deployment. Life is a series of greetings and farewells.

Hear the good news of what the earlier Christians found, what the Scripture records, and what we too may receive, of the meaning of love in the season of change.

"THIS IS MY COMMANDMENT THAT YOU LOVE ONE ANOTHER, AS I HAVE LOVED YOU."

First, the new commandment is known as a word, love. But what is new about this? Did not the ancient philosophers also acclaim the power of love? Did not the tradition Israel acclaim love of God and neighbor? What is new of this?

What is new is the community that carries the commandment to earth. Listen to John Wesley shouting at this passage: "Who then dares assert that God's love does not at all depend on (human) works?" This is a community—you are its offspring—that knows with confidence the experience of being heard, being heard by divine ears.

The passion narrative in John is greatly altered from his inheritance in many ways. Chief among them is its muting of the physicality and violence of the cross. John is writing at least eighty and maybe a hundred years later, but his reason for writing a milder passion is theological not historical. For him, the cross is glory. It is the completion of God's work. So he can use that lovely perfect passive third person singular verb, "it is finished," to summarize his gospel. What has needed or saying or doing now has been said and done. Loving and giving are permanently married. There is no love without giving, and there is no giving without love. You truly have what you have: the freedom and grace and love, to give.

So this is the community of love in transition, Always in transition: a day of new beginnings, time to believe what love is bringing, laying to rest the pain that is gone. Here is the commandment, new and spoken, that is, lived, in you:

- Continuous choices to live for others
- Continuous willingness to prefer the narrow and straight to the broad and wide

- Continuous reform of inherited patterns
- Continuous exodus from established positions
- Continuous connection of personal passion with human need
- Continuous improvisation in partnership.

"You are my friends if you do what I command you."

Second, the new commandment is known in friendship. Actually, the striking thing about this commandment in John is how vague it is. There is no fine print, no Leviticus. There is no illustration, no narrative, no application. The writer assumes that you and I will know love from non-love, when we see it.

That is, the meaning and nature of love are known in temporal, finite relationships. In what Paul called the "earthen vessels." In the April of life, in change, we learn about denial, anger, bargaining, and acceptance, as Kübler Ross summarized. We are reluctant to let go.

Did you ever try to put a grandson to sleep? They rage against the dying of the light. They know that good reluctance.

Robert Frost gave us such a feeling for friendship, for love in change, for reluctance:

The definition of friendship is the willingness to risk the friendship for the sake of the friend. You live and grow in this here, dear friends. You are aware, too, that this congregation will die or survive on two questions: Do we tithe? Do we invite? Tithe and you will live. Invite and you will live. And if not, you will not.

"YOU DID NOT CHOOSE ME BUT I CHOSE YOU AND APPOINTED YOU THAT YOU SHOULD GO AND BEAR FRUIT."

Third, the commandment is known in fruit. Greater love has no one than this. Bear fruit. Here is what the community of the beloved disciple discovered, not in theological disappointment nor in sociological dislocation, but in personal departure: the "meaning" of love.

This is what America learned on April 15 of 1865, when Abraham Lincoln's life ended, speaking of laying down one's life for friends, writing about malice toward none and charity for all. How often we think of him. When we are hurt. It is hard to have a dream die. Then we think of Lincoln: "I was too hurt to laugh and too old to cry." Or when we feel betrayed. Then we hear his voice, "with charity for all." Lincoln saved the republic from itself.

The Spirit of Truth: Commandment

This is what America learned again on April 12 of 1944, when Franklin Roosevelt's life ended, a life utterly changed in 1920 by polio. Henceforth a life and voice clearly connected to the hurt, the least, the last, the lost. How often we think of him, in seasons of change. Roosevelt saved capitalism from itself.

This is what the churches learned Aprils ago from Reinhold Neibuhr, remembered now by his daughter's book, *The Serenity Prayer*. That there is no reconciliation without the shedding of blood. That we are saved by hope. And that especially daily we shall need to develop that capacity, that spiritual discipline against resentment. Niebuhr saved the church from itself, for a time. But the rogue is an excellent swimmer, as Barth said of Adam.

This is what we learned again on April 4 of 1968, when Robert Kennedy spoke in the twilight of Indianapolis, lamenting Martin Luther King's death, quoting Aeschylus about grief, speaking to all of America, red and blue, and saying that he could understand those who might be tempted to violence. After all, "I, too, had a brother who was killed." Robert Kennedy tried to save liberalism from itself.

And who will save Methodism from itself? And historic Protestantism from itself? And a republic of laws and not of men from itself? And nationalism from itself? And who will work to save this world from its self-destructive tendencies?

This is what we learn with every self-giving act of love, the laying down of life in a pattern or a year or a moment. This is my commandment, that you love one another. Odd, isn't it, to hear this best in the hour of loss?

"WHEN THE COUNSELOR COMES, WHOM I SHALL SEND TO YOU FROM THE FATHER, EVEN THE SPIRIT OF TRUTH, WHO PROCEEDS FROM THE FATHER, HE WILL BEAR WITNESS TO ME, AND YOU ALSO ARE WITNESSES..."

Fourth, and last, the new commandment is known in spirit. John can find freedom in disappointment and grace in dislocation and love in departure, because he has sensed the free, gracious, loving wind of God, in the Spirit. And who needs Armageddon when you have spirit? And who wants family of origin when you have spirit? And who fears transition when you have spirit? Not you.

You only appreciate what you have when it is gone.

The iron matriarchy of our little village decreed that all activities would end when the streetlights came on, that all engagements would end when the streetlights came on, that all games would conclude when the streetlights came on. When twilight gives way to streetlight, the end is near.

Swing batter. Tommy come home. 3-and-1. Billy come home. Foul ball. Jimmy come home.

There were always men left on base, and contests unfinished, and matches unsettled, and things left incomplete. Walking home in the twilight, though, somehow, we knew the meaning of what we had.

We were at a party the other night, and a young woman called to her daughter, "Scout." Yes, she was named for Jeanne Louise, who knew her father's love as he departed the courtroom.

Even in a departure, sometimes, a kind of love emerges. One of my predecessors here was a Southerner, Andrew Turnipseeed, a friend of Dr King's. At his funeral T.L. Butts preached:

> Near the end of Nelle Harper Lee's wonderful novel, *To Kill a Mockingbird,* there is a touching and unforgettable scene. Jean Louise (Scout), young daughter of the courageous Atticus Finch, has persuaded her father to let her come to the courtroom to hear the verdict in the controversial case in which he is defending a black man. She chose to sit in the balcony with the black people. The inevitable "guilty" verdict is rendered. It is over. Atticus Finch gathers his papers, places them in his briefcase, and begins a sad and lonely walk down the center aisle to the back door. Scout hears someone call her name, "Miss Jean Louise?" She looks behind her and sees that all of the black people are standing ups as her father walks down the aisle. Then she heard the voice of the black minister, Rev. Sykes: "Miss Jean Louise, stand up, stand up, your father's passin.'" Can you hear that? It begs to be heard.

We visited a dear friend in hospital. As we took our leave, leave takings being so significant, she leaned up and said: "All of us are better when we are loved." Then, "See, Bob, I was listening!"

14

The Spirit of Truth: Catechesis
John 16

It is both the acute memory and the actual experience of the early Christian community for whom John is written, that the nature and measure of love are given, unexpectedly, in the hour of departure. We hunger for this good news! We long to discover, as did the ancients, that we may know love, best know love, when life is moving away from us.

Vernon Jordan stood surrounded by suitcases, on the steps of DePauw University. He was nineteen. He watched his mother and father and many siblings depart, driving an old station wagon out the drive in Greencastle, Indiana. He was weeping. Moments before, his father had said, through his own tears: "Son, we are going now. We won't be coming back. You know how much we love you. But now it is up to you. Read, Vernon, read. When others are playing, you read. When others are drinking, you read. When others are partying, you read. This is your life now. We will be back when you are finished." Did that feel good? No. Was it good? Yes. It was love in an hour of departure.

Throughout this year we have been learning together from the Gospel of John. We are almost through. Some will be sad, others glad. Some will arise inspired and others awake refreshed, as we like to say. Our passage today emphasizes the process of learning. Hence, the sermon title, "catechesis," or teaching. It is not a very good title. But it does begin with the letter

C (which is why it was chosen!). In the spirit, we are learning together. We may isolate three modes of teaching and learning offered us today.

EVERYDAY CATECHESIS

One is everyday experience. As Yogi Berra said, "You can observe a lot just by watching." Our Gospel neither fears nor disdains our daily experience. In fact, John lets into his teaching (or catechesis, the word beginning with C) all manner of experience. He happily pirates for use the religious, but not yet Christian, experience of his time. He steals the thunder of the Gnostics, his main competitors. His figure for Spirit, "Paraclete" or "Advocate" or "Counselor," is probably in origin a Gnostic figure. John takes this figure from his culture and uses it to preach his gospel. His language, especially through these five rare chapters, 13–17, he steals from the same Gnostics. This language is all departure language: leave. . . leave you. . . return. . . house. . . many mansions. . . rooms. . . go to prepare. . . knowledge. . . truth. . . way. It would be as if someone took the pervasive technical language of our time and filled it with good news. Our language is technical: connection. . . network. . . workstation. . . download. . . bandwidth. . . virtual reality. . . cyberspace. . . web. It would be as if someone today wrote a cybergospel, a modern, strange, technical proclamation. Maybe someone will.

Your acute memory and your actual experience matter. Your grief matters. Your loss matters. Your intimate longing matters. Your everyday hurts matter. Somehow, by a miracle, they are the medium, though not the source, of learning about love, especially as they are taken seriously, biblically, spiritually. Think this week about what you are going through. Monet was asked: "What do you mix with your paints to produce such beauty?" He answered: "Brains." Where your deepest passion meets the world's greatest hunger—especially at the point of your own strongest talent—there, you learn, is your calling. Sometimes this comes right in the heart of grief, loss, longing and hurt.

Every day we die a little bit. Something departs. Someone departs. Some bit of life moves away from us. We experience some denial, anger, bargaining, and then, perhaps, acceptance. Remember, for the disciples, and so for us, "Jesus is always the one who is taking his leave. If we do not know the grief of being left, we can never know the joy of union." Every day experience is catechesis.

ECUMENICAL CATECHESIS

A second mode of learning we may call the mode of ecumenical experience. We learn from the globe. John did not fear his culture. He decorated his home with Gnostic symbols. Then he subtly changed their meanings. It is a big world. And Jesus, or as John calls Jesus' Presence, "Paraclete," is not stable, not isolable, not confined. He is not confined. He is not confined to a Petri dish, nor a dusty tome, nor a precise dogma, nor a particular sect, nor a single form of service (not even your favorite or mine), nor to a single issue. He is risen! He is not here! In this season we have witnessed the departure of one pope, and the arrival of another. What do we learn? Our sister church, the Roman Catholic communion, a billion strong across the globe, seems to be moving further back, departing back into a certain form of tradition. We could continue to raise the doctrinal arguments that are as old as the Reformation. About the celibacy of the priesthood: are the gifts of celibacy and ministry always conjoined? About the sacrifice of the mass: is the Lord's Supper a matter of substance or of spirit? About the infallibility of the pope: what does this mean? About the sub-ordination of women: are orders limited to just one of the genders? Maybe, though, we ought to think ecumenically.

Maybe we also ought to look at ourselves. Maybe the problem with Catholicism is Protestantism. Maybe the Roman Church has just not had a strong enough dancing partner, a compelling enough perspective, a shining and imaginative enough alternative. Fifty years ago young Catholics were eagerly studying Protestant theologians. My mentor at Lemoyne College studied Tillich. Young Protestants were studying Catholic writings and events. So Robert McAfee Brown's bestseller, *The Ecumenical Revolution*. Today fewer folks from either flock are jumping over fences, not because the fences are higher, but because the grasses are not so compellingly and tantalizingly green. There is less to jump to. We learn ecumenically; we learn together. "The Spirit is the power of proclamation, grounded in Jesus, and at work in the community." Ecumenical experience is catechesis.

EXISTENTIAL CATECHESIS

A third mode of learning is existential. Existence involve choices. Think of Frost's *The Road Not Taken*.

Existential choices are hard to make. They always carry cost, risk and uncertainty. The good news from antiquity, and in the spirit today, is that we do learn in our decisions. The grief which drenches these chapters, John

13-17, harbors a beautiful insight. Jesus had to depart to make faith possible. Jesus' departure—his leave taking and his present absence—is the basis for our real freedom. The fact that the disciples no longer have him is his real victory.

You are a resurrection people! So you anticipate the future in faith not in knowledge. And that is the thing about faith. There is always, finally, a leap involved. Faith gives you the courage to discern deep love in the hour of departure. Faith gives you the courage to hear and heed a new calling. Faith gives you the courage to see and do the right, without primary regard for who will be disappointed, or what the timing is like, or whether others will understand. Faith gives you the courage to improvise. Generalize if you want. Specialize if you must. But existence, choice, means to improvise. Faith gives you the courage simply to be, and to have the daily stamina to peel off the false name tags that life pins on your sweater. Faith gives you the courage to change, to travel, to choose, to grow. Faith gives you the existential courage even to endure departure, even the departure of loved ones: parents, friends, lovers, children. Faith gives you the courage to discover there, in the grief of departure, the promise of learning in love. Existential experience is catechesis.

> "A new commandment I give you
> That you love one another
> Even as I have loved you
> You also ought to love one another
> This is my commandment
> That you love one another"

PART THREE

15

An Embraceable Variant

John 17: 1–11

> OCTOBER 16, 2011
> MARSH CHAPEL

SUMMIT

High atop the world's greatest writings sits our Holy Scripture. Such knowledge is too wonderful for us. It is high. We cannot attain it.

Within the Scripture itself are conjoined the sibling testaments, the older and newer, the Hebrew Scripture and the Christian Writings. For us just now, the twenty-seven newer books stand a little bit higher.

The Gospels and the Letters and the Apocalyptic Writings are all inspired and inspiring, all sufficient for faith and practice. The gospels though have a certain priority, in our liturgy, and in our hearts. They lie just a step or two higher, atop higher ground.

You love all the Gospels. One there is though which from antiquity has been known as the sublime, the spiritual gospel. We shall ascend today, on ascension Sunday, to the craggy paths and rarified air of the Fourth Gospel.

High above the rest of John, above the seven signs to begin and above the passion and resurrection to end, there lies the strangest moonscape in the Scripture, and so in all literature, and so in life. I mean chapters 13–17.

We are about to place our homiletical flag on the very summit, the highest of high peaks, the textual Matterhorn, Everest, Mount Washington, Pike's Peak: John 17.

And this is eternal life, that they may know you, the only true God, and Jesus Christ whom you have sent.

WHERE WE LEAST EXPECT TO FIND IT: FREEDOM IN DISAPPOINTMENT, GRACE IN DISLOCATION, LOVE IN DEPARTURE: JOHN

Your own participation in this sermon is cordially invited, and fully required today. We affirm, with the ancient Gospel according to St. John the Divine, that we find freedom in disappointment, we grasp grace in dislocation, and we learn love in departure. Look back at all your experience to date. What is your greatest disappointment? It is a clue to freedom. What is your hardest dislocation? It is a signpost for grace. What is your most grievous departure? It is the way of love.

The community of the beloved disciple knew about disappointment. After three generations, and some, the community had awaited the primitive hope of the church to be realized. They awaited the return of Christ. The resurrection of the dead from their graves. The end of time. The apocalypse of God. It did not come. He did not come, at least not in the way once hoped. I find it the most remarkable experience of the New Testament that John, rather than being lost in a sea of disheartening failure, in the very eye of his most stormy theological hurricane, found freedom. In disappointment he found freedom.

The community of the beloved disciple knew about dislocation. They had lost their family of origin. They were sent out from their mother religion. The church that wrote John had been thrown out of the synagogue. The life they grew up with had cast them out. It took three generations for them to grasp the joyful grace in dislocation. Count it all grace, brethren, when various dislocations beset you!

Our time has also known dislocation aplenty. We should hunt more for grace in the financial dislocation that is endemic in our time. I have yet to serve a church that was not financially challenged. Every religious institution in our region—church, conference, seminary, campground, school, all—is under water in financial terms. More: middle aged families are sinking into the quicksand of debt. They are buying groceries on credit. Debt is work undone. Savings is work done. We have work to do.

An Embraceable Variant

The community of the beloved disciple knew about departure. The layers of grief culminating in chapter 17, while ostensibly a rehearsal of Jesus' own departure, may also have been crafted by the heart and voice of their aged John, the other and beloved disciple, whose own departure, in the midst of disappointment and dislocation, itself provoked these layers of grief. Is it not ironic that the sharpest, most rarified language of love in all of the New Testament—in all of literature—arises in the hour of departure?

In our time, we are bidding a reluctant farewell to God. To a certain, junior, perception of God. God reigns. This we affirm with the church militant and triumphant. But God's way among us is away from us. He is risen. He is not here. See the place where they laid him. The measures of freedom and grace given to us become real possibilities, real freedom and real grace, only when we have the gracious freedom to decide for faith. The same is magnificently true of love. This is the message of John, at the end.

The departure of the Christ makes space for love. As I have loved you, so you also ought to love one another.

BROTHER JOHN

We are four siblings in my family of origin. The older three have brown hair. The youngest is a redhead, whose name is John. John's bright red locks are unlike, quite unlike, the less remarkable curls of Bob, Cathy and Cynthia. He stands apart, does John. It makes you wonder where he came from, with such a distinctive aspect. John is like his Gospel namesake, the Fourth Gospel. The youngest of the four, he stands out, so different from his synoptic siblings Matthew, Mark and Luke. They with their shared brown hair, their shared parables and teachings, their shared emphasis on the humanity of Jesus, their shared trips from Galilee to Jerusalem, they just don't look at all like their younger redheaded brother.

In the summer, it happens, as it may in your family, there is a family reunion for one part of our tribe. Occasionally, we would go, growing up. Like yours, ours is something of standard reunion. It is held on a farm near Albany, which has been in the family since before George Washington rode a horse. After the usual light meal of beef, corn, potatoes, bread, sausage, pies, and pickles and so on, the extended family (or those who having eaten so can still move) will sometimes stand for a photograph on the long farm house veranda. I ask you to look at the photo. I am holding it here. Can you see it? Well, even if you cannot see it across the radio waves, you can probably guess what it shows. Of these eighty people, do you see how many have red hair? About sixty—young or old, tall or short, heavy or slight, male or female, they mostly have red hair, like John. 75% are redheads. In fact, in the photo, it looks like a sea of red hair. Maybe a red heads convention out in the farm fields of Cooperstown, NY. John isn't the odd ball. His siblings are.

John is not the second century Greco Roman odd ball. His synoptic siblings are. When you put the Fourth Gospel, with all its red haired radical difference, on the farm house veranda of second century religious family literature, he fits right in. He stands shoulder to shoulder with all the Gnostic writings that are so like him, especially in these late chapters. It looks like a redheads convention. He looks and sounds quite like the rest of his second and third cousins, once or twice removed: The Paraphrase of Shem, the Treatise on the Resurrection, the Odes of Solomon, the Apocryphon of John, the Gospel of Peter, the Gospel of Mary. How else will we ever hear this voice of Jesus from John 17?

And this is eternal life, that they may know you, the only true God, and Jesus Christ whom though hast sent.

Six Synoptic differences! Eternal life, not kingdom of heaven. Know, not believe. The only true God, not Abba. Jesus Christ, not Rabbi or Master. Sent, not begotten.

This voice is *nothing* like that of the Sermon on the Mount, or that of the parable of the Good Samaritan, or that of the cry from Psalm 22 on the cross. Not human, but divine, here. Not earthly, but heavenly, here. Not low, but high, here. Not immanent, but transcendent, here.

The community of the Gospel of John had a radical experience of Jesus, as God on earth. To render that experience meaningful, they had the radical courage to take language from the heretics around them, the Gnostics, and use it as their own *because it fit*. It worked. It explained to the huddled humans clinging to Christ what they had experienced in him: divine grace and divine freedom. It rendered the sense of consecration, the sense of holy living and dying, the sense of consecrated joy, which they had found, with the Light of the World, with the Bread of Life, with the Good Shepherd, with the Resurrection, with the Word made flesh.

The community of the Gospel of John feared not the culture around them. They feared not truth, even when that truth was best expressed outside of their particular religious circle. They had the guts to use language belonging to pagans, outsiders, heretics, Gnostics to celebrate and consecrate their faith. In doing so, they opened up the church to the world, to the future, to the culture around them. They changed their way of speaking of Christ, and pointed to Christ above, in, and transforming the culture around them. They changed. They had the courage to change.

In age, our own, when the Gospel of John, served raw, without cooking, without historical interpretation, can be made to sound like the voice not of tradition but of traditionalism, we do well to remember John's courage to change, to reach out to the culture around, to put the gospel in word and music on the air waves of a pagan culture, out on the radio waves of a secular world, and where possible to use that same culture

Raymond Brown: "Some scholars may ponder on the luck of the Beloved Disciple that his community's Gospel was not recognized for the sectarian tractate that it really was. But others among us will see this as a recognition by Apostolic Christians that the Johannine language was not really a riddle and the Johannine voice was not alien. . . What the Johannine Christians considered to be a tradition that had come down from Jesus seems to have been accepted by many other Christians as an embraceable variant of the tradition that they had from Jesus."[1]

WHERE WE LEAST EXPECT TO FIND IT: FREEDOM IN DISAPPOINTMENT, GRACE IN DISLOCATION, LOVE IN DEPARTURE: TODAY FREEDOM

Bring to mind Robert Frost's "The Road Not Taken." A poor man went to a Methodist church for worship. The congregation welcomed him and he returned week by week. After a while the women's circle took up a collection and bought him a nice new suit, with a blue tie. He happily received the gift, but they never saw him in church again.

A while later, on the street, one of church members saw him and asked what had happened. Did he not like the suit? Did it not fit? Was he afraid to wear it?

"Oh no, I love the suit. I look great in it. When I say myself in the mirror, I looked so good I thought, 'I look like a million bucks. I look too good to go just to the Methodist church. I think I'm dressed well enough to go the Episcopal church. I think I will go there. And that is what I did"

Sometimes a dose of realized eschatology can clear the mind and strengthen the soul. In a way, every day is our last. In a way, heaven and hell are here and now. In a way, the end time is all of time. John puts it this way: the hour is coming *and now is*.

The freedom of the gospel has gradually embraced multiple variants. The poor. The immigrant. People of color. Those once enslaved. Women. Gay people. Others. The Other. In fact, the lesson of the gospel of freedom enshrined in John is the spiritual expansion of freedom found in the embrace of the embraceable variant.

1. Raymond Brown, *The Community of the Beloved Disciple* (Mahwah, NJ: Paulist, 1979) 18.

THE COURAGEOUS GOSPEL

Some years ago we sat at dinner with several other couples, in a beautiful home, over a majestic meal, graciously served. Because the couples new each other well, and were in trust to each other, there was the chance for hard and serious conversation, consecrated conversation you might say. This evening the debate swirled around gay marriage.

There are tipping points in the way a culture moves. Some of them occur at dinner, in beautiful homes, over majestic meals, graciously served. The host was opposed, to gay marriage that is. The conversation widened, and then narrowed, and then widened again. We can surely agree that there are many ways of keeping faith, and many honest, different, points of view, on this and on many issues.

Across the table sat Carol, mother of two fine teenagers, married with joy to a business leader, baseball player, Red Sox fan. She had battled cancer once before, and now it returned, and she fought it again. We could not see it then, but in seven months she was gone.

Over some heat and some laughter, much disagreement but little discord, the conversation, consecrated you might say, moved on. Carol spoke fully, and at one point said: 'You know, I have learned how precious life is, how fragile, what a gift every day is. Here is what I feel: if two people truly love each other, deeply commit to each other, and want to consecrate their vows, that is they want what Doug and I have, why would I ever want to stand in their way, why would I ever want to deprive them of that happiness that I know so well.' I heard some minds changing as dessert came that night.

At a wedding dinner this month, in a beautiful room, with fine food and gracious hosts, gay and straight danced the night away together, gay and straight. It was right, normal, easy, organic, natural—the way things are meant to be. The embodiment of the embraceable variant.

GRACE

Our churches are in the throes of dislocation. Lyle Schaller had our number twenty-five years ago when he said: "These denominations will gladly accept 2–3% annual decline in exchange for the tacit agreement that there be no significant change." And so, in twenty-fiveyears, in the Northeast, United Methodism has lost 50% of its membership. Today more; five hundred and eleven of the nine hundred pulpits in my home conference, Upper New York, are occupied by non-elders: the preaching and ministry are done by people without full or proper education, preparation, examination or ordination. In what other sector of serious life would we permit this?

Pasternak loved Shakespeare's Sonnett 66. It is said that whenever he read aloud the crowd would not let him leave until he had rehearsed it for them. "Give us the 66th. . ." Its evocation of daily anxiety bears remembering. The poem is unequaled in its announcement of trouble. When life gives you the 66th remember Shakespeare, especially his last couplet.

'Captive good attending captain ill. . .' Can you hear that? It begs to be heard. Stand with your people in tragedy, honest and kind in word and deed.

In grace, our healthy future will come from a resurrection of thought, word and deed: of traditional worship, of traveling elders who excel in preaching, and in tithing to support the church we love.

All of the lastingly good features of my life have come through grace in dislocation: name in baptism, faith in confirmation, community in eucharist, partnership in marriage, work in ordination, love in pardon, and hope in Christ for this life and the next.

Love

Be sober, be watchful. Your adversary the devil prowls around like a roaring lion seeking someone to devour." While we may shed the inherited demonic mythology in the verse, knowing and honoring its origins in the distant past, we nonetheless fully recognize the spiritual truth here: we know not what a day may bring, but only that the hour for serving is always present. Our dear Springfield mother, caught in a tornado, covering her daughter and so saving her in a bathtub, knew not what a day would bring, but only the presence of mind to save her beloved. 1 John 4: 7–12 captures love divinely: *Beloved let us love one another. . .*

We too want to discipline ourselves and keep alert. So we pray. Do you pray? So we commune. Do you receive the eucharist? So we study. Have you devotionally read your Bible this week? So we converse with one another. Have you opened home and heart recently in Christian conversation? So we fast—park your car, save your money, do not reply all: fight pollution, debt and dehumanization. We too want to discipline ourselves and keep alert.

16

An Introduction to Gnosticism for Students of John

—Jason Ford

SCHOLARS HAVE LONG SINCE spent their energies analyzing a form of religious thought coined "gnosticism." Ancient witnesses bear witness to specific groups in the second century that identified themselves as gnostics, a term stemming from their emphasis on knowledge (*gnosis* in Greek). Scholars today, with the benefit of hindsight, recognize the checkered past of gnostic studies—assumptions have been made, accepted and passed through much of the scholarly literature on the subject; an entire anti-Christian religion recognized; a suspicious categorization of ancient materials; and polemical, biased scholarship. It seems that gnostic studies has some problems. Despite such missteps in the field of gnostic studies there is much material that is worth continued study.

The topic of concern here has long been labeled "gnosticism," which more or less has been understood as a system of religious thought in the early centuries of the Christian era. Numerous ancient writers bear witness to a gnostic school of thought, though these writers are inherently biased and their writing is apologetic in nature. The recognition of this polemical tone in these ancient writers instigated the mutiny against acceptance of a system called gnosticism. One fascinating part of this puzzle is that even recognition of the biases does not prevent the acceptance of this bias in

An Introduction to Gnosticism for Students of John

favor of "traditional" beliefs over and against the "non-traditional/heretical/distorted" thought of the gnostics.

Most of the discussions on gnosticism betray the fact that no one seems to know what the hell we're all talking about. For example:

> There is no true consensus even among specialists in the religions of the Greco-Roman world on a definition of the category "gnosticism," even though there is no reason why categories as such should be difficult to define. In fact, a good argument could be made that the very function of categories should be to make things clearer and easier to sort out, and that if it proves to be the case that researchers have difficulty agreeing on the definition of a category itself, then that category should be the very first thing shoved out the door to make way for better ones before we get on with the business of sorting.[1]

Or try this one:

> The state of research into what is traditionally called 'Gnosticism,' a religious phenomenon of late antiquity, is opaque or even confusing at the moment.[2]

One being introduced to gnostic studies faces an immediate problem at the very outset of "introductory" texts. They are presented with the fact that even the subject of study [!] is somewhat nebulous. Amazingly, Michael Williams, author of the first quote states that his book is intended for a wide audience—not just specialists, or even people involved in religious studies at all—who could very well be a "general reader, who knows little or nothing about what is customarily called 'gnosticism.'"[3] But, would you be encouraged at the outset of the monograph when no one can even seem to agree on the point of academic study. It's crazy. It is for this reason that much of today's discussion about and concerning gnosticism moves quickly to the realm of abstraction, with specialized jargon, nuanced and narrow definitions, and too often near impenetrable academic prose. Several recent introductions to gnosticism try to clear a path by moving chronologically from the supposed time of the movement (or school, or proponents) up through modern day gnostic studies. The problem with such an approach

---

1. Michael A. Williams, *Rethinking "Gnosticism": An Argument for Dismantling a Dubious Category* (Princeton, N.J.: Princeton University Press, 1996) 4.

2. Antti Marjanen, "'Gnosticism,'" in *The Oxford Handbook of Early Christian Studies*, edited by Susan Ashbrook Harvey and David G. Hunter, 203–220 (New York: Oxford University Press, 2008) 203

3. Williams, *Rethinking*, xiii.

is that it often only makes sense in hindsight, meaning one only appreciates the figures, theories and writings once one *already* understands the whole.

Two goals guide the remainder of this essay. First, this is meant to serve as an introduction to gnostic studies for one with little or no immediate comprehension of the current scholarly discussion on the matter. The specific audience in mind is that of students studying New Testament. As best as possible, inundating the audience with names and theories with no frame of reference will be avoided.[4] (Here one might validly raise the question, "If the goal of present-day gnostic studies is to avoid unfair bias by separating material as either 'canonical' or 'traditional' from 'non-canonical' or 'unorthodox' doesn't analyzing the material *for the purpose of* better understanding the NT, in fact, create just such a bias?" Well, the answer is yes and no. Yes, in the sense that anytime one uses certain texts in hopes of understanding a different text, then one unavoidably takes away certain conclusions that may or may not be available when the original text is taken by itself. However—and more importantly—we can answer no to such push back. Simply using a certain text, or set of texts, to better understand an independent and different text does not remove the validity of understanding the original set on their own terms. Nor, by definition, does it create a superior (= text you are studying) and inferior (= text you are using to elucidate your study) hierarchy. Admittedly, one could (and often has) used texts for this end but comparison and evaluation of different texts do not require such privileging.)

In 2010 David Brakke published *The Gnostics: Myth, Ritual, and Diversity in Early Christianity*.[5] This book is the most recent text on gnosticism of which I am aware. It is also an incredibly helpful entry point to the discussion of gnosticism. Brakke, professor at Indiana State, was, too, disheartened by the lack of clarity revolving around this field. He proposes a simple, albeit nuanced, position on moving forward with gnostic studies. For Brakke, to make any sense of this situation, we must return to the beginning (or at least what we can identify as the beginning). Once returned to the beginning, he then performs some investigative work, deducing clues and patchworking material together to give us some, however vague, notion

---

4. Here it is recognized that part of the scholarly challenge is to produce material that is thorough in terms of accuracy but acceptable in terms of purpose. This introduction to gnosticism attempts to show the validity of gnostic studies, with or without any comparison to other early Christian literature, canonical or not. But the second part of this essay will demonstrate that even though gnostic studies is an important field in its own right, it also helps us better understand aspects of early Christianity, including those of New Testament texts, in this case the Gospel of John.

5. David Brakke, *The Gnostics Myth, Ritual, and Diversity in Early Christianity* (Cambridge, MA: Harvard University Press, 2010).

An Introduction to Gnosticism for Students of John

of who the Gnostics were, what was important to them, and what others' comments about them tell us.

The beginning of the gnostic story, then, begins with a fellow named Irenaeus. He was a church writer of the second century CE and of whom much original material is extant. The important volume for this discussion is *Against Heresies*, where Irenaeus sets out to show all the ways that Christianity *has been distorted*. Irenaeus claims—certainly inaccurately as modern scholars now recognize—that the *original*, single form of Christianity is twisted or perverted by various groups of people. His attempt is to systematically demonstrate their errors and show the superiority of *true Christianity*. Irenaeus is our most ancient witness to gnostics, writing: see *AH* 1.29–31; 2.1.1. Central to Brakke's thesis is the fact that Irenaeus calls them a "school of gnostics." Thus, we may conclude, however polemical the content of Irenaeus's characterization of them, that there were a group of people who called themselves "Gnostics" and held to some sort of belief system.[6]

Irenaeus identifies certain books associated with this school, as well as their mythology (here used with no pejorative meaning; it is comparable to the type of mythology and one finds in the book of Acts with its focus on "substitutionary atonement"). Of the books he names we do have some of these materials now available to us. Most interestingly is probably the *Gospel of Judas*, which we will return tot presently. What Brakke highlights as the most important feature, and what helps determine what is and is not Gnostic, of the gnostic system is its mythology, which focuses particularly on cosmogony. Irenaeus states that the Gnostics believe in some version of the following: There is an ultimate Unknowable God (= UG). This UG, through certain aspects such as self-reflection, created entities that did not entirely encompass himself—such as divine Thought, stemming from his reflection upon himself. Thus, the UG created certain emanations of himself that, though containing aspects of his character, did not constitute the entirety of him and thus contained smaller aspects of the divine in them. The last being of this system, often depicted as Sophia (from the Jewish Wisdom tradition) created an inferior emanation, though not by normal process. Instead she went outside the system and created another, lower tier of Being who she called Ialdabaoth. Immediately she recognized this was a

---

6. Brakke feels that the term "gnostic" is too flattering to be made up and therefore must be the *actual* name the gnostics used to refer to themselves. This reasoning is dubious to say the least. Is it not possible to use a positive term for the exact purpose of lampooning someone? It should be said that even though the argumentation for the specific name "gnostics" is weak the actual reasoning for identifying a certain school of thought, with its own mythological structure and specialized texts, is strong.

mistake and banished him from the divine realm (called Pleroma, meaning fullness). This particular divine entity contained even less of the Divine sprit than the previous emanations. He was jealous of power and, recognizing that he could create things, created the material world. According to gnostic mythology, then, this is the same being as the Creator God of the Hebrew Scriptures. To say the least, this is a radical reinterpretation of the standard Jewish conception of divine Creator; instead of being the God of Gods who gives life and is worthy of all praise, this God—Ialdabaoth—is a false god-like figure merely playing the role of God. Since Sophia recognized that what she did was wrong, she tricks Ialdabaoth into breathing his spirit into the original human beings (cf. Gen 2–3), which imparts them with a part of the UG. Sophia, the other emanations, and, ultimately, the UG engage in a warfare-like battle against Ialdabaoth for the human creations. Ialdabaoth repeatedly attempts to keep them in the dark (I alone am God, Isaiah) and the UK repeatedly attempts to show them the spark of true divinity that is held inside of them. Ultimately, a redeemer figure (in later Christian interpretation this figure is identified as Jesus Christ) enters material, human existence in order to give them the divine revelation—that this material is not their real home but merely a façade meant to imprison them (much like the world of *The Matrix*).

This complex mythological gnostic system recounted in Irenaeus is paralleled—almost exactly—in the Secret Apocryphon of John. It is for this reason that scholars conclude that Irenaeus was familiar with ApJn.

With the discovery of the Nag Hammadi codices in the 1940s scholars had their hands on material that reflected Christian thought but did not come down the channels of traditional, accepted texts by the Church. The vast material contained in these codices provided an insider's view into certain religious thought of late antiquity, long thought to be lost to the hazardous preservation of texts across history. The fifty-two tractates from this discovery cover a wide range of genres and religious positions. Once quick to be identified as a gnostic collection, these texts now seem like vagrants without any larger framework to be studied within, which is obviously problematic for scholars attempting to situate these texts.

Scholarship on the subject of gnostic thought (and related terms: gnosticism, varieties-of-ancient Christianity) is awash with definitions, explications, clarifications, and the like in order to provide absolute clarity. This emphasis on clarity is necessary for the academic enterprise—we must know as clearly as possible what it is that we are studying. Unfortunately, the result of this meticulous detailing of minutia is often incomprehensible—and worse, impenetrable—prose for the novice, and I suppose, even some experts. Clarity is important for scholars and future-scholars alike,

An Introduction to Gnosticism for Students of John

however constantly redefining and qualifying material makes it, ironically, more opaque. Such opaqueness is what a student interested in gnostic studies finds with much of the current scholarship.

Given the current confusion and lack of unanimity on what is- and what is not gnosticism, many current introductory texts move chronologically to show how "gnostics" has been used, what we know about them (and from whom), what has been said about them (polemically, accurately), and so on, up until the point of where we are today. Such chronological reports are completely necessary; but speaking as one immensely interested in gnostic studies I found that this kind of text is much more valuable to me once I already understand where we are at today and then am I able look back and see that, yes, Harnack had good reason to suppose that was so but it makes sense why we no longer follow that view. Such a task as I'm proposing, starting from the other way around, does not mean we are free from the thicket of obscurity. One must still introduce foreign terms, discuss old and new scholars in what often results to be a smorgasbord of names and ideas, and do so in a way that introduces the beginning student to the necessary material, all the while remaining accessible.

One of the tasks in this essay is to do just that: to introduce the current state of gnostic studies, alerting the reader to the important scholars and their perspective. This introduction is specialized though, for it addressed primarily to Johannine studies students (in say a seminar) who are interested in pursuing research on the relationship (if any) between gnostic and Johannine thought. The nature of this essay, then, will fall neatly into two parts: 1) an introduction to the current state of gnostic studies, highlighting the most important ideas and people; 2) the areas of fruitful study between gnostic and Johannine ideas and presentation. This approach is advantageous to me as one who thinks "archeologically," meaning one who makes the most sense of the preceding material by recognizing that I am contextualized thinking, looking back—with all the biases that contains.

ON GNOSTICISM

Antti Marjanen called the current state of research on gnosticism "opaque, or even confusing at the moment."[7] I see no need in repeating the manifold descriptions, clarifications, and correctives offered by scholars in many current essays and monographs. Scholars who reach quite divergent conclusions proceed by stripping away the chaff and methodologically clarifying

---

7. Marjanen, "'Gnosticism,'" 203.

what we—they—understand gnosticism (or gnostic, or ancient Christianity, et. al) to mean.

Most recent introductory essays and monographs on gnosticism (Marjanen and King to name but two) proceed by providing a chronological history of sorts describing how people have understood and studied gnosticism over the years. Such a survey identifies many of the problems related to this field: who were the gnostics; were gnostics united or divided in thought; what characterizes gnostic thought; were there enough gnostics to be considered a religion? sect? were they simply likeminded folk; was gnostic thought pre- or post-Christian; should one locate gnostic background in Jewish, or Iranian, or Platonic thought; did (some, all?) gnostics identify themselves as Christians; was there a gnostic religion; and on, and on we could go.

Today scholars are a little more tentative to attribute a widespread gnostic religious or philosophical movement. Since the origins and nature of gnostic thought is more trying than that of, say, Christianity, scholars take different paths in identifying and discussing gnostic thought.

Some scholars reject entirely the title 'gnosticism' as a misleading scholarly construct (i.e., Michael Williams); others wholeheartedly embrace the term and identify it as an ancient Mediterranean religion alongside, say, Christianity or Judaism (i.e., Birger Pearson). With such problems of even the most basic terms related to the study of gnostics and gnosticism there is a potential to get lost in a track of a certain school of interpreting gnostics and miss out on the larger discussion, or worse, be unaware that such a view is the minority.

The most recent introduction to Gnostic thought I am aware of is David Brakke's *The Gnostics*. Brakke looks at the claims of Irenaeus, whose surviving work *Against Heresies* is the most important ancient witness to Gnostics. Irenaeus, when speaking of the Second-century teacher Valentinus, said that Valentinus "adapted the fundamental principles of the Gnostic school of thought to his own kind of system."[8] Irenaeus's writings have long been identified as polemical and therefore distorting, possibly quite significantly, the picture of second century Christianity. However, the result of this consensus by scholars is that Irenaeus's accounts are often totally dismissed (or conversely, as King points out, sometimes reproduced by current scholarship unintentionally). Brakke clearly identifies the problem with Irenaeus's account and so much subsequent scholarship: that there was a single, original orthodoxy and a single, multifaceted gnosticism. This is an

---

8. Quoted in Brakke, *Gnostics*, 31.

An Introduction to Gnosticism for Students of John

untenable position and needs to be rejected. However, Brakke finds much value in Irenaeus's thought, particularly his emphasis on a Gnostic school.

Brakke takes Irenaeus at his word that there was a *haeresis of gnostics*, literally a Gnostic school of thought. He uses examples from Josephus and others in demonstrating that when Irenaeus used the term it did not mean anti-orthodox, the way "heresy" is invoked today. Irenaeus's witness here is crucial for Brakke's argument. He finds it completely improbable that Irenaeus would have invented the name "Gnostic" for a group of people he was refuting. Brakke states that the term gnostic was just too flattering to be applied by Irenaeus polemically. Whether this reason is justified is debatable, but in a field of studies with such differing viewpoints and understandings of the material, there is surprising consensus over the existence of such a school and the writings they produced in the early second century; this group is most commonly referred to as "Sethian Gnosticism" (though Brakke says that we should drop "Sethian" and the suffix "ism," but it is this group that can be identified as Gnostics).

Irenaeus provides a summation of the Gnostic cosmological myth. Though not quoting the text, his understanding of this gnostic myth seems to derive from the *Apocryphon of John*. The *ApJohn* (= *Apocryphon of John*), then, is an incredibly important document for understanding gnostic thought. In it, there is a detailed account of a (the?) gnostic story regarding the creation of the world. This myth goes generally as follows: There is a single, unknowable God. This God produced a divine realm for himself. Emanations, or aeons, came from this unknowable God and filled the divine realm, which is called "Pleroma," meaning Fullness. These divine emanations are called such things as "Thought," and "Life," and are created in male/female pairs, often totaling twenty-four (for there are variations of this myth in other texts). According to *ApJohn* the last emanation, Sophia, attempted to create another divine being without the assistance of her male counterpart. Thus, the being she created, whom she called Ialdabaoth, was imperfect and Sophia was ashamed of such a creation and sent him outside the divine Pleroma into the lower realms. This Ialdabaoth is identified as the Creator God of the Old Testament, YHWH. Ialdabaoth creates lesser divine beings that contain less and less of the true Unknowable God in them. Eventually Ialdabaoth creates the material world. He creates humans and Sophia tricks him into blowing spirit into them under the premise of giving them life but really imparting part of the divine spirit into them, which provides humans with the capability, if they experience revelation, to realize that Ialdabaoth is not the true God. Ialdabaoth does everything in his power to keep the humans from knowing the truth: that the material world is a not reality, that deep down they have a divine aspect of them that is awaiting liberation from the earthly and material world so they can return to the divine Pleroma.

This creation account is incredibly complicated but is found in numerous other documents now available to us. This raises the question of whether or not those other texts originate from the same school, that is the Gnostic school. Attempting to limit or identify certain texts typologically is often problematic. However, Brakke argues that this type of creation myth was typical of the gnostics and therefore other texts of the same time period that betray, either explicitly or implicitly, this myth can be categorized as gnostic. This myth, then, is one of the principle aspects of importance to the group of Gnostics. It is in this way that this group differentiated themselves from other Christian groups. Therefore, "Gnostic" was a self-referential term, based on their claim to special gnosis, for a group of people who developed and interpreted the world within a certain mythological structure. One could draw a parallel here to the self-references of the followers of Jesus in Acts who call themselves 'people of the way' and articulate a mythological system involving Jesus, the crucifixion, resurrection and a restoration of people to God.

The discovery of the Nag Hammadi library in 1945 provided scholars with fifty-two ancient works written in Coptic from roughly the second through the fourth centuries. Many of these texts were quickly identified as "Gnostic" based on their "distortion of Christianity." But Brakke's argument is that such a group of texts must not be identified based on "distorting" Christianity but of their acceptance of the gnostic creation myth. Some of the texts found at Nag Hammadi Irenaeus and other heresiologists (define) referenced as gnostic: *Apocryphon of John*, *Zostrianos*, and *Allogenes*. Others reflect the same or similar myth of *Apocryphon of John*: *Apocalypse of Adam*, *Hypostasis of the Archons*, *Trimorphic Protennoia*, *Gospel of the Egyptians*, *Three Tablets of Seth*, *Marsanes*, *Melchizedek*, *The Thought of Norea*. Other texts, such as *The Thunder: Perfect Mind* and the untitled Bruce Codex, are debated as to whether they fit this gnostic categorization.

Though not discovered at Nag Hammadi, perhaps the most interesting Gnostic text is the recently published *Gospel of Judas*. This text is referenced and named by Irenaeus and was published in 2006 by National Geographic amidst a swirl of controversy. The controversy on a popular level stems from some of the claims of this text, namely that Judas is a hero doing the pre-approved work that Jesus asked him to do in his betrayal of Jesus. Widely enough, his aspect of the text is also controversial in scholarly circles because there seem to be questionable translation choices made to portray Judas in this positive way.[9] Regardless of the hype and controversy, most scholars are willing to include *Gospel of Judas* in the grouping of gnostic texts.

Brakke's text is immensely helpful to the world of gnostic scholarship. There is now a group of material that can best be described as gnostic (since, following Brakke, this is their own name). Brakke's position can be called a mediating position. It is important to now turn our attention to the two "poles" one could arbitrarily state that Brakke is found between.

Another recent and important introduction to gnosticism is Birger Pearson's *Ancient Gnosticism*. Pearson thinks retaining the term "gnosticism" is valuable for scholarship. Like Brakke, Pearson highlights that the term was not originally pejorative, though it has consistently been used that way in scholarship in the past couple hundred years. Again similar to Brakke, Pearson begins with the *ApJohn* as the starting point in identifying the school of gnostics. From the Nag Hammadi library we find that "there are a number of other texts we now have that are very closely related, in terms of myth and ritual, to the *Apocryphon of John*."[10] The characteristics, then, of gnosticism are: emphasis on gnosis for salvation; a dualistic way of looking at God, humanity, and the world; the construction of elaborate myths through which revealed gnosis is transmitted (theosophy, cosmogony, antrhpogony, soteriology).

Pearson's list of "Sethian Gnostic" texts is exactly the same, save one, as Brakke's group of texts attributed to the Gnostics. The one exception is the addition of an unpublished text from the same codex as *Gospel of Judas* that "is reported to be in very damaged condition."[11]

Based on Pearson's typological definition of gnosticism he includes different groups than just Sethian gnosticism. For example, besides Sethians the next best attested group of gnostics is the school of Valentinus. Brakke excludes this group from his category because they do not explicitly teach the myth found in *ApJohn* and related texts, rather they adapt parts of this myth and other Gnostic material with much more focus on Christ; he calls them "Valentinian Christians" comparable to "Johannine Christians." Irenaeus stated that Valentinus adapted and included the gnostic materials in his own teaching (Ag Her 1.29–31). Valentinus claimed apostolic authority from Paul through Theodas. This model of apostolic succession became very important to heresiologists refuting other Christian groups and the gnostics.

---

9. See April DeConick, *The Thirteenth Apostle: What the Gospel of Judas Really Says* (New York: Continuum, 2007) especially 45–61 on mistaken translations.

10. Birger A. Pearson, *Ancient Gnosticism: Traditions and Literature* (Minneapolis: Fortress, 2007) 10.

11. Ibid., 97.

There is one text presumably written by Valentinus preserved at Nag Hammadi, *The Gospel of Truth*. In addition to this, there are six fragments of his writings preserved by Clement of Alexandria. It seems at some point the followers of Valentinus split over their understanding of his teachings. Certain texts from these camps are referred to by ancient witness (Western: Ptolemy's Letter to Flora; Heracleon's commentary on John quoted in Origen's commentary; Eastern: Theodotious's writings). There are several Valentinian documents from Nag Hammadi besides *Gospel of Truth*. These include: *Prayer of the Apostle Paul, Treatise on the Resurrection, Gospel of Philip, Interpretation of Knowledge, Valentinian Exposition,* and *Tripartite Tractate*.

In addition to Valentinian and Sethian Gnosticism, Pearson also identifies two other "branches," Basilidian and Three-Principle Systems. Only one document from these groups appears at Nag Hammadi: the *Paraphrase of Shem*. Particularly important about this text is that it "lacks any Christian features, though some knowledge of Christianity may (or may not!) be reflected in the text."[12]

The field of gnostic studies was revolutionized with the discovery in Nag Hammadi. Scholars now had access to ancient traditions and writings preserved only in scanty detail by opponents. But the texts from Nag Hammadi have presented many complications and problems, none more so than classification. A number of texts from Nag Hammadi reflect influence and dependence upon Sethian and Valentinian forms of Gnosticism. But many of these texts also reflect Christian authorship. The following list are texts Pearson refers to simply as "Coptic Gnostic Writings of Uncertain Affiliation": *Eugnostos the Blessed* (and its Christianized form *Sophia of Jesus Christ*), *Apocryphon of James, On the Origin of the World, The Exegesis of the Soul, Apocalypse of Paul, (First) Apocalypse of James, (Second) Apocalypse of James, Thunder: Perfect Mind; Concept of Our Great Power, Second Treatise of the Great Seth, Apocalypse of Peter, Letter of Peter to Philip, Testimony of Truth, Hypsiphrone, Gospel of Mary, Pistis Sophia, Books of Jeu*.

Before finishing up our discussion on Pearson's presentation of the material we must mention briefly his understanding of Thomasine Christianity. Despite the *Gospel of Thomas's* emphasis on gnosis, it does not fit even Pearson's broad, typological definition of Gnostic (for it lacks the doctrine of pleromatic emanations, Sophia myth, and a Demiurge). There seems to have been a Thomas school of Christianity that produces the *Gospel of Thomas*, as well as *The Acts of Thomas, Hymn of the Pearl*, and *Book of Thomas the Contender*, but based on these texts this was not a gnostic group.

---

12. Pearson, 208.

An Introduction to Gnosticism for Students of John

On the other side of the spectrum from Pearson are Michael Williams and Karen King. Williams wrote a book titled *Rethinking Gnosticism: the Dismantling of a Dubious Category*, where he argues that scholars have obscured the texts and traditions under the title of gnosticism. He thinks scholars should reject the category of gnosticism altogether because the types of "gnosticism" often referred to (like Pearson's categories) do not share the same traits or features. He opts for dealing with a category entitled "Biblical Demiurgy" because this term is specific, a wholly modern scholarly construction, and free from patristic and other prejudice. Williams insists that the so-called gnostic texts be viewed as versions of religious creativity and most certainly not as parasitic to "orthodox Christianity." This said though, Williams recognizes that there are undeniable connections between the Sethian texts.[13]

King wrote a very important book entitled *What is Gnosticism?*. In this monograph she follows Williams in critiquing scholars' treatment and analysis of texts and thoughts commonly associated with gnosticism. In particular, King feels that scholars have too often followed the early polemic against gnostics by some Christian writers (most importantly Irenaeus, but Justin and Tertullian and others). Clearly King is right that we cannot possibly accept the simplistic explanation of gnosticism by Irenaeus, namely that it misrepresented and misused a previous, standard Christian position. All-around King feels the treatment of gnosticism (if there is such a thing) has been unfair. For example, one prominent characteristic that receives widespread scholarly acceptance is that gnostic thought is syncretistic. She accepts this because "all religions are syncretic."[14] Her problem is that "Modern discourse about Gnostic syncretism has been thoroughly negative, replicating to a large degree the polemicists' indictments of heresy."[15] King's great strength is in raising our awareness to the ways that scholars have continued to characterize and treat the texts and communities of the gnostics. She also provides an extensive history of scholarship and writing on gnostics and gnosticism. She does not go as far as Williams in suggesting that 'gnosticism' as a whole be rejected. Instead, she argues for more careful and less bias when approaching ancient texts.

King and Williams help balance the focus and scholarship of gnostic studies. They remind us that there was no such thing as "gnosticism" as a unified, ancient religion; so too, Christianity was multiform and contained

---

13. Brakke, *Gnostics*, 46.

14. Karen L. King, *What Is Gnosticism?* Cambridge, MA: Belknap of Harvard University Press, 2003) 223.

15. Ibid., 223.

many voices and interpretations. Pearson, on the other hand, argues that the materials traditionally grouped together as Gnostic share many characteristics and scholars can continue to group them this way as long as they don't follow Irenaeus and others in saying that Gnosticism is really nothing but a distortion of the true form of Christianity. Brakke's position is most appealing, in part because he so adequately deals with the observations of different scholars and lucidly highlights their weaknesses. He offers a persuasive account of the Gnostics, including their writings and their rituals.

There are many other texts that are essential for the study of the Gnostics. Paving the way for much of the scholarship today was Walter Bauer. Before the discovery of the Nag Hammadi texts he published a book titled *Orthodoxy and Heresy in Earliest Christianity*. Bauer had scanty evidence available to him but argued that the long-held convention that heresy follows from and distorts orthodoxy was inaccurate. Though most scholars refute his specific arguments for this conclusion they nonetheless agree with his argument. In this way Bauer makes me think of Bultmann's commentary on the Fourth Gospel. Most scholars reject every facet of Bultmann's argument except a *Semia* source but Bultmann still "got" the text and the message of the Fourth Gospel. Bauer, too, understood well the original diversity in early Christianity but his particular arguments for such diversity are rejected.

There are two other very important works of the twentieth century that must be mentioned. Hans Jonas's *The Gnostic Religion* argues that gnosticism was a religious movement with its symbolic universe and certain main tenants. He defines gnosticism typologically and discusses various systems of gnostic thought. Another important introduction to gnosticism is Kurt Rudolph's *Gnosis*. He includes many quotations of primary material and discusses the nature and structure of gnostic thought and language and a chronological history of Gnosis.

CONCLUSION

The category "Gnostic" is particularly helpful for scholars and is used in much the same way as "apocalyptic Judaism" or "Johannine Christianity." There are many areas of Gnostic scholarship that require further study: the origins of gnostic thought, though one should be aware of the warnings of King on associating origins with essence; what are the connections between Gnostic thought and other similar religious/philosophical movements of the time (i.e. Persian, Iranian, Indian); what relationship did Gnostic groups have to the New Testament texts both in their construction and in their use;

to what extent can we uncover the social environment of the communities that produced the texts (can we make similar discoveries to the Martyn–Brown hypothesis that identifies the *Sitz im leben* imbedded in the Fourth Gospel); further work on the interrelationship between certain Nag Hammadi texts.

17

Book Review: *Understanding the Fourth Gospel*
BY JOHN ASHTON
OXFORD: CLARENDON PRESS, 1991
PAPERBACK 1993
OCTOBER 12, 1994

THE RECENTLY RELEASED PAPERBACK edition of Ashton's outstanding book carries on its cover a commendation from Wayne Meeks: "The sight of yet another book—and such a big one—about this baffling Gospel is more likely to evoke groans than gratitude. That reaction would be a mistake. Leave all the rest on the shelf and read Ashton." To Meeks's accurate accolade one might add: for the preacher who enjoys the Fourth Gospel and yet is often puzzled regarding its interpretation, Ashton's work is essential reading. Several striking features of the book make it so.

One is Ashton's judicious, critical use of R. Bultmann as his point of departure. Bultmann remains unsurpassed in his interpretation of John. Ashton, more than most other Johannine scholars—particularly British scholars—acknowledges the great German existentialist's ongoing preeminence. How refreshing it is to follow a British scholar's critical yet appreciative review of Bultmann: "the uncompromising starkness of Bultmann's theology may cause one to miss the sheer elegance of his total solution. . . Bultmann's commentary is so much more urgent and exciting than run-of-the-mill commentaries that have followed it."

Book Review: Understanding the Fourth Gospel

Ashton also builds upon the seminal sociological analysis of J. L. Martyn (*History and Theology of the Fourth Gospel*). In the twenty years since Martyn's groundbreaking exegesis of John 9 and other passages, no other Johannine scholar has had the courage strongly to advance the "two level drama" interpretation, to take the next step. Ashton does so with brilliance. He argues that the very Christological titles so central and yet so "baffling" in John (Messiah, Son of God, Son of Man), can finally be partially understood against the background of the community's history. This history, as Martyn showed, is one of progressive conflict with Judaism. Ashton argues that the various Christological titles come from different stages in the life of the Johannine church, as it fought, stage by stage, with its parent synagogue: "the dispute is conducted close to the borders of a shared faith in which both parties had claim to the exlusive possession of the truth—a classic instance of *odium theologicum*, though not one that the evangelist's absolute partiality allows him to acknowledge. . . The community's concern for its own survival found expression in a series of allegories (door, shepherd, vine) which are eloquent testimony of the sustenance it continued to derive from its total commitment to Jesus." The Gospel is rooted in a series of sermons, prepared and delivered in the course of this controversy. Many of us have stood in grateful awe at Martyn's work. Few have taken up the search where he left off. None has cut trail like Ashton. Ashton reminds us just how exciting a lifetime's work of exegesis can be.

A further aspect of *Understanding the Fourth Gospel* significant to the preacher lies in its bold reckoning with the background of the gospel. Bultmann's hypothesis of a gnostic background (the evangelist is thought of as a convert from gnosticism) receives due consideration here, and is not finally rejected. However, the author argues forcefully for a minority or counter-cultural Jewish background, which also would have included the dualism, the emphasis on revelation (apocalypse), and the pessimism of John. "All early Christians were converts and John was no exception. Bultmann thought he was a Gnostic; I believe he is more likely to have been an Essene, simply because this is the easiest and most convenient explanation of the dualism that is such a notable characteristic of his thought and marks off his Gospel from the other three. . . what looks like and has often been interpreted as a cosmological dualism close to Gnosticism is really a moral dualism: the good versus the wicked." Gradually our understanding of the background to the New Testament allows a view of the fluidity between so-called Jewish or apocalyptic background and so-called Hellenistic or gnostic background.

The fearlessness of Ashton's analysis does not, thankfully, die before the conclusion. The author's nerve and pluck carry through, to the end. Since

F.C. Baur, the "difference" of John from the Synoptics has been admitted. However, the very magnitude of that difference has seldom been conceded. We still tend to read the Fourth Gospel as "fourth" first and "gospel" second. It is hard to elbow our way through Matthew, Mark and Luke to see the face of John, and to hear his radically free sermons. We have much history, tradition, reason and experience which caution us not to get too close. But John baffles still, and the gospel baffles because it is so different, and so free, and so "other": "If this is not gnosis it is remarkably close. Where the Fourth Gospel diverges from Gnosticism is in its insistence upon the salvific will of God. There is only one God and only one world, the object of his love. *The message is not inconsistent with Christian belief; Paul's teaching on the cross, for example. But it is not tied to this, or only by the slightest and slenderest of threads. . . It is as if the gospel story has been filtered through a fine mesh; all that is left is a lingering essence of revelatory discourse, exuding nothing more tangible than a persistent and quite distinctive aroma.*" (emphasis added). Ashton's fearlessness matches that of his subject. Maybe some of their bravery will rub off on modern preachers. John, like the rest of the Bible at its best, is about freedom. What a saving word for a time in which bibliolatry and fundamentalism have made it seem like a book about religious slavery.

In sum, leave all the others aside and read Ashton.

18

Teaching through John Ashton
Understanding the Fourth Gospel (1991)

BEFORE BULTMANN

What is the book's content, author, readership, nature? Bultmann addressed all, but not John's situation. Clement called it 'the spiritual gospel.' Barrett says it was detached. Before Bultmann, there were various insights: von Weizsacker (anti Semitism); Wrede (polemics); Bornhauser (jewish and anti jewish); Dodd (Hellenistic); Many on (authorship—and authority); history of religions, so Michaelis (gnosis)—"to a conservative Christian opinion this could seem both shocking and frightening"(21); Bousset (Hermetica); Bultmann (Mandaism); Harnack ('the most marvelous enigma in early Christianity"); Oderberg (mysticism); Bauer (Ginza); Meeks ("John: stylistic unity, thematic coherence, and bad transitions"); Faure (miracle source, otherwise 'go from string of sausages back to a pig'); Strauss (myth); Baur (non historical); Bacon (either synoptic or John—not both true); Hoskyns ("fuses history and interpretation into an indissoluable whole"). This last is Ashton's key. Conceptual world, six options: synoptics; Paul; Judaism; Hellenistic Judaism; Hellenism; Gnosticism. Sources: displacement (3:31–6); ur John; source-evangelist-redactor; Myth: ideal, philosophy, allegory, mysticism, meaning, theology.

THE COURAGEOUS GOSPEL

BULTMANN

Read aloud 44-45. "Penetration" is Bultmann's essence (w\Hoskyns, both H&T). Bultmann drew from many: Baur, Bauer, Hirsch, Wellhausen, Faure (e.r.), Bousset, Dibelius, Percy, Kierkegaard, *History*. Always for Bultmann three layers: redaction; evangelist; sources (sign, discourse, passion). *The more Ashton assaults Bultmann, the better Bultmann looks.* John outside big three (Hellenism (Paul); Jewish Hellenism (1 Clement); Palestinian (Synoptics)). "Jesus reveals one thing only: that he is the revealer." Myth, not dogma cult or mysticism, is the answer to riddle one. *Key*: 28 themes (Read Aloud 55). "Jesus' words are interpreted in terms of the Gnostic myth." (JA: RB is 'tidy but wrong,' 57). *And* RB: "John older. . .Jesus close to Gnostic\ baptist movement." John took over 'a non Christian source, one steeped in Gnostic mythology, and adapted it to his own purposes, so as to convey a message which is neither myth, dogma nor mystery, but radical challenge' (58). Bultmann's evangelist has demythologizes his source (the origin of the myth). "The gospel. . . must be stripped of the clothing borrowed from the Gnostic source." Sorrows for RB: no consensus about gnosis; chicken and egg; ignores other possibilities; *Theology*. Revelation is the central theme. Faith, not religion. 'Bultmann sees the central message of the Fourth Gospel (and the NT) as a call to faith, and does not wish to permit this message to remain unencumbered by its grosser Gnostic accoutrements' (63). Faith means to believe in Jesus Christ (Luther). A Call to Decision. Revelation is warning. Christ is no more than a voice—Word. John is not like Paul or Synoptics. So, if Gnosticism is out, one must find something else. . .

AFTER BULTMANN

Future eschatology is almost gone. Early church debates move from soteriology to Christology. Kasemann: 'eschatology has turned into protology.' *Scholars*. Kasemann, Kummel, Mussner, Meeks, Martyn, Fortna (signs source), Hoare (displacement), Brown (who does not let composition influence interpretation), Dodd (stay with text—odd man out), Wilkensn (multistage), Lindars (short collections—*Gospel began life as separate homilies. . . Audience asks John to put homilies into some permanent form*), Boismard (*urjohn* and multiple stages), Shcnackenburg (syncretism), Hoskyns (reluctant to admit non-biblical sources), MacRae (patchwork quilt—diversity as expression of universality), Schulz (theme history), Meeks (prophet King, and Gnostic myth), van Unnik (Jewishness), Robinson (Messiah), Martyn (*read aloud* 107-111), Berger (cognitive minorities) After RB, 'the majority

Teaching through John Ashton

have either stuck rigidly to the order of the received text, or confined their suggestions regarding structure to a few passages'; 'Lindars picture of the Johannine preacher composing his homilies for an attentive audience must be fleshed out by (86 a consideration of the differing situations to which these were addressed'). Still: "the truly inspired writing, according to this rather romantic conception, occupies the middle ground between source and redaction." Displacement theories and the revelation source are blind alleys. "If the Gospel was indeed composed over a period of years, years in which the situation of the Johannine group was never altogether stable, then it seems certain that the Gospel must have grown *pari passu* with the community whose faith it expressed." Influences vs sources. Kasemann fails. "Jews had long been exposed to Hellenistic influences" (97). So: "no need to search outside the world of first-century Judaism for such Greek traits as are exhibited by the Fourth Gospel" (*Ashton whistling past the graveyard*). (97: 'the origins of the Gospel were 'Jewish' in some broad sense' ?: John's readership: universal or particular, Jewish or Gentile, Christian or non-Christian?);Martyn: "The gospel tells the story of an actual event in the life of the community in such a way that it may be seen to re-enact an episode in the career of Jesus. He begins with chapter 9...(108). Meeks: 'coming to faith in Jesus is for the Johannine group a change in social location' (cf B Stone). Ashton: John... "written for the encouragement and edification of a group of Jewish Christians who needed to assert their identity over against the local synagogue... these findings... assured." Aristotle (forget this).

GENESIS

Scholars

Fitzmeyer (Melchizedek); Josephus (Pharisees); Segal (Scrolls); Bornhauser (Torah Fanatics): Dodd (form); Culpepper (school); Kuhn (Scrolls); Brown (scrolls and stages); Meeks (Heaven, best since Bultmann); Talbert (anti-gnostic); Borgen (Jewish exegetical tradition)

Dissent and Community

"In accounting for the genesis of the Fourth Gospel, one must focus primarily upon its ideas. These are what singles it out from the other gospels and makes it so hard to explain." 123. "It is necessary to ask the position of the gospel in the history of Jewish thought" 124 (*So, the fix is in*). Sources no help. Factors in origins: 1. Jesus tradition. 2. Johannine Community.

THE COURAGEOUS GOSPEL

3. Author (s). 4. Heterodox Judaism (why not Gnosis?)—"broadly speaking, the influences on the Fourth Gospel are all Jewish. . ." 129. Philo. Josephus. "The Gospel as we know it was largely inspired by the traumatic experience of the community's expulsion from the synagogue. It tells with graphic symbolism of the birth, the very painful birth, of a new sect, or, to slant the matter differently, a new religion." *Odium Theologicum.* "The essentially religious character of the Gospel's anti-Semitism is inescapable." READ: Bultmann on the Jews (135); anti-Semitism, 5-8-10. Synoptic Sabbath legal debate becomes an affirmation of Jesus' divinity. He claims equality with God.140: "The dispute is conducted close to the borders of a shared faith in which both parties had laid claim to the exclusive possession of the truth—a classic instance of *Odium Theologicum,* though not one that the evangelist's absolute partiality allows him to acknowledge." (Ditheism). *Special pleading:8:58–59.A is close to attributing gnosis to Judaism.146. Angels.Goes to great lengths to stretch Judaism to cover Gnosticism.* Gospel in finished form for Christian readers. *Family Row.* So: 1.Origins of John lie in heterodox Judaism 2. "The Jews" are the post 70 authorities (aka Pharisees). John fights the new establishment. 159. It was Christians who preserved the literature of heterodox Judaism. Again, sources: 1. Displacement. 2. Grundschrift. 3. Multiple source. 4. Multiple stage. "At one vital stage the gospel consisted of independent homilies" 162. "Certainly the great revelation discourses are best thought of as built upon the words of a preacher addressing a responsive audience and not simply the work of a writer toiling away.." Ashton's theory: 1. Signs source. 2. Passion source and sayings traditions (?). 3. Synagogue and dissenters. 4. Traditionalists attack. 5. So JPreachers were both apologists and preachers. "It seems that between the signs source that preceded the birth of the community and its expulsion from the synagogue not one of the dialogues or discourses in the Gospel was originally composed in precisely the form we now have it" 165 6. Expulsion from synagogue (5-8-10-9). End of material in 'first edition' (without 6, 15-17, other). 7. Second edition: 6,11,15,10,2. 8. Final redactor. 21, other. "Thus the only major sections of the gospel that cannot be directly accredited to the evangelist are the signs source and 21." Martyn's three periods: early (messianic synagogue group); middle (excommunication and martyrdom); late (firm social theological configurations). (Martyn thinks the gospel was written, stages 1 and 2, in the late period. Ashton thinks charge of ditheism preceded expulsion. "To make sense of the evidence we have to postulate a. . . move. . . from low to high Christology." "The growing awareness that Jesus was in his own person the fulfillment of much more than the messianic claims that had originally been made on his behalf. . . the shining silver of the finished product also carries the hallmark of genius,

most probably an individual genius who may or may not have drawn upon the work of other, less gifted preachers" 171. From Christian Jews to Jewish Christians. 10:1–18. Sheep=Johannine community. Thieves etc: Jewish authorities. Hireling: cowardly cryto-Christians. Shepherd=Jesus. Bultmann: general. Martyn: particular. John: universal, particular, polemical. Did "I am the light of the world" come from the memory of a sermon in which the preacher said, "He is the light of the world"? Amen, I Am, Riddles.

Dualism

*World. LightDarkness. Life. Judgment. Trial.Division.*Bultmann: John a Gnostic convert. Ashton: John an Essene convert. (Essenism is the easiest and most convenient explanation of the dualism in the gospel.) Dualism itself had three stages: signs, first edition, late. Vertical opposition. Dualism moral not cosmological. Like Scr.olls)('an affinity of thought and feeling' 214). "The new life enjoyed by the faithful is more than an ordinary existence: it is the life of faith." Eternal life: Jewish esch atoogy and Synoptics. Light treatment of Odes. Judgment is found in acceptance\rejection of Jesus. READ aloud 225 (on my thesis, eschatology). Bultmann comprehensive— and wrong (count # of times Ashton says this). "the fundamental bipolarity of John's vision of the world. . ." (231) *Best accounted for in gnosis.* Good summary found in 237.

Titles

Messiah. (*The best two paragraphs in the book,* 238). *Read these two pages to class.* Messiah is a title from the early period. (Key: the titles give clues to the stages, Ashton argues). Evidence? 1. Acts. 2. James Jerusalem. 3. Pseudo Clementines. Messiah;Elijah; Prophet; Chosen One; Lamb ofGod; Son of God; King of Israel. Church: incomprehension and compliance. 279: Bultmann elbows out OT. *Son of God.* Samaritan connection. ? 4:42 is a *hapax legomenon* in NT. "chief priests and Pharisees'"—odd because one could be both. Words outlast deeds. "The fourth evangelist's insistence that Jesus enters the world as a stranger and is never truly at home there runs counter to the whole Synoptic tradition. . . Such a formal contradiction of the traditions concerning Jesus himself as well as those concerning the Messiah he claimed to be is hardly conceivable without appeal to an equally powerful tradition, on that so far has eluded us." Ashton's partial proposal: the mission of the prophet, and, the law of Jewish agency. 313. 'an agent is like one who sent him.' Mission and agency. "Is there anything more to Christian belief which may help to explain why no other Jewish group before the advent of true Gnosticism made such extravagant claims on behalf of its leader?" Add: 'transmission of authority." "To consider the Christology of the Fourth Gospel in the light of these juridical concepts is like being given another eye. Suddenly the whole relationship between the Father and the Son stands out in startlingly fresh perspective" 323. John 5:19–30. The Jewish legal system may furnish a plausible background for this Christology, but not a source. *Son of Man*. Divine being whose true home is heaven. 13 uses. Daniel. Meeks: for the ascent\descent of the redeemer, there is no closer parallel than in the Mandeaen writings. 3;13, etc. The strongest support 'for the hypothesis that the Johannine Christology is connected with Gnostic mythology.' 342: *read aloud*. Even here: Jewish tradition, Jewish writers, Jewish legend, Jewish myth. . ."What Jacob concluded about a place, Bethel, is transferred by the evangelist to a person who, as the Son of Man, is the locus of revelation" Surely the Lord was in this place and we knew it not. 355: "What we have in the gospel is a fusion of two mythological traditions, one angelic, starting in heaven, the other mystical, starting from earth. In Jesus, angel and seer are one ('one of the most significant advances in all Christian thought") The blending of the two meant a new religion. "The conviction that the heavenly being was human and the human being heavenly was the conceptual hub round which the huge wheel of Christian theology would revolve for centuries to come."

REVELATION

An exegete takes the entire text. "The particular focus given to the uncompromising dualism which makes the fourth gospel so different from the other three is best accounted for by the bitterness and fear with which the members of the Johannine group regarded their Jewish neighbors. The direction taken by the evangelist's thought was determined by his experience and that of his community" 382.

Apocalyptic

Kasemann. Usual: apocalyptic\eschatology tussle. John profoundly indebted to apocalyptic. *Mystery*. Heart of the gospel genre. John's dualism not radical enough to be Gnostic, thinks Ashton. I Enoch. 4 Ezra. Pseudonymity. Pesher technique. "Consciously tendentious re-reading of biblical texts." Pesher is midrash squared 'by insisting that the whole meaning of the ancient text has been unavailable until now.' NT is one. Gospel not fulfillment

Teaching through John Ashton

of prophecy but revelation of mystery. *Visions and dreams.* Paraclete: *angelus interpres.* Cognitive minority. *If riddling discourse and apocalyptic are so important to John, then why are there no actual parables? Is riddling discourse truly more apocalyptic than Gnostic?* Read aloud 404, JLM on the two-level drama. John is an upside down apocalypse. Four intimations: mystery, vision, riddle, correspondence.

Genre

In the gospels, 'every saying or story is intended to be heard or read in the light of the resurrection.' The paradox of discontinuity (Bultmann) and continuity, Jesus and Christ, is the heart of the gospels. Neither biography nor theological treatise, nor compromise nor amalgam. Sui generic. John creates continuity by operating at two levels of understanding. JLM: *John speaking to his own first hearers.* Two level drama, crucial. Riddles galore. "The key turns surprisingly well in the Gospel wherever we insert it" (418). Examples from art and literature: Verdi, Stanze. Spirit (required for other generations—hence importance to late John). Spirit=passion, resurrection, Pentecost, life. For John, given his theology of the cross, resurrection is superfluous, and given his theology of incarnation, the cross is nearly so too. Story and interpretation are indissoluably locked together (hence the structure of our course in John). Wittgenstein: "Christianity is not based on a historical truth: rather it offers us a historical narrative and says, now believe! But not believe this narrative with the belief appropriate to an historical narrative, but believe through thick and thin." John wants to keep the tradition, but his main interest is in offering a *new reading* of the tradition. The evangelists are not writing history at all. Creed. Proclamation. Call. John desires to draw attention to the implications of the gospel genre (Don Quixote, Don Juan, Milton, Rossini, Strauss, Beethoven, Manet, Picasso, Rembrandt. . .). "John the Evangelist who also distrusted direct vision would have appreciated the force of Picasso's misgivings." Importance of his own pseudonmity. "Where faith is concerned, physical vision is a handicap rather than an advantage." Lessing's ditch.

Departure\Return

Exegesis of Farewell Discourse. We still do not understand the background of the Paraclete. Testament Form. Testament of Moses. John moves from death to departure. John is story and interpretation. *Sondersprache* (Ben Hill, Susan Shafer). Death is a return from a mission, in John. *(But this very*

THE COURAGEOUS GOSPEL

material is utterly Gnostic). So: presence in absence. Jubilees. Chpt 15, originally quite a separate homily. Keep word: preach, and write\keep written gospel. "The tradition of the Second Coming is irreconcilable with any final goodbye" 460. 'The whole gospel is permeated by an awareness of what is available to the believer here and now.' Read 461, explain according to Hill. Three consolations: the coming of the Son; indwelling of Father and Son; gift of spirit. Spirit is Jesus' alter ego, shadow. Spirit=Truth=Church=Dream. Comparison to Deuteronomy. Second Moses. 'What Jesus surveyed on the eve of his death was a domain which, in the eyes of the evangelist, held out more promise than the land of Canaan did to the Israelites: it was 'the truth,' a territory whose boundaries were already clearly defined as the revelation of Jesus, but the extent of whose riches had yet to be discovered—under the guidance of the Paraclete." 476. Martyn the linchpin. 'For this discourse to be fully understood it must be read on two levels: what was true of Jesus is also true of the Johannine prophet: his death is a departure but his 'spirit' will live on,' *two level drama.* Jesus' words, but the 'voice' of the Johannine prophet (his valedictory).

Passion\Resurrection

John: incarnation is glory and cross is exaltation (contra Paul). Kasemann: John's acceptance into the canon was a mistake. Cross: cry, word, prayer. Even passion unnecessary, so John imprints victory on top of passion. John suppresses the painful and the violent and the shameful (no cry of desolation in the garden). Cross=throne. Death: crucifixion of the Messiah; departure of the Son of God; exaltation of the Son of Man. (Realized, horizontal, vertical). See past the cross to its meaning. John: three titles, three deaths. Three Christs? John is more than a theologian. He is an evangelist. "He will not be properly understood unless he is seen to be wrestling with the problems and paradoxes inherent in his own genre." 501. "resurrection is not another event, but a form of thinking that permits Christian faith to find expression." Four episodes, chapter 20. Thomas is closest to John's thinking. Excellent exegesis of John 20. Four separate endings, two of presence and two of absence. Faith. Recognition. Mission. "Neither the resurrection itself nor the stories told to illustrate its significance are historical in any meaningful sense of the word" 511.

Medium\Message

Revelation. Johannine cognates: word, glory, truth, words, signs, witness, testify, say, speak, proclaim, teach, remind, expound, believe, know, hear. John is not a dogmatist, but an evangelist. What he writes is not doctrine but gospel. *Bultmann fares well even here in the teeth of Ashton's rebuttal.* Truth is self-authenticating. God's action is carried out in Jesus' words. "In the descent of the Son of Man and the mission of the Son of God two originally distinct Christological developments stand side by side." 8:28 *represents the final stage of the Evangelist's theological reflection.* "In the farewell discourses the world replaces the Jews as the general term for Jesus' adversaries." The gospel as revelation... "If this is not gnosis, it is remarkably close. Where the Fourth Gospel diverges from Gnosticism is in its insistence upon the salvific will of God. There is only one God and only one world, the object of his love. The message is not inconsistent with Christian belief; Paul's teaching on the cross for example. But it is not tied to this, or only by the slightest and slenderest of threads. In fact, there is not mention of the cross in any of these (revelation) passages: death is conceived as departure, exaltation, or ascent... It is as if the gospel story has been filtered through a fine mesh; all that is left is a lingering essence of revelatory discourse, exuding nothing more tangible than a persistent and quite distinctive aroma." For Bultmann, revelation came from a source, for Ashton, from the community's struggles... after prolonged and sometimes painful reflection in the course of a struggle with the establishment party in the synagogue. Rejection (cross and synagogue) is culpable blindness, judgment; the cross is above all the pain of being repulsed and expelled by one's own people." 547. "The spiritual lesson of the resurrection, spelled out in the Lazarus story, is summed up in the term, eternal life, the life of the new age." John focuses not on the event, but on its enduring significance in the experience of the community. Odes of Solomon! (*too little, too late*). His voice remains, 'equable, serene, assured. There is no other voice like it in literature.' 551. Jesus reveals that he is an enigma. "His own understanding was acquired gradually and painfully from a profound reflection upon his faith." *The meaning and message of John is that it is a gospel.*

19

Summary

Raymond E. Brown, "The Gospel According to John," ch. 11 of An Introduction to the New Testament (New York: Doubleday, 1997) 333–82.

STYLE

John employs a poetic format, misunderstanding, twofold meanings, irony, careful inclusions and transitions, and parenthetical notes.

Outline: Prologue, Signs (1:19—12:50), Glory (13:1—20:31, inc Passion), Epilogue

The beginning. John 1: 19 to 2:11 is set in a pattern of days (4). Then the signs begin, 2:11. Cana, Temple, Nicodemus, Samaritan Woman, Healing follow (note 3: 31–36, a puzzlement).

OT FEASTS

Chapters 5–10 are arranged around OT feasts and their replacement (Sabbath, Passover, Tabernacles, Hannukah). A lethal antipathy to Jesus appears

Summary

early. Jesus causes people to judge themselves. The scenes portray how one comes to faith.
Lazarus. Resuscitation not resurrection. The light has come into the world constituting the occasion of self-judgment.

LAST DISCOURSE (14)

A testament (Jacob, Moses, Joshua, David, Paul, Peter). Paraklete: has a hostile relation to the world, teaches the implications of what Jesus said. 15-16 (is 16: 4 ff a repetition of 14?). Love one another. Here: the world (not 'Jews'); no BD; 17. Prayer, assurance.

PASSION (18/19)

Arrest, interrogation, trial, crucifixion. Here John is closer to Mark than elsewhere. John accurate: only the Roman governor could order execution. John is more dramatic than the synoptics, making major theological episodes out of details. 20. 4 scenes, 2 garden, 2 house; 2 individual, 2 group. Ironically, Thomas utters the highest Christological confession. Conclusion (purpose).

EPILOGUE: 2 PARTS, FISH AND SHEEP

Sources or Stages? To 18th century, John supposed author. Then the understanding that John used nonhistorical sources (Bultmann 3: signs, discourse, passion). But style is consistent. So, John like others (3 stages: Jesus, Church, Writer). The theological difference (John vs others) is only one of intensity. *John vs. Synoptics.* Many differences (preexistence, ministry in Jerusalem (not Galilee), no kingdom language, long discourses but no parables, no diabolical possessions, only a few miracles (7). Some similarities (JBap, feeding of 5000, some phrases, passion details. REB: Mark and John shared common preGospel traditions (middle ground between much and none)

UNITY

Many aporia (4/5, 14/15, 20/21). Someone was responsible for the gospel in its final form. Theory of the redactor (Bultmann: Ecclesiastical Redactor). More likely: redactor agreed with John and was of the same community of thought. Added: omitted material (20:31), duplications (3:31ff.), (16:4ff.), epilogue.

Author and BD. Irenaeus (BD author, and Ephesus place). BD? John of Zebedee? Pure Symbol? Minor follower but central to John community? (REB view). John familiar with Palestine and with Judaica. The tradition about Jesus coming from the BD has been reflected on for many years, and expanded in light of the community's experience

Influences. Hellenism (abstract ideas, dualisms, Word. Philo. Gnosticism (savior from above, not of this world, return to heavenly dwelling, syncretism, NHL, Mandaens. Meeks, Bultmann, Haenchen). For these, John did not stem from the Palestinian world. Judaism (diversity of OT, Wisdom, DSS and its dualisms. The resemblance in vocabulary and thought between the DSS and John should banish the idea that the Johannine tradition could not have developed on Palestinian soil.

Community. REB reconstruction. 1. Phase before writing (70–90). JC Davidic Messiah, BD present; then some Samaritans (more Mosaic), Jesus with God, high Christology, ditheism, expulsion from synagogue (not dependent on Birkat ha-minim), anger with contemporaries (devil), realized eschatology to compensate for what they had lost in Judaism, need for public faith. 2. Writing of Gospel (90+). Ephesus, Hellenistic atmosphere, Greeks see but Jews are blind. 3. Epistles I and II (100). Split community (no longer fight with 'Jews' but internal), stressing JC humanity and ethical behavior, with some secessionists. 4. III John and redactor (21). Need for human authority, not just Spirit (Peter returns). Those who left went on to docetism\gnosticism\montanism. First commentator on John in 2nd century was Heracleon, a Valentinian Gnostic.

Issues: John 8. Love. Sacraments. Word+Table. Exegesis+.

20

"The Word Being Made Flesh, and the Priesthood of All Believers"

STH Commencement Sermon—Ray L. Hart

Marsh Chapel
16 May 2008

SCRIPTURES

Genesis: 2:5–13 "The Spirit was moving over the face of the waters... and God said.."

Philippians 2: 5–13 "Let this mind be in you which was in Christ Jesus..." (*kenosis*: the self-emptying of deity in the likeness of man).

Acts, chapter 9 (not read today): Saul on the Damascus road... (Pentecost).

John 1:1–5 "In the beginning was the Word... and the Word was with God and the Word was God... and the Word became flesh.

GRADUATING CLASS

As befits this ceremony of your passage, a celebration central to a Christian theological school at home in a research university, my remarks today comprise some features of a *sermon* but also some of a *lecture* or address. A sermon because it is fundamental in the passages from the Bible just read, but also because it is not free of *exhortation* and *personal address*. A lecture because it is not in entirely free association with some central doctrines of our faith, notably those of creation, providence, and Incarnation, and especially of that teaching central to all Protestant Christianity, the priesthood (both clergy and lay) of all believers. It will be *unlike* a typical sermon in that it has not *three* points but really only *one*. And it may well be like some of the lectures you have heard here, from which you conclude that it has no point at all! Let us open ourselves to the moving Spirit. Will you pray with me?

PRAYER

Lord God, you are yet brooding over the face of deep waters, those outside us, those underneath us, those within us. Stir our depths and continue saying us, speaking this muddy clay we are into the fleshed Word you are fashioning, that your Spirit may be as palpable as the muddy clay we are without your creating and redeeming presence. Amen.

WATER AND THE WORD: THE TWO BECOMING ONE IN FLESH.

I said that as sermon my words will have one point, not three. But I will begin with two themes in order to come to one. These are *water* and *word*. I very much hope some of you will have read Norman MacLean's book, *A River Runs Through It,* or at least have seen the movie. This is a book about the two sons, a veritable Cain and Abel, of a Presbyterian minister in Missoula, Montana. The Reverend Dr. MacLean tutored his sons at home in what he took to be the fundaments of a classical education: Hebrew, Greek and Latin; they read the primary texts of the Bible, Homer, Plato, Aristotle, Shakespeare and Milton. Knowing these languages and texts, said Dr. MacLean, you can learn everything else on your own. They studied from 8 a.m. everyday until 2 p.m., each student required to write an essay of two pages, which was criticized by the father, then reduced by one half, ditto, until there was a half page of compact prose. Following a quick lunch, the three headed to the Little Blackfeet River for the enacted poetry of addressing trout through the presentation of flies which they had tied. Throughout the remainder of the day they debated the question: in the constitution of the world, which is more primordial, water or the Word? I shall claim that

"The Word Being Made Flesh, and the Priesthood of All Believers"

water and Word are equiprimordial, in tensive, dialectical relation, the very process of continuing creation.

WATER

Henry David Thoreau, the American prophet a century and a half ago in this region over at Concord, reminded us "it is always well to have some water in your neighborhood, if only to know it is good for something other than to keep your butter cool." In the American epic, *Moby-Dick*, Ishmael said of Ahab he said he was "the meditative Magian Rover of deep waters." The opening lines of *Moby-Dick* tip us off: "Whenever I find myself growing grim about the mouth, whenever it is a damp, drizzly November in my soul, whenever I find myself involuntarily pausing before coffin warehouses, and bringing up the rear of every funeral I meet; and especially whenever my hypos get such an upper hand of me, that it requires a strong moral principle to prevent me from deliberately stepping into the street, and methodically knocking people's hats off—then, I account it high time to get to sea as soon as I can." Water, there is magic in it.

We here are fortunate to have here a river running through it: the Charles, and I hope you maguses saunter along its banks (Thoreau's derivation of "saunter" in his discourse on meditative walking: from French *Sainte Terre*, so a *saint-terre-r* is a "holy lander," one on the way to the Holy Land). Only two or three decades before Thoreau wrote *Walden* the Charles was flowing under us, right where we sit, under Marsh Chapel (it then wended northeast to flow under what is now Hillel House). Thoreau said: "they are leveling the hills of Boston to fill up a morass in the Milky Way." And that is why the Charles now flows by us instead of under us.

Water: what kinships there are in it! Or is it of us in it? That was the eternal conundrum of *Narcissus* in Greek mythology. This beautiful youth could not pass water without being mesmerized by kinship: water was the *spaeculum* (the mirror) of the ancients: in water I see my likeness. But water gives us back in a way that a modern mirror does not. Before still deep water my question is that of Narcissus: am I outside looking in, or inside looking out? In theological terms, we have here the double reflexivity of the image, and we don't have to skip many steps before we are in the middle of the problem of the *imago Dei*: is the human person the image of God, or is God the image of the human person? If you insist on a literal answer you can do as Narcissus did and dive in. But he didn't come up. We know in our toenails that water is kin to both death and life: Christians know this from baptism. Or, as I recommend, before the kinships that water arouses in our souls, you can live in the tensive power of the figure. How much of the spiritual life is born in figure and communicated amongst us by figuration? There is a latter-day expression I cotton to: Go figure! But beware: figuration is tensive, tactile, and tenuous. And that is why, if one dwells on and in the figure of water, Norman MacLean says: "I am haunted by waters."

This double reflexivity is not just a matter of reflection or rumination: it is our life. Water is outside of us and inside of us. We know this in our very body: water outside comes inside through daily drafts—first through mother's milk, then by the glass, the faucet, the brook. Conceived (con-ceived) by the joining of liquid sperm and coagulated egg, our first months are spent in the amniotic sea of our mother's womb. Organs emerge to circulate this internal sea within and among the forming microcosms of the organism that we bodily are. The body of each of us is an endless co-evolving of larger and larger macro-cosmoi internally related to the formation of smaller and smaller micro-cosmoi—the systemic process of continuing creation. And all this is parabolic of how Water is becoming flesh.

As a boy I was chagrined that my Daddy could catch fish and I couldn't. When I asked why, he said simply, "Because you don't think like a fish." Without knowing it, he announced a central dictum of all epistemology, that "like knows like." If I do not know something it is because there is unlikeness between me and it, and that unlikeness must be lessened or attenuated if I am to know it. (See, we are creeping up on Incarnations—for surely God and the human person are unlike?) That is why ontology precedes epistemology: the very being of the knower must change, as must the very being of the known, so that they are more adequated, more like than unlike. The fish I want to catch is outside me, but I can think like a fish because there is one inside me. Every flyfisherman knows the critical nature of the backcast: as Thoreau said, you must first catch the fish in the air before you can catch the fish in the water.

If you remember anything from freshman High School Biology, it will be this: "Ontogeny recapitulates phylogeny." A freewheeling translation: the origin of what *is* traces the origin of kinds (something Plato already knew). That means: our very bodies, our very corporation, incorporate many other kinds of bodies: their outsides are my insides. The first homes of settlers on the western American prairie were dug-out cellars, and my family was at home with salamanders, water-dogs, snakes. I never knew why, like all children, I loved to hide in the dark, unannounced and unseen, and peer out at an unsuspecting world; nor why I loved caves and burrowing underground. I was a snake. But I was a bird as well. I spent endless hours astride Ole Granny, my mare horse, herding cattle. In the heat of the day I would lie on the rimrock, watching eagles and hawks rising and falling on updrafts

"The Word Being Made Flesh, and the Priesthood of All Believers"

and downdrafts. Which was it, that I lay on the ground and looked up, or that I was an eagle looking down? I was and am morally certain I was and am both. I am still a bird, a multiply locative bird with many nests, and I still soar.

If the fish inside me was underdeveloped as a child, well, there wasn't much water outside to stir the fish inside (northwest Texas was a dry & barren place). But inside there were and are vestigial remnants of the fish I am: there are simulacra of gills, and my limbs are vestiges of fins and tail. The bird inside grows weakened as well: my bones are too dense to encompass sufficient air to bear me aloft. But I am gifted with the wings of imagination, that infinite capacity for the exacerbation of likeness and the lessening of unlikeness, that capacity not only for knowing but also for *becoming* the other without *being* the other. William Blake knew this bird on intimate terms: in the first Memorable Fancy of The Marriage of Heaven and Hell: "How do you know but ev'ry Bird that cuts the airy way, Is an immense world of delight, clos'd by your senses five." Who has such birds in the aviary of her mind will not require much prompting to set them free. That is how the Word uses this natural cage of animals that I am to turn the eternal Word into temporal flesh, so that St. Francis could preach to all creatures and speak them into existence as the Word made flesh.

The *Word*; the creating power of words. "The Spirit of God was hovering over the face of the waters. Then God *said*. . ." Have we thought enough, if at all, about what it means for God to create by *speaking* the creatures into existence? And let's get one thing straight—as the so-called "creationists" have not—viz., that God is *Creator* and not *cause*. In no defensible sense of causation is God the efficient cause of the universe or anything within it. As Creator God establishes the conditions under which anything other than God is and becomes. We humans are subject to all the conditions for the emergence of sentient animate creatures. What then distinguishes Mary from John?. A human infant is like every animate other: you shovel food in the front and the residue out the back. The child emerges in its uniqueness with *voice*: from gurgles (always thought by parents to be happy cooing) to yelling and screaming. But with words personhood emerges: personality, character, *this* person, not *that*. There are many deprivations, but the most fatal is not scant food or shelter; the greatest deprivation of all is that lack of love evident in not being spoken with and to. Children are spoken into existence: by parents, teachers, friends. This process of being created by the Word through words never ends. We are unfinished. Behind every new word, behind every language we don't understand, stands a world trying to become the Word made flesh in our own tongues. The continual and continuous Word never ceases to reduce and attenuate the unlikeness between us and all things holy—whether fascinating or daunting.

Okay, I said that unlike the typical sermon this one has not three points, but one. I must now regroup the three briefly, in order to come to the one. The three are temporal exstases of the Word especially but not exclusively honored in the Christian traditions, but all of them depend upon a fundamental distinction no longer much discussed in theology. That is the distinction between eternal and temporal creation, much observed in the early Church and in medieval theology. Eternal creation refers not to the emergence of the universe and the divine providence within it, but to the internal organization or economy of the Godhead. Only in that internal systemic context does the Prologue to John make any sense: "in the beginning was the Word, and the Word was with God and was God. . .and the Word became flesh and dwelt among us."

From the narrative of our salvation-history, let us settle on three temporal exstases of the Word. The first is that of *dabar* as embodied in Torah, the sign of the Covenant, and preserved in scrolls and tablets. No doubt it is necessary to put things into writing, but there is something terrible and terrifying about that too. The creating Word is a speaking, not a written word. The prophets knew this, as the rabbis came to know this: yes, the *dabar* of Torah is written, but it is also and necessarily *sung* and *danced* and renewed every Shabbat through the midsrashim of rabbinic interpretations. But humankind is always messing up, preferring some settled text or practice to being constituted by the living Word. The second is the Word made flesh in Jesus of Nazareth, in the words and deeds of his life. But Jesus was crucified and his followers left in despair. Were, that is, until there were manifest appearances of the Spirit of God, at first anonymously but then as the selfsame Spirit that was in Jesus. (Remember: today is Pentecost. But so is every day that the Lord hath made!)

The third is the spiritual birth of the Word in the human creature irrespective of time, place, or salvation-history narrative: which is why Pentecost is as central as Advent and Easter in the Christian calendar. Our own salvation-history is replete with instances of the Word becoming flesh among us, and none since biblical times is more powerful than that of Meister Eckhart. We are arrived at the one point of this exhortation, and remember it if you remember nothing else. Said Eckhart: "If the Word is not born in the ground of your own soul, it is nowhere born." (repeat) Do beliefs, doctrines, theories about God, the Word, Incarnation matter? Of course they do, but only if the Word is born in the ground of your own soul. Only if the Word suffuses, imbues your own soul's flesh are the gears of the living, speaking, creating Word engaged, the "talk" "walked."

"The Word Being Made Flesh, and the Priesthood of All Believers"

And only if the Word is being born in the ground of your own soul are you the bearer of that Word to your neighbor, only so are you priest to every other soul with whom you come into contact. In the ground of every human soul is the "spark," the trace of the Eternal Word. We never know, and need not know, when the flame within us fans the spark in the ground of another soul. God moves in mysterious ways His wonders to perform.

"If the Word is not born in the ground of your own soul, it is nowhere born."

If you bear what is born in you to your neighbor, it will not be triumphaly, but anonymously. Let it name itself. Let it speak your neighbor into existence, as it has you. This is your only glory, and your burden. We have it on high authority that the yoke is easy, and the burden light.

21

Notes on *The Community of the Beloved Disciple* by Raymond Brown[1]

INTRODUCTION

Welcome to the most adventuresome body of literature in the NT! (5) The word church never appears in John. We must read the Gospel on several levels: evangelist, community, Jesus. We read the Gospel as we have it, not relying on reconstructed sources. Four phases: pre Gospel (to late 80's), Gospel (90's), epistles (100), secession (110). John is cited earlier and more frequently by heterodox than by orthodox writers (24).

PHASE ONE: ORIGINS

For John the higher Christology of his community has brought out the true, deeper meaning of the original confessions. The claim to possess the witness of the Beloved Disciple (BD) enabled the Johannine Christians to defend their peculiar insights in Christology and ecclesiology. BD not one of the 12. Chapter 4 shifts attention from John the Baptist (JBap) and his followers to the Samaritans—did they influence the move to a higher Christology? Moses not David. Did they influence the harsh "Jews" language? In the

---

1. Raymond Brown, *The Community of the Beloved Disciple* (Mahwah, NJ: Paulist, 1979). Page references given in parentheses.

Notes on *The Community of the Beloved Disciple* by Raymond Brown

Fourth Gospel the vocabulary of the evangelist's time has been erad back into the ministry of Jesus. Some Johannine Christians had been executed by the authorities of the local synagogue (Martyn), like Stephen, James and James. Battle over Christology. John prefers the glory of God to that of men. Replacement nor refreshment. A new religion. John thought synthetically, though, not dialectically (key difference of Brown from Bultmann). New insights reinterpreted old. The Hellenistic features of the Fourth Gospel tell us more about its final audience than about the background of its author or its tradition. While phrases like Son of God and I Am have a distinctive OT and intertestamental background, their usage in John could be appreciated by pagan Greeks. John may have been uniquely universalist in presenting Jesus in a multitude of symbolic garbs, appealing to men and women of all backgrounds, so that they understood that Jesus transcends all ideologies (MacRae).

PHASE TWO: EXTERNAL STRUGGLES

Johannine misunderstanding functions like Synoptic parables. Opposition to the Jews, 5–12, to the World, 14–17: a chronology in relationships. The dominant dispute in the gospel is over the divinity of Jesus. Scriptural arguments meant to help crypto Christians leave the synagogue. Some left, some stayed to work for reform from within. The new answers John proposed were "true to the direction of the Scriptures." Orthodoxy is not always the possession of those who try to hold onto the past. In 5 of 6 passages in which he is mentioned the BD is directly contrasted with Peter. In counterposing their hero over against the most famous member of the 12, the Johannine community is symbolically counterposing itself over against the kinds of churches which venerate Peter and the 12. (Throughout, Brown downplays sources). John deemphasizes resurrection and highlights crucifixion. No clear evidence that John is condemning apostolic succession, church offices or sacramental practice. (Really??). "Some scholars may ponder on the luck of the Beloved Disciple that his community's Gospel was not recognized for the sectarian tractate that it really was. But others among us will see this as a recognition by Apostolic Christians that the Johannine language was not really a riddle and the Johannine voice was not alien. . . What the Johannine Christians considered to be a tradition that had come down from Jesus seems to have been accepted by many other Christians as an embraceable variant of the tradition that they had from Jesus" (18).

THE COURAGEOUS GOSPEL

PHASE THREE: INTERNAL STRUGGLES

The Gospel deals with outsiders, the Epistles with insiders. Both point to specific situations, but have wider import. Stage trumps source, history trumps literature, for Brown. Battle with Bauer (105): "A more important question, which Bauer never really answered, is whether what won out in orthodoxy was truer than its opposite to *the implications* of what was held from the beginning." Epistles show fight with those who left (secessionists). The Gospel stressed that Jesus is the *Son of God*. The Epistles stressed that *Jesus* is the Son of God. 4;2–3. This leads to some consideration of who these secessionists were. Docetists? Trimorhpic Protenoia, Apocalypse of Peter, Tripartite Tractate: they believed that the human existence of Jesus while real was not salvifically significant. John after all relativizes Jesus humanity, and also makes less important the public ministry of Jesus. John alone does not describe Jesus' baptism. For him the cross is the glory: death is revelation, not moral example. The Jesus of 1 John though is a redeemer as well as a revealer. I John brings back ethics, and argues about ethics. John is notably deficient on precise moral teaching when compared to the Synoptics. I John is a sermon about love spoke in anger, with a dose of hatred (RAH). Love, by the way, not for the neighbor, but for one another. In 1 John we see that the dualistic language once employed by Jesus in his attack on the world and the Jews hs been shifted over to an attack on Christians with whom the author disagrees. John attacks the Jews. 1 John attacks the Gnostics. The dualism of John over centuries has had a deletrious effect, supporting people who hate others for the love of God.

PHASE FOUR: DISSOLUTION

Some go to the Great Church, others to the Gnostic movement. Heterodox groups championed John. Oldest commentary: Heracleon, 170. Loved by Valentinus and Ptolemy. Similar to Odes of Solomon. Logos in Tripartite Tractate, IAM in Second Apocalypse of James, Thuder Perfect Mind. By contrast, more orthodox knew him not: no mention in Ignatius or Justin Martyr. Ireneaus reads the Gospel through the Epistle. I Johns saved John for the church. The Johannine stress on the pre-existence of Jesus and on his SOnship as the model for the Christian's status as child was the matrix out of which a Gnostic thesis could be shaped. John's portrait of Mary Magdalene at the tomb allowed the Gnostic Gospels to make her the chief recipient of revelation and rival to Peter. 'The ultimate check on John has been the church's hermeneutical decision to place it in the same canon with M\M\L,

Notes on The Community of the Beloved Disciple by Raymond Brown

which implicitly advocate the side opposite to many Johannine positions." The church chose to live with tension. The presence in our Scriptures of a disciple whom Jesus loved more than Peter is an eloquent commentary on the relative value of church office. The authoritative office is necessary because a task is to be done and unity is to be preserved, but the scale of power in various offices is not necessarily the scale of Jesus' esteem and love (164). "While the Gospel was capable of being read in a gnostic manner, it was the Johannine secessionists, mentioned in 1 John, who first began to go down the path toward gnosticism, and that at no period documented in either the Gospel or the Epistles can one yet speak of a real Johannine Gnosticism" (182)—*His last sentence.*

22

The Gnostic Worldview

Frederik Wisse Lectures: As Noted by Robert Allan Hill

Winter 1984
McGill University
Montreal

JANUARY 17, 1984

The following comments are general reflections on Hellenistic religions.

Overview

The Greco-Roman world harbored a yearning for ancient wisdom. The interests of their religious perspectives were typical of religious interests like those seen in Hinduism, for example, and elsewhere. There was a vast, eclectic syncretism at work in the ancient world, a unique phenomenon. This made possible an abstraction of common themes out of and from different traditions. Philosophers, popular and otherwise, did this and had a wide influence. For those "rootless" types in the population there was and admiration for those who had an ancient, living tradition... like the Jews.

The Gnostic Worldview

The Old Testament was widely available. Similarly, the Egyptians had ancient wisdom, ancient mythology, ancient manuscripts, ancient practices. Isis and Osiris became popular broadly across the Mediterranean at this time, and were written about by Greek authors. The Isis cult itself continued in a modified form for a long time, in a recasting of the ancient myth.

The Greeks and Romans took interest in Judaism, Egyptian religion, India, Persia, Mesopotamia and the Sumarians. Some of the Canaanite religious lore had been made available earlier. Slowly, these concepts, names, and themes became prevalent. Plutarch discussed Isis and Osiris. By way of literature, these things came into the hands of those who wanted to make use of them. (This is not unlike what happened with *Pistis Sophia* and other such books in religious societies set up in the 19th century.)

Aesclypius saw ancient Egypt as the land of the Gods, as described in one of the hermetic tractates. Religion was purer, piety was better, it was thought, in ancient times. The Greco-Roman culture was in part trying to recover the "golden age of religion." Egypt is the dwelling place of heaven! Temples, History, True Religion! A time will come when Egyptians will have served the gods in vain, and religion will have become vain. All activity of divinity will flee to heaven (really this is somewhat nationalistic). Foreigners will come! Egyptians will be prohibited from worshipping God. The future life will become prominent. In Judaism, Hades and Gehenna are recast in terms of a hope for a blessed life after death. Could this life be an end in itself? The Epicureans said "yes." But most others said "no," because there are too many negatives in this life. The Platonic contrast between matter and spirit, mind and body abetted this. Paul's image of the runner and the race, with the crown as fulfillment, fits in here. No, real freedom to pursue one's own interest is only possible for the immortals, who possessed all the positives: perfection, incorruptibility, and so on. Death cast a long shadow and made immortality extremely desirable.

The Gnostics took it for granted that this life and this body were foreign and oppressive, and that there was no way to justify this life as an end in itself (cf. M Aurelius, *The Emporer*). This is a place of suffering, and suffering with, and suffering through, not a place of high expectations (cf. The Sentences of Sextus). Judaism and Christianity stand in this lineage. One seeks to be saved from this world, this body, this cycle, this experience.

Mystery Cults

Lohse is sufficient for an understanding of the mystery cults. Gnosticism is a similar solution to the human predicament. You can escape, they taught.

The mystery cults (Apuleius, Metamorphoses, the Isis cult) offered a sacramental escape. Baptism. Sacred Meals. Initiation rites and stages. The Gnostics were very suspicious of sacramentalism. To find escape through a sacrament, but not through life or belief—this, they denied. No, there is no short-cut, the Gnostics taught. In fact, after baptism, the moral burden of the believer becomes extremely heavy. It would be incomprehensible why or that a mature Christian could or would sin. The goal, the Gnostic goal, was perfection. So, life and lifestyle were very much involved. Sacramentalism can lead to a great deal of laxity in one's lifestyle and moral life. Mystery cults (like that of Mithra) were like the Masons, and had that kind of attraction: don't think about things too much, be non-exclusive, be a member of as many as possible, maybe all of them. Stoicism as a philosophical school hardly existed, but its influence as an ethical system was of major importance. Its worldview was quite influential. Stoicism and Platonism supplied the basic worldview of the Greco-roman world. The divine logos is understood as dispersed throughout the universe—a kind of pantheism. The cosmos had a divine imprint. "If I get in tune with the cosmos, then I can live a life of inner freedom, in spite of my circumstances." Epictetus comes to mind here. He was a traveling preacher who extolled inner freedom from the pressures of life. The body. The passions. The buffeting of fate. None of these can touch you if you have inner peace. Paul's teaching on freedom is similar. Circumstances should make no difference. This kind of creed is not for the many, not for the masses, but for those who have the leisure and freedom to consider it. If one is other directed, one is a slave of circumstance, but if one is inner-directed (like the Stoics), then one has peace. Christianity was the harder way. And the Gnostics were the elite who alone could reach perfection. Philo could interpret the OT allegorically, as was done in Christian circles, too. A community of sages: a loose, scattered, small group held together by a spiritual bond. There were also a few who called for a revival of the old Greek religion (Appolonyius and the Neopythagoreans and Epictetus).

Early Christianity

How shall we describe it? There are various possibilities. One is the traditional view, which was dominant until 1850 and is still strong. Jesus Christ is the founder, the head of the church, and the Pope stands in the place of Christ. The tradition is transmitted to and through the apostles. Who? Paul, James, the twelve, Jude, Mark, Luke. Authority and leadership are given to the apostles, along with the right and perfect doctrine, in the Scriptures,

The Gnostic Worldview

within the canon, the perfect rule of faith and practice. All were unified; there was no serious disagreement (cf. Acts 4:32). Gifts of the spirit were shared, there was not a single needy person among them, and the apostles defended the truth. They did so against religious charlatans like Simon Magus, Lucian, and Marcus the Gnostic. "Simony" is the buying of spiritual gifts and religious offices.

JANUARY 25, 1984

The following comments are general reflections on the life of the early church.

Let us review the traditional view, that of the church fathers. First, there is Jesus. Second, there is the kerygma, the preaching of the gospel. Third, there is the oral tradition of Jesus' words and deeds. The first grows into Jewish Christianity. The second becomes Pauline Christianity. The third develops into non-Pauline Gentile Christianity.

One: Jewish Christianity.

Jewish Christianity is a source and issue of endless speculation and consideration. On the original view, this is the "first generation," which set the norm for teaching, practice, ritual and polity. However, the basis and support for this argument (from Judaism to Christianity) are questionable. We know there were Jewish Christian sects by the second and third centuries, groups that were ethnically Jewish, and did not recognize the validity of Gentile Christianity. They were later called Ebionites or Nazarenes. *We simply lack the evidence we need to support much of this speculation.* Our speculation continues even in terms of the sources identified and used in this set of arguments. *None of the usual N.T. sources are certainly, without any doubt, Jewish Christian (including Matthew, Hebrews, and the Apocalypse).*

Two: Pauline Christianity

Paul understood himself as the Apostle to the Gentiles. He went first to the synagogues, but was not there accepted. He understood his mission to be among the Gentiles. Paul's theology is a theology *apart from the law.* Now, to be sure, there is a real tension between One and Two. The church of the second and third centuries understood themselves though to be within the Pauline tradition.

THE COURAGEOUS GOSPEL

Three: Gentile Christianity.

Here we think of Roman, Syrian and other Christianity across the Mediterranean. The Roman church was basically a Gentile church. Rome was non-Pauline church as well. How are we think numerically of Jewish and Gentile Christianity in the period of the early church? For Paul, Jewish Christianity is only a remnant, and a very small one at that. Jerusalem had a population of fifty thousand in the first century. Did three thousand become Christian in one day? It seems unlikely. Paul sees the rejection of Jesus by Israel as a hardening of Israel that is according to God's purpose and plan. Now, in contrast to other ages, God is moving to, toward and through the Gentiles. This is not merely a *pragmatic* move on Paul's part. Paul talks of harvesting among the Gentiles. By the years 50 to 60 CE Christianity has become a Gentile affair. Jewish Christianity is tiny, stagnant, isolated and forgotten. *The community of the Gospel of John would clearly be a part of this group—Gentile Christianity.*

What this amounts to is a highly heterodox, pervasively pluralistic situation. What is orthodox on the one hand is not heterodox, but what is heretical on the other hand is not heterodox either. This rather, is a time period during which very important differences about Christ, about organization, about Spirit, and about many other things *are not settled, and are far from being settled*. A number of widely divergent views could and did exist side by side. This heterodox pluralism was greatly aided by the geographical isolation of the churches, the communities, from one another.

As the church grew, and as groups thus came into contact with one another on a more regular basis, there was increasingly more chance of conflict. And conflict ensued. Teachers came to Rome for a fee, to speak either in a private home or in a public setting. They came to expound on the deeper truths of the Christian faith in the midst of a tolerant, pluralistic, heterodox setting. Here the story of Valentinus comes to mind. Of necessity, the setting in second century Rome was a highly heterodox situation. Ignatius, writing as a Bishop, as a defender of the faith, expects a following and finds one. Still, his too is a highly heterodox, highly pluralistic situation.

In such a fluid situation, conflict, when it came, tended to be conflict in terms of people, of individuals. The whole career of Paul's ministry itself comes to mind here. "Why do you think you can push your teaching on us, Paul?" Likewise, conflict, when it came, tended to be conflict in terms of practice, of behavior, of individual behavior. It is much easier to fight about people and practices than it is to fight about doctrine. It is easy to fight about circumcision, about law and laws, about taxes, about eating customs, and so on. But to prepare to fight about doctrine, teaching and dogma took and

The Gnostic Worldview

takes a whole lot longer to work out. Think for example about the Trinity. This was finally a very painful, controversial issue over which the church split.

Our picture of the early church and its heterodox, pluralistic condition can be illustrated with reference to A. Early Catholicism, B. Montanism, C. Marcionism, D. Valentinianism. By the way, how many Christians were there in the early second century? We do not know. Perhaps 50,000? It is only a wild guess.

A. Early Catholicism

Here our examples are found in the Pastoral Epistles and in Luke-Acts, both "orthodox" if you will.

B. Montanism

We have evidence of Montanism in Phrygia, and in Asia Minor. Montanism is an expression of religious enthusiasm. It was created and lead by a prophetic figure, Montanus, with the support of many "prophetesses." Montanus and his followers maintained a very fervent hope and expectation of the return of the Lord in the very near future. They were seen as a threat to the church. They supported both the office of Bishop and the role of the prophetesses Priscilla and Maximilla. Asia Minor had the most Christians for a very long time The Nicaean list of Bishops is the longest.

C. Marcionism

Marcion basically belongs to the Gnostic movement. He was Gnostic, with this difference: he set up churches. Our knowledge of Marcion is limited. In a way, his church was a counter-church. Marcion, from Asia-minor, was excommunicated. We know though that he had followers, and his churches had adherents in Rome and in Carthage. Marcion's father was a wealthy Bishop on the Black Sea. Marcionism continued well into the fifth century. Marcion believed that the God of Jesus was not the God who demanded the annihilation of the Amalekites. These two Gods cannot be the same God, he argued. They just cannot be identical. *His primary proof texts were found in the Gospel of John.* In a way, Marcion propounded an extreme Paulinism. His *Antitheses* is his most distinctive work. Marcionism was a highly ascetic movement, more dedicated and less compromising than the great church, which was much larger in numbers. Marcion made his appeal to the discipline of the Christian lifestyle: piety, dedication, Godliness. The desert fathers, the monastics, were kindred spirits to his and to him. They longed for the ideal way, celebrated encratism, the rejection of marriage.

D. Valentinianism

The Valentinians were found in North Africa, in Asia Minor, and in Mesopotamia (they were thus far less of a political threat, because they wee on the periphery to a great extent). This too was a form of Christian Gnosticism. The Valentinians made room for the exploration of Christian faith by Gnostics. They too were disciplined ascetics. They taught and practiced a sex-less marriage, a kind of brother\sister union, which was successful and genuine. Virginity was in some places a condition for baptism. The Valentinians taught a radical dualism and engaged in much imaginative and creative speculation.

Summary

A tension in the early church quickly developed between the uncompromising perspective and the more moderate view. Paul and the N.T. writers are moderates. It would be wrong, they thought, to require and demand asceticism of all. They may have admired and preferred asceticism, but they could and would not demand it. You can be saved without being a monk. This has always been a bitter struggle, between those who charge others with fanaticism, and those who charge others with corruption. (You are a fanatic! You are corrupt!). The gnostics and others like them tended toward anti-authoritarian perspectives, and had strong tendencies toward asceticism. They made no compromises with the world. They also developed strong tendencies toward speculative theology.

Let us say a word about the Gnostic documents.

The Nag Hammadi library was found in December of 1945. It only became available in translation in 1976. A whole issue of Biblical Archaeology was then devoted to the discovery. At about the same time, the facsimile edition began to appear, with Codex VII. Bookmaking was a relatively new art (the codex) at the time of the composition of these documents. They were contained in a leather envelope, and bound. Rodents and moisture can often destroy these. Goat and sheep skins were often used. For binding they used cartonnage, and papyrus as a filler and for cover. For example, a Coptic translation of Genesis, and letters is very interesting for historians. Dating is possible in terms of the kind of ink (i.e. did it have a metallic base, or was it plant-based?)

Coptic is an Egyptian language in Greek letters, plus a few others. Fifteen percent of the words are Greek. They used a *T* not a *PI* ending to make recitation easier. They provided readers aids for eyes and for pronunciation. The documents were made out of papyrus, a choir. Only one codex out of the thirteen made use of multiple choirs. The fold in the document is very important. They only started to write on the document after it was already bound (you can tell by looking at the margins).

JANUARY 31, 1984

The Gnostic Worldview

Lifestyle rather than doctrine determined inclusion or exclusion for Pachomius. He was the father of alphabet mysticism, had an interest in heterodox, curious thing. Pachomius was the father of orthodox monasticism. The burial of the books was due to the Alexandrian Patriarch Athanasius, who sent out a letter to churches up and down the Nile, warning about apocryphal books (like the NHL). The Pachomian monks studied them privately in cells, and judged that they "could be used with profit." Perhaps a cell search was organized, and perhaps the intention was to bury the books for a while, and then to dig them up later. We do not know. Unlike the Dead Sea Scrolls, they cannot be assigned to the archaeological discovery of a community. Any volume containing heretical material was thrown out. The tie-in with the monasteries is a very important point. If these assumptions are true, then maybe some Anchorite brought them in.

Were these monks then Gnostics? Well, St. Anthony was as orthodox as they come. Hieracas\Ephiphanius wrote and made use of apocryphal material. There was perhaps a great deal of tension between the village Bishop and the monastic hermits, who were outsiders both physically and theologically. Their life practice was more pious, more dedicated. Orthodoxy has no control, and the monastic life is necessary, says Hieracas. Athanasius says it is not necessary for all. For Hieracas, if you are married, and if you die before practicing asceticism, you will not inherit the kingdom of heaven. The ascetic lifestyle is God's demand for all! Compromise with this world is excluded. A faithful remnant must struggle to remain. The purpose of this life is a moral battle. It is not to raise children, settle homes, go to college, and so on. Rather, the purpose of this life is to learn to fight demons in the desert. The move from "a better way" to "the only way" is a very small step. Chastity, poverty, obedience, the narrow gate. Many NHL documents exclude martyrdom, as "the easy way out." One is to reject the world and so imitate the heavenly life. Sex is evil, and there is no sex in heaven. Try living the angelic life now.

Conclusion

All the NHL codices are *heterodox* (neither orthodox nor heretical), *esoteric* (inside group, elitist, secret, meant for a small group), *ascetic* (the more Christian the document, generally, the more ascetic), used by *monks* in the early monastic movement, and used generally for *private meditation* (so they were not equivalent to Scripture). They were used to reinforce the ascetic ideal. The monks also used the wilder parts of the OT and NT in support of their own speculation. In church history, when the accent falls on asceticism, then usually there is less emphasis on teaching. These monks practiced an "ascetic syncretism." A book is acceptable if it supports right practice, "orthopraxis." Orthodox teaching led to pre-marital sex in high proportion. Where interest in doctrine is high, rigor in practice is low, and vice-versa.

The Gnostic Myth

Sophia is to Eve as Christ is to Adam. The "fall" happens in the heavens, "up there." There never was a paradise on earth. The fall is the escape of some light from the fullness of eternal light. Salvation is the return of the light to the realm of light. How did the light get out? This is a tough problem. There are two possibilities. One is dualism, found in Manichaeism. Light and darkness are co-eternal. Another is that a lower being within the Godhead (Sophia) makes a mistake. She wanted to create without the help of her companion, like the Father. She wanted to be equal to the supreme God. So she creates. . .a monster. Once she sees it, she throws it out. But, unfortunately, since the monster comes from Sophia, some light comes with it. Yaldabaoth is the chief archon. But since the verse says "let us. . ." there are more and other archons, evil demonic beings. Creation is the product of Yaldabaoth, who is a horrendous, horrible being. So, creation is a rotten place: hades, hell, not just hell on earth but hell as earth. This is hell. Yaldabaoth is tricked into transferring light particles into Adam (blowing in his nostrils), then into Eve. Sex is the way in which light particles are spread out. Seth is the traditional hero of the Gnostics. Seth and his race and seed fall into forgetfulness, and they need to be reminded of their knowledge of their heavenly origin. They need to be shown the way back, through an ascetic life style. For when the pleroma is restored, then the archons will be destroyed. There will be no way for the whole thing to start over. The Apocryphon of John is an excellent instance of this.

The Gnostic Worldview

MARCH 27, 1984

The Gospel of Thomas: the issues here include its relationship to Jewish Christianity, to the Gospel of the Hebrew, to other sayings, to the synoptic tradition, its independence, or dependence on gospels or traditions.

Purpose and Intent

The author compiler mentions the twin in the first sentence, and has an interest in asceticism and encratism. He holds in check, controls, and denies the bodily passions. Food (vegetarianism and never eating to full satisfaction). Clothing. Sex. Sleep. Encratism, idealized in monasticism, is against marriage. Marriage is a creation of evil powers. In the Acts of Thomas, he comes to a wedding and converts the couple to an encratic lifestyle. The books that bear Thomas' name have in common this emphasis on encratism, so perhaps it is not accidental that Thomas (Acts, Contender) is mentioned here.

Hermeneia is essential to salvation, but this is in contrast to "gnosis" as it generally came. Still, it is a kind of knowledge. Jesus speaks in parables in order to fool. There is an elitist aspect with this ascetic emphasis on preparation, on the narrow gate, on self-denial, on salvation through interpretation.

These are secret sayings because, though they are public, they are still mysterious. On this view, only a very few sayings are immediately clear, but most are enigmatic, riddles. In the early fourth century began the tradition of cenobitic monasticism with St. Pachomius, who started a community, with a rule, like that of St. Benedict. We have a number of letters about this, thanks to Jerome in the late fourth century. They are translated into Latin, which itself is strange. Hard to make sense of it. Then some Coptic and Greek fragments were found, which were very curious, full of enigmatic speech, cryptograms, allegories, coded language, sacred purposed, coded letters, and so on. Often, a prayer came out of it. Or, there was no code at all.

There are many parts of these documents that are out of reach, where understanding cannot be put into words. Did the author know the meaning of all these passages? No. What was the theology of Thomas? Was there such? Can we distil a Gnostic theology from this, like that of Jonas. These texts were never intended to be studied the way we do now. We can say, though, that the author-compiler takes very seriously the tradition of Jesus. The author does not deny the eschaton, but takes the emphasis away from it, not denial, but reduced influence. H. R. Niehbur: "heresy is absolutizing the relative." *There is an interesting overlap with Gnosticism in this heterodox, early Christian piece of literature.*

The constant suspicion is that there was never any definitive meaning for these sayings. It is Zen-like, a mystical Christ. So it is the seeking of the interpretation, rather than its finding, that comes to the fore. So, for scholars, there is less work to be done. It was used for devotion by Pachomian monks of curious tastes: Thunder, Thomas, Letters, Meditation, Enlightenment, Heavenly World. Many of Thomas' sayings are early monastic, an early form of Syrian monasticism. Thomas is clear on ethics, mysterious on all else.

23

The Jewish Background to the New Testament

Opening Lecture

FAMILIARITY WITH ANCIENT HOLINESS is a tremendous and terrifying thing. Of course many students of ancient religious literature attain no such thing. They glance over these old writings, turn in acceptable work, and move on—remarkably untouched by the pain and glory, the holiness, behind the writings. Familiarity with this holiness is tremendous and terrifying. For this reason: it brings the student within earshot of another world, a world quite unlike the smug, cold, and self-sufficient world in which most modern western people live most of the time. Ancient holiness introduces the student to another world—a world disturbed by the question of God: a conceptual, social, historical, literary world profoundly unlike, different from, foreign to, alien to ours. A world grounded in the possibility that our world, both secular and religious, largely deems impossible: the possibility of the Holy One of Israel. A vision, like that of Isaiah, of the invisible. "I saw the Lord sitting upon a throne, high and lifted up; and his train filled the temple. Above him stood the seraphim; each had six wings: with two he covered his face, and with two he covered his feet, and with two he flew. And one called to another and said: 'Holy, holy, holy is the Lord of hosts; the whole earth is full of his glory.'" The high and Holy One of Israel. Familiarity with ancient holiness... that is the hidden treasure before us.

This holiness, however, died with the men and women who practiced it and believed it. Only in their institutional documents (e.g., synagogue) or in their remaining writings (e.g., 1 Enoch) can we hope as moderns to encounter it. This course follows the latter path. It is a course focused on ancient literature, literature from the period 200 BCE to 100 CE, with some a little later. At this point the major "anthropological" question of the course arises. If we are interested in ancient holiness and the people inspired by it, why then do we concentrate merely on the literature? Indeed, even in the bibliography assembled for this, many students of the Jewish background to the New Testament have gone well beyond the literature of the period. Simon's book, Jewish Sects at the Time of Jesus, is a good example. He feels confident and free to speculate widely about his topic. This is precisely the point: the difference between primary source material and secondary appropriations of it, although basic and well-known, is all too easily blurred. St. Paul admonishes us to "test everything" (1 Thess 5) and in this case we do well to heed his advice. In this course you must develop some capacity for judging what is good and what is bad secondary literature. As has been the case with Jesus himself, all kinds of pictures can be drawn of the social, historical and theological background of the N.T. You find these pictures—very different from one another—in the secondary literature. Which ones are true to their subject? Only a solid grasp of the primary literature will help you begin to answer this question. The difference between what we know and what we think we know needs constantly to be kept before us. Therefore, we concentrate on the primary source material, mainly as it is found in C. K. Barrett's The *New Testament Background: Selected Documents*.

On the other hand, cautious as we must be in claiming too much certain knowledge too quickly, we are vitally interested in the "holiness" behind these writings. We want an understanding of intertestamental Jewish theology. We want descriptions of the sociology of the period, including accurate pictures of the main sects, Pharisees, Sadducees, and Essenes. We want, too, a grasp of the history of the period stretching from the Maccabean revolt down to the destruction of the temple: both dates, facts, events, and so on; and, a hold on the process of history weaving its way through 300 years in the life of a small, minor, state located on the fringes of the world's greatest empire. Theology, sociology, and history, now lie just beneath our primary interest in and focus on the literature of the period. But we seek the truth of these things, without distortion. Both to teach by example by showing you how I handle primary literature in order to distill background information,

The Jewish Background to the New Testament

and to teach by whetting your appetites for further study, I want to offer you three glimpses into the Jewish background of the N.T. These three short essays (about ten minutes each!) constitute what on the stage would be called cameo appearances of one historical, one social, and one theological issue. May I warn you that the themes here chosen are the most important ones in each of the three areas making up the Jewish background to the N.T. (so have your pens poised!). In history, the most important theme is that of political conflict, tension, and rebellion. In sociology, the most important theme is the question of the Pharisees. In theology, the most important theme is that of apocalyptic. Would that we knew all we want to about political turmoil, the Pharisees, and apocalyptic in the Jewish background of the N.T.! What we do not know of each far outweighs what we do know. Perhaps, though, these short glimpses of each will stimulate some interest for the months to come.

A.

Of the three areas, we are on the soundest ground in the area of history, proper. Yet we must not think of Jewish history of 200 BCE to 100 CE as of earth-shaking consequence for world politics. Nothing could be further from the truth! The little Jewish "nation" was a political backwater in the great Roman empire, a vassal state presided over by a combination of third-rate Roman civil servants and quisling native royalty. Pilate and Herod were not exactly Maggie Thatcher and Queen Elizabeth. "How odd of God to choose the Jews!" But brief survey of historical development of the period, focusing on political conflict, is essential to an understanding of the Jewish background to the N.T.

In the third century BCE, the Ptolemies, benevolent despots from Egypt, controlled Palestine. The encourage Hellenization of culture and the Septuagint (Greek O.T.) came into being. The native priestly group in Jerusalem emphasized the Pentateuch in religious instruction, and wide latitude when no absolute rule could be found. Things considered "*adiaphora*" were many (explain). Among the leadership, at any rate, Hellenization went a great way (See Hengel, *Judaism and Hellenism*). After 200 B.C.E. it is questionable how accurately we can speak of a "Hebrew" culture. A gradual process of benevolent hellenization is taking place. But in the years 200–198 another foreign power, the Seleucids of Syria took over. They were less benevolent. Antiochus Epiphanes (175–163), one of the Seleucid rulers, was not satisfied with the slow pace of hellenization in Palestine. He forced hellenization at a much faster rate with edicts regarding the Sabbath, pork, circumcision, and the temple. A tremendous political reaction came—not from the upper class priests, but from the country priests. The reaction soon swelled into a revolt centered around the Maccabees, a family of many brothers whose name means, "the hammerers." Through this revolt Israel gained independence and a fierce sense of nationalistic pride. Our primary sources of knowledge for this period are the intertestamental apocryphal literature like 1 and 2 Maccabees, and Josephus.

Judas Maccabeas reconsecrated the temple in 165 (This event is still commemorated today by a feast). His followersand successors, however, the Hasmoneans soon began to fight among themselves; they were keenly interested in securing power. (The origin of the Pharisees may well lie in the early Hasmonean movement.) Nationalistic fervor continued to increase. Alexander Janaeus ruled Israel from 104–78 BCE. His territorial domain exceeded that of Solomon. But the internal Hasmonean squabbles continued, and finally led to an appeal, by one faction, to Rome. Roman response was swift. Pompey simply marched in and took over in 63 BCE. Following Roman practice, he set up a puppet government under the Edomite Antipater (Herod's father). The Pharisees opposed this move. Herod became king in 37 BCE and died in 4- BCE At this time the Romans and Jews shared an awkward balance of power in Palestine. The Roman appearance did not squelch revolutionary feelings. It led, rather, to a resurgence of hope for an independent state. This fervor finally culminated in the Jewish War of 66 CE, sparked by the refusal of a priest to sacrifice to Caesar. The Roman eagle in the temple exercised equally Zealots, Pharisees, and Saducees at many levels of the population. In 70 CE the Romans put an end to the revolt by sacking Jerusalem and burning the temple. With the burning of the temple this period of Jewish political history comes to a close.

B.

To domesticate the tangled and obscure history of apocalyptic literature is at present an impossible task. Questions abound regarding the origin of apocalyptic, the number and dating of intertestamental texts to be assembled under this rubric, its relationship to prophecy on the one hand and gnosticism on the other, the exact boundaries of its extent and content, the sociology of its actual utilization, its confusion with eschatology, and its precise relationship to the New Testament writings. We are not yet out of the woods. Many studies eschew, therefore, any detailed discussion of the history of apocalyptic, and dive in, in mediares, overcharged with major undefended assumptions. In particular, questions about the dating of apocalyptic texts remain unresolved. In such a situation, a cautious and minimal assessment of the raw material available, and interpretations thereof, probably makes the most sense. If 4 Ezra (2 Esdras) was written in 100 CE, just how valuable can it be for background to the New Testament? Was "The Assumption

The Jewish Background to the New Testament

of Moses" written during Jesus1 lifetime? And what about the apocalyptic features of the Dead Sea Scrolls? Do they encourage us to judge that, "what we have in Mark, therefore, is a foundation document for an apocalyptic community?" Only with Enoch do we seem to be on utterly solid ground with regard to intertestamemtal apocalyptic literature.

Assumptions must then be made gingerly about particulars. Nevertheless, we have to have some idea of apocalyptic in general in order to approach many N.T. passages in a historical fashion. Any such review has to begin with the issue of origin. For some time the origin of apocalyptic was posited in Iran. "Persian cosmological dualism" was depicted as the seedbed for Jewish apocalyptic. Some still hold tightly to this view today. But the crucial problem with the hypothesis of Persian origin was spotted early on. In recent years, the origin of apocalyptic has been sought in the Old Testament itself. Chief among these attempts is P. D. Hanson's *The Dawn of Apocalyptic*. It is a common failing of academic theological writing that historical questions are immediately pushed well back into the time of King David, if not into the Garden of Eden itself, when no cause for such excessive historical concern is apparent. Perhaps we repeat that failing here. Nevertheless, Hanson's argument is important for this essay for one theological reason and one historical (sociological) reason. Behind the literature in 3 Isaiah Hanson sees a growing conflict in the post-exilic community, a conflict between "visionaries" and "realists." The "visionaries" stand in the tradition of 2 Isaiah. Perhaps they include members of the disenfranchised Levitical priesthood, or persons who remained in Judah during the Babylonian captivity. They confront the ruling party with a Utopian vision of what the real "restoration" entails—mainly, the action of Yahweh himself. The "realists" on the other hand probably come from the line of Zadokite priests who, since the time of Solomon had controlled the temple. Their idea of restoration centers almost exclusively on the temple (its rebuilding, arrangement, and the religious practices intended for it). Through the years from the time of the return until sometime in the first half of the fifth century, the rift between these two groups grows ever wider, until at last it devolves into the most acrimonious sort of conflict. Out of this sociological setting, Hanson argues, apocalyptic eschatology is born. For Hanson, prophecy gives way to apocalyptic as vision and reality separate, as the prophet feels less bound to apply his vision to mundane politics, and as any "realistic optimism" about deliverance in the present age declines. When hope is unhinged from history, prophecy becomes apocalyptic: this is the theological point of interest. Historically, it is noteworthy that Hanson at least sets the dawn of apocalyptic in connection with a communal dispute which is visible behind the polemical literature of 3 Isaiah. (This argument depends heavily on Karl Mannheim's sociological treatise, *Ideology and Utopia*.) Hanson writes, "already at the end of the sixth century the basic schema of apocalyptic eschatology has evolved in Israel . . . The whole development is perfectly comprehensible within the history of Israel's own community and cult. Hasty recourse to late Persian influence is therefore unnecessary and unjustifiable in the search for the origins of the basic eschatology of Jewish apocalyptic."[1]

These apocalyptic texts, however, did not arise in a sociological, political, or historical vacuum. The turmoil of the later second temple period permeates the whole of the literature, especially regarding the fourth point of contact which Vielhauer mentions, that of determinism and imminent expectation: "the pitcher is near to the well, the ship to the harbour, the caravan to the city, and life to its conclusion." This sort of expectation arose over against the national eschatology. We are reminded somewhat of Hanson's portrait of 3 Isaiah. Again a polemical background to the literature makes much sense. Vielhauer notices this point but within the bounds of this writing does not pursue it. For instance, Vielhauer writes: "we may therefore designate apocalyptic as a special expression of the Jewish eschatology which existed alongside the national eschatology represented by the rabbis." Here again we see an official ideology, focusing on the temple, set in tension with a Utopian vision, focusing in apocalyptic fashion on the imminent end. We witness a polemical polarity in intertestamental apocalyptic that has formal similarities to the polemic Hanson sees at the dawn of apocalyptic.

C.

Who were the Pharisees? If fate or the Paraclete could bequeath Biblical studies with one all-important gift, we might well wish it to be the answer to this question. How much more we would know about Oesus, Paul, and the early church, if we were more familiar with the Pharisees! It would be difficult, in terms of this course, to overestimate the importance of the Pharisees. Let us then turn to a look at Pharisaism in the first century.

A few things are fairly universally asserted about the Pharisees. The *fons et origo* of the Pharisaical movement was the Maccabean revolt. Some sort of proto-Pharisaical activity perhaps took place in the third century, BCE, under the influence of the *hymnasia* and hellenic culture in general My judgment regarding the study of the origin of the Pharisees would be to look less toward the O.T. and the second temple and more toward post-Alexandrian culture for sources and influences. The root of the name refers

---

1 Hanson, *Dawn of the Apocalyptic*, 160.

The Jewish Background to the New Testament

to the "separated ones." Over the course of time this originally scornful epithet came to be used in a positive way of the group. (The parallel with Methodism is often invoked at this point.) The Pharisees dissented from the political maneuverings in the late second temple. On the basis of Torah and an expanding body of traditionally transmitted "oral law," the Pharisees attacked foreign influence in the temple and among the priests, The Pharisees seem to have been very popular with the masses. They seem to have enjoined the average layman to practice priestly piety. They seem to have sided with the common people over against the mighty. The Pharisees had made inroads into many walks of life in Palestine, but—as far as we know—had no highly developed internal organization of their own. (Parenthetically, this is a good example of scholarly confusion vis. the Pharisees. On the one hand, it is widely and generally asserted that the Pharisees held great sway over the people, to the extent, for instance, that the temple hierarchy unwillingly followed their instructions regarding temple practice, for fear of the people. On the other hand, it is widely and generally asserted that the Pharisees had no very powerful organization of their own. This is a non-sequitur!) Doctrinal questions concerning the Pharisees are much more difficult to answer. At least we may attribute to them a focus on the Torah, though not to the exclusion of the temple, and along with this focus a development of exegesis. Finally, and perhaps most significantly, the Pharisees gave birth to rabbinic Judaism. All this, as little as it is, could fairly safely be said about the Pharisees.

The major scholarly problem with regard to the Pharisees is the question of the proper assessment of the rabbinical literature, and its relationship to Josephus. Josephus says only a meager amount about the Pharisees, but he is consistent. In the rabbinical literature, however, "pharisee" can refer to both devil and hero, but almost never to those who gave birth to rabbinic Judaism: there is no uniform use of the root, *prsh*. The middle of the first century, reflects a transitional stage. Here "pharisee" refers to the tendency in the hakamic movement to move to extremes of holiness. Nowhere is this more evident than in Mark 7:1. Thus it may be that we have in Mark, and particularly in Mark 7:1, a part of the solution to the problem raised by the differing uses of the term "pharisee" in Josephus and in the rabbinical literature. If this is true, then the picture that Mark presents of Jesus surpasses anything we have yet seen: Here Jesus points out to the Pharisees the inevitable internal development of their sect, and its tendency toward extremism.

Familiarity with ancient holiness, by way of the study of ancient literature, is the goal of this course. In these first days, I have given you a glimpse of how we will approach the literature. Good luck in your study!

24

The Two Level Drama

FORTY YEARS AGO J. L. Martyn found the magic key to open and unlock the door to historical, situational understanding of the fourth gospel.[1] He found the key hidden in chapter 9, lying under the single greek word, *aposynagogos*, "out of the synagogue." This one word, unknown in Greek literature before John 9, and used twice again in the gospel, unlatched the portal of interpretation. Ashton: "The lock turns surprisingly well in the socket wherever you insert it."

John 9 describes the healing of a man born blind, and the communal controversy surrounding the healing. Like the rest of the Gospel, read in light of Martyn's hypothesis, this passage reports two layers of healing, of blindness, of community, and of controversy. On one hand, the pericope remembers, perhaps by the aid of a source or as part of a source—the so-called signs source, a moment in the ministry of Jesus, in which a man is given sight. On the other hand, the pericope announces the spiritual unshackling of a hero in the community who bears witness to what Jesus has done for him, no matter the repercussions from others, from parents, from family, from community—from synagogue. For his courage, he is thrown "out of the synagogue." This word Martyn finds constructed for the very announcement in question (in his dating somewhere near year 100). Martyn finds that the expulsion so named may have been codified in Judaism, near the same period in time, with the proclamation and publication of a ban on

---

[1] This entire chapter summarizes and reflects on J. Louis Martyn, *History and Theology in the Fourth Gospel*, 2nd ed. (Nashville: Abingdon, 1979).

The Two Level Drama

heretics, which then became a part of the daily Jewish prayer, the indictment against the "Nazarenes."

The preacher in the Johannine community of the 2nd century is telling the story of the Son of Man. To do so, he celebrates the courageous witness to healing, and the courageous endurance of expulsion, of a man born blind. Here, he says, is what I mean by faith. The story he uses comes, through untrackable oral and written traditions, from 30 CE. The story he tells comes from 110 CE. Every character in the story has two roles. Jesus is both earthly rabbi and heavenly redeemer. The blind man is both historic patient and current hero. The family is both Palestinian record and diaspora synagogue. The Jews are both the adversaries of Jesus and the nearby inhabitants of the synagogue, the Johannine community's former home. When Jesus gives sight, Christ gives freedom. When the blind one is cured, the congregation sees truth. When the man is cast out of his synagogue, the community of the beloved disciples recognizes their own most recent expulsion. When the Jews criticize Jesus, the synagogue is criticizing the church. When the healing story ends, the life of faith begins.

Suddenly the otherwise opaque account of John 9 makes sense. It is a two level drama. To see it and hear it requires stereo-optic vision. Unconsciously, preconsciously, the preacher who narrated the healing for the health of his hearers brought two levels to bear on his drama. The key turns surprisingly well in the lock.

The exegetical power of this hypothesis arises from a cluster of discoveries. The genius of the insight itself, its imaginative burst, is at the heart of this. The careful attention to textual criticism, and the uncovering of "*aposynagogos*," is crucial. The nearly contemporaneous "benediction against the Nazarenes" brings historical support. The manner in which the hypothesis makes sense of an otherwise unwieldy passage is part of the equation. The fact that such a two level drama is regularly, if semi-consciously a part of any preaching gives the thesis practical affirmation. Perhaps most tellingly, this thought illumines the central struggle of the community—their bitter spiritual itinerancy from the familiar confines of Christian Judaism, out into the unknown wilderness of Jewish Christianity. History and the history of religions bear manifold witness to this kind of crisis in communal identity, and the long hard trail of travel from primary to secondary identity. In retrospect, as the community gathers itself in its new setting (the pilgrims in Boston, the Mormons in Utah) the story of the tearful trail itself becomes the heart of communal memory and imagination.

What Martyn unearthed in John 9 can also and readily be applied to the rest of the Gospel as well: to the wedding at Cana, to Nicodemus, to the woman at the well, to the healing on the water, to the feeding of the thousands, to the controversies with the Jews, to the raising of Lazarus, to the farewell discourse, to the trial and passion. All of these reflect the experience in dramatic interaction between the synagogue and John's church. The phrase "the Jews" then refers, in its second level of drama, to that authoritative group within Judaism which, before John's time, pronounced a ban on Nazarenes. Over against these authorities, John's community understands itself, though they were expulsed, as those who left.

With less and more success, Martyn traces some historical roots and sources for his argument: in third century patristic literature, in Pauline material depicting his withdrawal from synagogues in Corinth and Ephesus, in Acts 18 and 19, in the history of the Council of Jamnia, and in the Benediction against the Heretics itself.

Against this historical backdrop, Martyn sketches a communal trajectory. To a synagogue there came some Christian missionaries. Perhaps they had or had with them a document portraying the miracles of Jesus. Some from the synagogue may have responded. Perhaps a group, a messianic group, formed within the synagogue. It may have been that they gathered for Eucharist. For some time they fairly contentedly lived as Jews who were disciples of Jesus. They were both.

But then the leadership in the synagogue began to view the fledgling Christians as apostates. Perhaps they are influenced by the benediction against heretics, or perhaps there are more local motives. Tensions rise, even to the point perhaps evidenced in John 16:2 at which there is mortal danger for those who confess Christ. Debates over Sabbath observance may well have entered in, as John 5:1-18, the healing of the lame man, shows. More significantly, the gradual elevation of Jesus in the minds and hearts of these Christian Jews becoming Jewish Christians, his gradual elevation to something like divine status must have provoked some communal, some theological, response. In John 7 the crowd, here almost like a chorus in Greek drama, is split between those who see Jesus as a good man and those who see him leading others astray.

(There is little other record of Jesus, in good Socratic fashion, leading others astray, neither in Paul nor in the Synoptics, nor elsewhere. Justin Martyr, in the second century reports that the Jews called Jesus a deceiver, a beguiler, but he may have John in view here.)

In this context it is interesting to note the differences between John and the Synoptics at the point of his arrest. First, and at first, the arrest fails, not as in the Synoptics because of individual fear, but because it is not yet God's time. Second, the Synoptics show no immediate second attempt at arrest, but John does. Third, Jesus' popularity becomes in the Synoptics a reason for the failure of the arrest, but in John his popularity is a reason for the arrest attempt itself.

The Two Level Drama

When John refers to 'chief priests' and 'elders' (a historical conundrum because any individual could have been both), the first may refer to the original story level of drama, and second to the Johannine drama. Did someone come from the Jewish authorities to arrest a person in the Johannine community? At every point, in any case, the author of John has a bi-focal vision, one eye on Jesus and one eye on the contemporary drama of his own day.

There are seven affirmations of Moses in John. John has some of the most accurate statements of Jewish thought in the NT. Furthermore, the figure of the eschatological prophet, present in Jewish messianic speculation, is also present in John. This figure is distinct, though, from the Messiah. Argument may have focused on the differences between inherited Messianic expectations and the record of Jesus. The Davidic Messiah is to defeat the enemy, to cleanse Jerusalem, to gather the holy people, to shepherd the Lord's flock. Does Jesus? To some degree, the whole discussion becomes a midrashic debate. Particularly the Nicodemus episode seems to fit this possibility. Nicodemus desires midrashic evidence, but Jesus offers him 'a dualism of election.' John increasingly contrasts Moses with Jesus, and argues that God still gives manna, from which one cannot hide in midrashic speculation. Oddly, Jesus here uses midrashic discourse and discussion in order to terminate midrashic discussion. The Johannine preacher is trying to lead his people forward from an understanding of Jesus as a prophet, or prophet-Messiah, toward a more adequate faith. Messiah is a wayfaring term, on the road toward Son of Man\Son of God (terms which Martyn, in contrast to others like Ashton) sees as interchangeable.

The two level drama is prevalent in Jewish apocalypticism. The Revelation to St John operates consistently on two levels, those of earth and heaven. In John both levels are on earth, and they are unconsciously presented. They share a use of the figure of the Son of Man. For John, the Son of Man is a heavenly figure representing judgment and the future. The figure of course is also found in Daniel and Enoch. But John's portrayal continues the authority of the figure found there, like that of a judge, and binds the Son of Man to OT figures, to the redeemer, to the language of sacramental ministry, to the motifs of being lifted up and being glorified. For John, Jesus is the Son of Man because in him the Son of God comes to man.

We come now to the strange, mysterious figure of the Paraclete (actually the second Paraclete, for Jesus himself is the first comforter). The Paraclete functions as Jesus' eternal presence in the world, Jesus on earth. In this way, the Paraclete himself creates the two level drama. Where the world is mono focal, and can see only the historical level of Jesus in history or only the theological level of Jesus in the witness of the Christian community, the Paraclete binds the two together. The Word dwelling among us, and our beholding his glory are not past events only. They transpire in a two level drama. They transpire both on the historical and contemporary levels, *or not at all*. Their transpiration on both levels is itself the good news.

Martyn's hypothesis has won the day and has been able to stand the test of time. While several points of criticism have arisen,[2] still, the key turns very well in the lock. Interpretation of the fourth Gospel not only deserves but requires acknowledgement of the two-level drama, acknowledgement of the historical movement from Christian Judaism to Jewish Christianity, and acknowledgement of their homiletical embedding in John.

What Martyn describes is the way the community was 'pushed out.' He depends on the Jewish background to the NT, and to the sources for John in his reading, his constructive and imaginative reengagement with the text. Apocalypticism, broadly construed, provides the language and imagery for his interpretation. What Martyn's thesis does not address is the foreground not the background of the Gospel. John was not only pushed, he also was pulled. The two go well, and surprisingly well together. The expulsion from the synagogue pushed John forward. But what pulled him? From the outside, from the Gnostic foreground of the NT, John was pulled forward. Gnosticism, broadly construed, provides the language and imagery for this further interpretation. Gnosticism provided the speculative intrigue that equipped the community in its primitive Christological imagination. Gnosticism provided the communicative connection with the new wilderness, the non-Jewish world and thought world for life outside the synagogue. Gnosticism provided the audacity of hope in a new language, not that parousia but that of Paraclete, not that of the end of the age, but that of the realm of light. Gnosticism especially provided the language and imagery of new identity, the confidence of identity in the face of alienation, which pulled the community along in its growth and change, even as they were pushed out of the synagogue. Hence, the fourth Gospel is not only a two–*level* drama, it is also a two–*stage* drama. In its first stage, that robed in Apocalypticism, the community is expulsed from Judaism. In its second stage, that robed in Gnosticism, the community is drawn to Hellenism. To understand both its history and its theology, both its origin and its meaning, the Johannine interpreter will need both Apocalypticism and Gnosticism. You cannot understand John 9:1 without the former. You cannot understand John 1:9 without the latter. To date, from Bultmann to Brown, we have had one or the other. We need both in order to do justice to the interpretation of what Clement rightly called "The Spiritual Gospel."

2. See John Ashton, *Understanding the Fourth Gospel* (Oxford: Clarendon, 1991), 343.

25

The Insights of George MacRae
—*Jason Ford*

GEORGE MACRAE WAS AN apparent jack of scholarly trades: he taught New Testament, Homiletics, and Pastoral ministry classes; served as editor on numerous boards (Society for New testament Studies; *Catholic Biblical Quarterly*); was a leading scholar of gnostic studies; was active in the translation committee of the Nag Hammadi literature; etc. Though passing before his time, MacRae left behind material whose fruit has still yet to bud (e.g., his work on the Thunder, and other texts) but for our purposes his work on John and gnosticism remains important and a helpful starting point. One of the areas MacRae left tantalizingly little behind is in the area of Johannine studies. He produced but a brief lay commentary, an equally brief introduction to the issues related to Johannine studies, and a couple journal articles. Like in the rest of his scholarship MacRae had a way of cutting through material, leaving behind unnecessary or unhelpful information and highlighting the most important. It is for this reason that MacRae's work, though largely ignored, is still worth engaging to this day.

In *Faith in the Word*[1] MacRae comments on the most challenging features related to Johannine scholarship —date, author, sources, redaction, and background. Most of these issues are notoriously difficult for scholars

---

1. George W. MacRae, *Faith in the Word: the Fourth Gospel* (Chicago: Franciscan Herald, 1973).

to reach consensus on but MacRae's perspective is balanced, incredibly nuanced and might offer a way forward in the scholarly discussions.

The problem of dating the Gospel of John, or any of the Gospels, is that exactness is impossible. That said, scholars generally agree on dates within a given decade. Most scholars date John's gospel to the 90s CE. The discovery of the Dead Sea Scrolls (DSS) demonstrated that the thought world of certain elements of the Fourth Gospel (FG) need not be late but could in fact be pre-70. There is also the connected issue of the FG relationship to the SG and one's position here could shift the dating slightly earlier or later. "For all the discussion of modern times, there is no substantial change in the dominant view that this work, at least in the form in which it entered the New Testament collection, belongs to the last decade of the first century."[2]

Discussion over the author of the FG continues but ultimately does not affect one's interpretation of the Gospel. "It is best to admit that the author is simply unknown, and that the validity of traditions contained in the Gospel does not hinge on apostolic authorship."[3] A more fruitful discussion for the interpreter is that of the source material the evangelist made use of. For any discussion of Johannine sources Bultmann's theories must be addressed and taken seriously, even if one dismisses his conclusions. Like most commentators MacRae sees no evidence for a written source behind the Johannine discourses, whether gnostic or not. If such a source once existed it cannot be recovered from the material we now have for it is too permeated with the evangelist's own style and theology.

The issue of the signs source remains the most plausible explanation of the miracle stories in the first half of the Gospel. Alongside the enumeration of the first two signs the Evangelist views the miracle stories as inadequate as the catalyst of belief. MacRae finds this the most compelling feature of the signs source. The Evangelist recognized the legitimacy of the miracle-working tradition of Jesus but in his own theological view find signs–faith inadequate. Not only is there good support for sources behind the Fourth Gospel but there is also some redaction that took place to reach the final stage of the text as we have it. MacRae follows modern scholars in his discussion of interpolated texts (7:53—8:11; 5:3b–4), the ordering of material in chs. 5 and 6, and later additions (ch. 21; 1:1–18; 12:44–50; 6:51–59)

As is pointed out in every discussion on Johannine and gnostic parallels, Bultmann remains the starting point. Bultmann's theories were offered without the advantage much of the source material we have today (notably the Nag Hammadi and the Qumran texts). Since gnosticism is such

2. MacRae, *Faith*, 10.
3. MacRae, *Faith*, 12.

The Insights of George MacRae

a nebulous term to define, Bultmann's theory of gnostic influence on the Fourth Gospel is not widely held today. That, and of course, his theory of a gnostic revealer/redeemer source has not borne results worthy of acceptance. However, as George MacRae noted, Bultmann was on to something. The Jewish background to the FG goes a long way to explain its origins, thought world and religious system. The work of Martyn and Brown shows the rewarding conclusions one can draw from studying the FG in its Jewish context/background. However, this background does not explain the FG in its entirety (which is probably a given if one does even a brief survey of the vast ink spilled on this Gospel and the plethora of opinions about guiding themes, backgrounds, sources, etc.).

It is to this discussion that one can look at gnostic thought and its relationship to the FG with some rewarding results. Before such discussion though, a brief word is necessary on categorical terms such as "Jewish" and, say, "Hellenistic" used in this essay. Such categories are heuristic terms employed by scholars to help classify ancient material. The more we learn of late antiquity the more amorphous the boundary lines seem to have been. Terms like these allow scholars not to over-define their subject but to work from a certain starting point.

The Johannine Christ is a described in a way almost wholly different than elsewhere in the New Testament. Most stark about this depiction of Jesus is his otherworldly nature, including the language used of him and by him. He is the heavenly revealer come to reveal his role as heavenly revealer. Bultmann recognized that a parallel development of a heavenly revealer could be found in the Mandaean literature. Though quite late in extant copies, Bultmann felt this literature provided evidence of a gnostic redeemer myth from the time of John's Gospel. John adapted this myth in a kind of gnostically anti-gnostic manner, meaning he took the concept from the thought world of gnostic myth but transformed that myth by infusing it with the story of Jesus of Nazareth. (Part of the problem here is that Bultmann assumed that *gnostic* could in some sense be equated with anti-flesh).

The Gospel of John remains a text viewed darkly. Scholars catch glimpses of meaning, influence, background, etc. and run wild with elaborate speculations on the Johannine author, community, and thought-world. Often such insights are helpful in clarifying *aspects* of John's presentation of Jesus. In Johannine studies we find arguments for and against influences such as: Hellenistic thought, Judaism, Jewish wisdom tradition, Jewish apocalyptic tradition, Greco-Roman legal traditions, etc. MacRae, as most scholars, recognized that no single tradition itself seemed to adequately explain the thought world of the Fourth Evangelist (FE). MacRae ingeniously argued that this incorporation of multiple traditions (sometimes called "syncretism") is the author's background and was utilized by the Evangelist with rhetorical force. MacRae's essay "The Fourth Gospel and *Religionsgeschichte*," concisely puts forward this theory and need not be reproduced here. My interest is in what we can say of a "gnostic" influence on Johannine thought.

The aspect of MacRae's work I find richest and most rewarding is his ability to recognize the plurality of backgrounds informing the FG. There are elements present in John that more explicitly betray their background than others (e.g., The OT background is more readily apparent than that of Hermetism). Like most scholars of late, MacRae finds a Jewish background to the Fourth Gospel supported by the strongest arguments. This is especially true of the Jewish Wisdom tradition; though, he is reluctant to argue that this particular tradition (or any tradition for that matter) can account for the FG's soteriology and Christology. Whereas certain elements of the FG have often been used to support a "Hellenistic" background (e.g., light/dark dualism), the evidence from the Dead Sea Scrolls now allows scholars to recognize that these aspects of the Evangelist's thought world (light/dark) are as likely to be influenced by Judaism as they are the greater Hellenistic world. Lest we get to caught up on the black-and-white categories of "Jewish" and "Hellenistic," MacRae says that what the Qumran texts have done is contribute to a "break-down of neat and clear distinctions between Hellenistic and Palestinian Judaism" and the result of this is "that it is increasingly difficult to assign a locus to the Johannine traditions or their development."[4] Other possible backgrounds include Jewish Wisdom tradition, Hermetism, Mandaeanism, and Gnosticism. MacRae sees something in scholars' inability to identify the background to the Gospel. He asks, "is it not possible that the Fourth Evangelist may have tried deliberately to incorporate a diversity of backgrounds into the one gospel message precisely to emphasize the universality of Jesus?"[5] Essential to MacRae's argument is that the FE was not content with any of his sources' presentation of Jesus. Central to the FE's portrayal of Jesus is his universality and the inclusion and adaption (and also inadequacy) of multiple presentations of Jesus demonstrates this. In this discussion MacRae avoids dealing with the thorny issue of the "ecclesiastical redactor." He states this is not an attempt to deny its validity or importance but to emphasize that the redactor's purpose was not to change a previous theological perspective but to highlight the universality of Jesus. Such universality is present in the juxtaposition of the Johannine

---

4. George W. MacRae, "The Fourth Gospel and Religionsgeschichte," in *Studies in the New Testament and Gnosticism* (Wilmington, DE: Michael Glazier, 1987) 17.

5. MacRae, "Fourth," 18.

The Insights of George MacRae

problem of both futurist and realized eschatology. MacRae sees it likely that the redactor left both eschatological views in the text to say that Jesus is the fulfillment of hopes, whether in the present or the future. The FE "was mainly concerned with asserting the universality of Jesus in the context of a growing divergence of eschatological viewpoints in the second- or third-generation Church."[6]

Besides this eclecticism, or possibly because of it, the other theme that MacRae identifies as paramount to the FG is its reinterpretation. For example, he finds the FE's reinterpretation of traditional material repeatedly through the Gospel. Just as Mark had a break in his story splitting the public ministry of Jesus from his private one with the disciples, so, too, does John. In fact, John's distinction between the two sections is much more sharply depicted. Chapter 12 ends on a note of failure (12:37–43) and Jesus's attention shifts to his disciples from 13 on. All of the miracles and symbols of Jesus (bread, life, light, etc.) are contained in the first twelve chapters. (Though, this observation is nothing new since the two sections have been called the "book of signs" and the "book of glory" since Dodd's time.) However, in MacRae's reading of the FG, this division and the multiplicity of symbols contained therein is exactly the point. Just as Mark had a three-fold passion prediction, so, too, does John, albeit reinterpreted as the three "raising up" sayings of 3:14, 8:28, and 12:34. Such reinterpretation allows the author to take over traditional material "without actually following Mark in any literary way."[7]

Whether it was through traditional Jesus material or through varied religious traditions, the point for MacRae is that the FE utilized them all to point people to Jesus, for none of them captures the meaning of Jesus in his entirety. He says, "For John there are many ways to Jesus: Jewish Messianic and prophetic expectations, basic common religious symbols such as life or light or bread, the recognition of the miracle-working 'divine man,' and the like. Any of these can be an avenue to faith, but Jesus is not bound up in any of them... For the Fourth Evangelist, one can approach Jesus as a Jew or a Greek, a Samaritan or a Gnostic, but one can have life in him only as a Christian."[8] Here is the crux for MacRae: "John deliberately uses whatever religious backgrounds he knows, though I remain convinced that his own is primarily in the wisdom tradition. He deliberately incorporates sources as disparate as the sings-source with a *theios aner* Christology and

---

6. MacRae, "Fourth," 23.
7. MacRae, "Fourth," 25.
8. MacRae, *Faith*, 58.

the Passion-narrative gospel, but he also subsumes all except the theme of love in action under the condemnation of their failure to reveal adequately what God is."[9]

These two Johannine features, eclecticism and reinterpretation, go a long way to helping us grasp the Johannine message of Jesus. MacRae's argument for the eclectic background to the FG is really quite important: for John, more than for the other Gospel writers, something is missed if we are unfamiliar with numerous background material to the FG. "In the end, John's message is that Jesus can be approached in many ways, but he can only be understood on Christian terms, not Jewish or Greek or Gnostic. That is why the Fourth Gospel was accepted as a Christian book: not, as Käsemann suggests, because its Gnosticizing trend was misunderstood [74–5], but because despite its Gnosticizing trend it is the Christian gospel that it proclaims."[10]

One element that is missing from much of the conversation on John today is the role of gnostic (or proto-gnostic, or nascent gnostic) thought on the FE. MacRae thinks there is some relationship between the FG and gnosticism. However, he does not think that the FG is either a gnostic or an anti-gnostic work. "It is rather an independent reinterpretation of the Jesus story on the part of a gifted Evangelist who was strongly influenced by the multiple currents of his syncretistic world including Gnosticism. His Gospel represents in part a gnosticisng of the tradition, which, however, stops short of absolute dualism and its corollary, Docetism. Thus, despite the attempt of the Valentinians to appropriate John as their Gospel because they rightly recognized its tendencies, the Fourth Gospel is not a Gnostic work."[11]

MacRae's comments on the background of John had a different effect on the scholarship of his day (the seventies) than it does for today. For his time, MacRae's work served as a "voice calling in the wilderness" not to lose sight of the forest (i.e. purpose of John) for the trees (i.e. some particular background as the answer to every Johannine question). Today, MacRae's work serves as a reminder that certain elements of John's gospel are best studied within a varied background. For example, one might not be able to "get" John 17.3 if they are unfamiliar with the developing gnostic traditions of the late first/early second centuries. On the areas of required study for gnosticism and its influence on the FG are the following:

---

9. MacRae, "Fourth," 28.

10. MacRae, "Fourth," 31.

11. George W. MacRae, "Nag Hammadi and the New Testament," in *Studies in the New Testament and Gnosticism* (Wilmington, DE: Michael Glazier, 1986) 168.

1. The relationship between the language and imagery of the Johannine Prologue and the Gnostic mythological structure of the Nag Hammadi tractate *Trimorphic Protennoia*.
2. The genre of revelation discourse which is shared by John and many Gnostic writings.
3. Patterns of Gnostic and Johannine Christology and soteriology.
4. The theme of becoming children of the Father by virtue of revelation of the Father in the Son, a theme common to John and the *Gospel of Truth*.
5. Johannine and Gnostic dualism, which of itself and in isolation is not seen as compelling evidence of Gnostic influence.
6. The possible Gnostic interaction of the Johannine Christians who were rejected by the author of the First Epistle of John.
7. As a suggestion for further study, the relationship of the Gnostic and the Johannine debt to the wisdom tradition.[12]

MacRae identifies several aspects of the Johannine Gospel where gnostic characterizations are most evident: the Prologue, Revelation discourses, Christology and soteriology, dualism, and identifying people who believe in Jesus as children of the Father. The *Trimorphic Protennoia* parallels the Prologue to the Fourth Gospel's presentation of the Logos as a divine revealer. It is not believed that the *Trimorphic Protennoia* influenced the Johannine Prologue but rather both texts were relying on a similar wisdom tradition.

The *Apocryphon of John* is often highlighted as the early attestation of gnostic thought in some sort of fully formed presentation. Irenaeus speaks of the gnostic school of thought and tells of their cosmology, describing a creation story found in almost exact parallel in the *Apocryphon of John*. *Apocryphon of John* is extant in four versions, longer and shorter. The long version, found in the Nag Hammadi library (Codices II and IV), concludes with a monologue by Mother Barbelo. She speaks of her descent as divine *Pronoia* (II 30.11—31.25). This descent to the lower realms is salvific in purpose and speaks of thrice descending.

The three-fold descent pattern is one that has been identified in other Sethian texts, most importantly the *Trimorphic Protennoia*.[13] John Turner

---

12. George W. MacRae, "Gnosticism and the Church of John's Gospel," in *Nag Hammadi, Gnosticism, and Early Christianity: Fourteen Leading Scholars Discuss the Current Issues in Gnostic Studies*, edited by C. W. Hedrick and R. Hodgson Jr., 89–96 (Peabody, MA: Hendrickson, 1986) 89–90.

13. See the work of John Turner on *Trimorphic Protennoi* in *Nag Hammadi Codices XI, XII and XIII*, edited by C.W. Hedrick; The Coptic Gnostic Library Edited with

dates the *TrimPro* early in the second-century, ca. 125 CE. He also identifies a three-fold stage of development. The earliest version *TrimPro* consisted of a first person monologue by Protennoia, similar to that of *ApJn*. She, too, speaks of three descents: first as divine *Voice*, second as divine *Speech*, and third as divine *Word*. During the second stage of development, certain narratives were added to monologue (overthrowing celestial powers, baptismal ascent ritual). Turner suggests that the document circulated as a complete text during this second stage. However, due to conflict among Christian groups, Christian Sethian added polemical Christological statements to the text to distance themselves from other branches of Christianity.

The prologue of the FG is recognized as a pre-Johannine hymn that the FE or redactor added to his gospel. Certain elements of this hymn (notably verses 6–8, 15) were inserted to emphasize Jesus's status over that of John the Baptist. It was for this reason that Bultmann argued that the prologue was originally written and circulated in a community that followed John the Baptist. The Prologue provides an interesting parallel to the *Pronoia* monologue and *Trimorphic Protennoia*. Though not written in the first person, the Johannine prologue speaks of three descents of the *Logos*. The Logos is said to have: a) appeared as life and light in the darkness but was not recognized; b) appeared to his own people but was rejected; c) became flesh in the person of Jesus and received by those believing in his name. These three documents, then, provide information on the developing traditions of Christian thought in the second-century.

In their final form, *Trimorphic Protennoia* and the *Pronoia* monologue of *ApJohn* contain polemical information toward the fourth-gospel. The prologue states that *In the beginning was the Word*. But *TrimPro* pushes the timeline back further. It asserts that *the Word* did come and did exist with God but that it was a later manifestation of the divine first thought.

REVELATION DISCOURSE: *EGO EIMI*

MacRae suggests two possibilities for further research on the relationship between *ego* proclamations in Gnostic sources and the Fourth Gospel (215ff). First, Bultmann drew comparisons between John's *ego* proclamations and those of the Mandaean writings. Since the Mandaean writings are quite late the Nag Hammadi library provides a (possibly) closer parallel to John. Bultmann's point is still worth pursuing, though by focusing on the NHL and not necessarily on the Mandaean literature. Second, the format of

---

English Translation, Introduction and Notes; Nag Hammadi Studies 28 (Leiden: Brill, 1990).

The Insights of George MacRae

several of the gnostic ego-proclamations (such as The Thunder) is paradoxical in nature, which possibly betrays influence from the Isis literature. The point of the ego-proclamations, according to MacRae is to communicate the speaker's transcendence and universality. Typical of gnostic thought, these first-person discourses emphasize revelation. As Bultmann has argued, the focus of the Johannine Gospel is also revelation.

There are numerous ego-proclamation texts one should look at. Some of the gnostic texts are written almost entirely in this style (The Thunder: Perfect Mind; The Three Appearances). A possible background for the self-identification feature of *The Thunder* is Jewish wisdom tradition. Specifically, Proverbs 8 contains self-identification and invitation on the part of the hearer. Another possible influence is the Deutero-Isaiah *ego eimi* sayings: Isa 45.5–7. The Thunder is spoken entirely in the first person with no structural divisions. The kinds of statements the speaker uses are: self proclamation, exhortations, and reproaches for failures. There are only minor parallels to the content of *Thunder* in other biblical or gnostic literature (e.g., "first and the last," Isa 44.6; 48.12; Rev 1.17; inside/outside, GosThom 22; 37; 26–27). The bulk of what the speaker says is contradictory and nonsensical (i.e. strength/fear; shameless/ashamed). The FG contains no parallels to this kind of paradoxical revelation discourse, unless you consider the phrase "resurrection and the life" to be such. "It may be that the Fourth Gospel, taking into consideration its over-all structure and its techniques, uses the form of *ego* proclamation not merely to assert that Jesus must be recognized as or identified with the variety of human religious symbolism: bread, light, shepherd, life, etc., but that Jesus in his truest reality *transcends* all of this and is revealed only in the moment of his return to the Father, through death and resurrection, as the love of the Father for men."[14] This parallel is "not so much in words or explicit allusions, as in religious outlook and religious discourse."[15]

Revelation Discourse is common in Gnostic texts, where the Revealer speaks in "I-style," calls the audience to a decision, and promises reward or judgment. MacRae identifies numerous passages of Revelation Discourse in the Fourth Gospel—6.35–51b; 8.12–47; 10.7–18. Contrary to Bultmann's opinion, the Fourth Evangelist (likely) did not rely on a Discourse source but was influenced by the genre of Revelation Discourse.

The Isis aretalogies also provide repeated *ego eimi* sayings. (See Kyme inscription, lines 3a–6). Hippolytus preserves some of the Heraclitus

---

14. George W. MacRae, "The Ego-Proclamation in Gnostic Sources," in *Studies on the New Testament and Gnosticism* (Wilmington, DE: Michael Glazier, 1986) 216–17.

15. MacRae, "Ego," 217.

tradition, which does not attest to the *ego eimi* formula but does describe the deity in terms of opposites. (God is day night, winter summer, war peace, satiety hunger).[16] These *ego eimi* statements are similar in *form* to the Fourth Gospel but not in content because they do not contain the antithetical material (again, unless you include 11:25)

Though recognizing similarities between Johannine and Gnostic Christology and soteriology, the Fourth Gospel's presentation of incarnation and the physical death of Jesus distances the Fourth Gospel from Gnosticism. 1 and 2 John are texts that can further enhance our knowledge of Johannine Christianity and its relationship to Gnosticism. In addition to those, the *Gospel of Truth* provides another helpful tool in analyzing Gnosticism and Johannine Christianity, especially if one concludes that the *Gospel of Truth* is free from Johannine influence.

MacRae identifies the central issue in Johannine studies going forward: "is the Fourth Gospel an independent development from the wisdom tradition or is it part of a larger movement of speculation in which Gnosticism also reinterprets wisdom?"[17]

---

16. MacRae, "Ego," 217.
17. MacRae, "Gnosticism," 95–96.

26

Gnosticism

Gnosis, the New Testament, and the Gospel of John

"THE TRUE LIGHT THAT ENLIGHTENS EVERYONE WAS COMING INTO THE WORLD." JOHN 1:9

This is a familiar verse to us. What does it mean? How does the preacher interpret its past significance in a way that tells truth today? What does mean and what did it mean? Our familiarity, or faux familiarity, with the verse is our worst ally here. Every single word in this well-known and well-worn passage presents an interpretative thicket of thorny problems. True? Light? Enlighten? Every man? World? While there are many other fundamental issues at stake in the rendering of this verse today, the weightiest is the question of what world this sentence comes from. Understanding about worldview, about perspective, about philosophical sphere will guide every other exegetical decision. The difficulty of exegesis itself confounds and compounds the problem.

The source critic will identify the seam at John 1:18, and so will define these opening verses as an extra or later addition to the full gospel. But the writer-redactors of the book included this verse at some point, so the value of this distinction is limited. The form critic will compare these same verses favorably with other examples of early hymnody, and so will call the passage a hymn, and see it 'formed' perhaps in the liturgical life of the church, or perhaps in the music and song of another religious community. But the fact that 1:9 is part of a hymn does not clarify its meaning, past or present. The literary critic may connect this beautiful haunting hymn with others like it, whether from the Oxyrynchus Papyri or from William Blake. Still, its standing among the great oaks of fine poetry does not cut into its meaning then or now. The redaction critic may conclude that 1:1–18 was added to the narrative body of the gospel at a later date, and may further link the hymn's praise of *Word* to the high Christology of the later chapters. Here we come a little closer to home, but the actual valence of the verse and its particular words are no clearer to us, even though their connection to the rest of the gospel may be. The canonical critic will wrap this verse and its hymn shell in passages from the Hebrew Scripture, Psalms, Proverbs, Prophets, and other, and in the other direction will wrap the verse and its hymn shell in neighboring, similar verses from Paul, from the Epistles, and, though lightly, from the Synoptics. But these comparisons can beg the real question. Just how, if at all, is the thought world of John connected to these other perspectives? We are left holding the bag.

Is true light meant in intentional contrast to false light? Is this light, the light, not just light or a light, but part of the one light that is all light? What does it mean for a man to be enlightened? Is this understood figuratively, metaphorically, literally, or theologically? What does the author, do the authors, have in his or their mind with the use of this one word, light? This light illumines every one. Every one? Every man. Every man? Idolaters? Slaves? Dead people? Perhaps most strangely, the light enters the world. Is the world dark without it, or just a bit brighter for its arrival? If there is no other light than this, how are we to understand, to know, what it is? If there is other light than this, is this then not a second source of wattage? 'The true light that enlightens everyone was coming into the world.' What does that mean? Without a sense of the lexicon from which these words are drawn, and the vocabulary from which these terms are taken, and the language from which these utterances are hewn, and the philosophy from which these thoughts are constructed, we are at sea. Help!

Here is one port in the storm.

The light entering the world is true in the sense that it is not a material part of the world entered. It is light, eternal. Tragically, and disprovidentially, this light was by accident broken away from the full light of eternal heaven, light perpetual, everlasting light. The personification of this light, the true light, is come into the world on a scouting mission to link up with other shards, fragments of light, cast adrift on the sea of darkness, also known as life as we know it. The world is dark, very dark, unutterably dark.

Gnosticism

It is a world created, but created by ill not good, by demi-god not God. How else do you explain its tragedy, sin, death, and meaninglessness? All who are enlightened are enlightened by the light that lasts, and the true light is coming into the world. Once TL, true light, gathers all remaining and real light to himself, he will take light to himself, that where he is, *lux perpetua*, they may be also. He comes, he sees, he names, he gathers, he draws, he goes, and he will return to take light to the room with many mansions. That is the original meaning, one could argue, of John 1:9, 'the true light that enlightens everyone was coming into the world.

Christ the true light, enlightening all, is cosmic freedom. There is a limitless expanse to this vision of the divine, an expanse in some dissonance with other more space and time bound aspects of the biblical witness. Christ the true light, enlightening all, is cosmic truth. There is a sobering, hard unmaskability to this reverence for truth, wherever it is found. There is a self-correcting spirit of truth, loose in the universe. Christ the true light, enlightening all, is cosmic life. Light does not darken, die, or end. Freedom, truth, life—the gifts of John 1:9.

But is this reading free of error, true to the text, true to life?

The answer depends upon our understanding of the worldview that produced the verse, in and through which then the verse may be interpreted. The harbor in the hurricane just offered supposes that Gnosticism is the worldview in and through which to interpret John 1:9. Which raises a three-part question. What is Gnosticism? How is related to the New Testament? How is it involved with the Gospel of John? To these three issues we now turn.

GNOSTICISM

What is Gnosticism? The term itself is an anachronism, since those who may have shared this perspective in antiquity did not use it. The Naasenes did call themselves Gnostics, and that term is also found elsewhere, but the larger construct, Gnosticism, is a modern creation. Some have argued that Gnosticism 'is not,' that there never was anything like a religious perspective, however loosely described, to which the term might refer. Moreover, the major cache of ancient documents, discovered in 1945 and finally published in 1976 does as much to loosen and explode our definitions of the term as it does to root and ground our terminology and understanding. To make matters still worse, the menagerie of versions, views, and evaluations of Gnosticism on offer today, by library and internet, defies ready focus if it allows any focus at all. We may simply need to admit ignorance, seeing

THE COURAGEOUS GOSPEL

all this, and quote Flip Wilson's character Geraldine, who told her\his boyfriend, memorably named Killer, "Honey, what you see is what you get." You see nothing, you get nothing.

The pessimism above, however, is not the whole story. Fashions come and go, as fashions are wont to do, in scholarship as in other fields. We have been for many decades focused on blur, so committed to diversity that any and every unifying field theory or definition is rank and suspect, including that of Gnosticism. For one thing, the early Christian writers, though they use not the word Gnosticism, know and name Gnostics. While his own understanding of the Gnostics may in many respects be no more accurate than our own, and while his writing on them may present us more woe than weal, Irenaeus tracks and identifies individuals, multiples of individuals, documents, concepts, and perspectives that can readily amount to a worldview, indeed a Gnostic world view. G. B. Caird gave his inaugural lecture in Montreal under the title, "The Unity of the New Testament." We have warrant to stretch toward such a unified theme with regard to the Gnostics.

Likewise, while the bounds and fences of Gnostic expression are loose and porous, with rails failing and posts in need of repair, and cattle drifting regularly from pasture to pasture and beyond, there is nonetheless a describable phenomenon, from the past, studied in the present, to which a term like Gnosticism, or one very much like it, may readily be applied.

Gnosticism was a religious perspective, pervasive in the Greco-Roman world of the first three centuries of the Common Era. We may begin with one definition and conclude with another. To begin, Gnosticism was a "pessimistic enthusiasm." Its perspective on the world, the life of the senses and the flesh, the human body, and what we would today call, simply, experience, was utterly pessimistic. The Gnostics believed that the world of experience, our world, was created out of malevolence and by accident. Miscarriage, abortion, mistake—for all its wonders, this world is not God's world. With regard to the created order, they were pessimists. They were enthusiastic optimists, however, with regard to hope for deliverance from this mess of earth. In fact, they were given to various sorts of conviction that amounted to certainty about the eternal, heavenly, light filled escape which would be theirs, following this squalid sojourn of life. For those who knew where they came from, who they are, where they are going, and how to get there, enthusiasm did and ought to have abounded, on the way "up yonder."

Gnosticism was a literary phenomenon, in the main. Evidence for Gnostic communal life is scant. Their perspective appealed to and was appealed to by wise and sensitive souls across the Mediterranean basin. In fact, given that our evidence for Gnosticism is entirely literary, whether patristic or Coptic, we should probably cleave to literary expressions and

Gnosticism

explanations of and for our understandings, rather than those more social, cultural, communal, cultic or ecclesiological. In the main, we are exploring a literary phenomenon. The sub-themes in its plot include a focal myth, a menagerie of teachers, a venerable opposition loyal to the great church, a form of philosophical dualism,

The Gnostic pessimistic enthusiasm, with roots in Plato and blossoms in Mani, with roots perhaps in Zoroaster or Enoch and blossoms perhaps in desert monasticism, has generally been understood to include a certain philosophical perspective, symbolically conveyed in a Gnostic myth. Some scholars would like to sharpen and narrow the focus of this claim, while others would like to broaden and un-focus it, sometimes to the point of denying the reality of Gnosticism in any meaningful sense. An earlier (mid-20th century) view propounded the former, and a later (late 20th century) view propounded the later. One easily recognizes the parallels to and influences out of the modern, later modern and postmodern hermeneutical positions. Now, for the 21st century, and given the passage of time and the inadequacies of the earlier combatant views, and given the further work on the Coptic Gnostic texts, and given the settling of dust that sometimes comes with partial settling of political and cultural scores, we may be ready to venture a newer, moderate description, that includes both the untenable yet alluring sharpness of Harnack's definition, "the acute Hellenization of Christianity," and also the more tenable and yet frustratingly tantalizing definition, that of Wisse, offered above, "pessimistic enthusiasm."

A global age definition of Gnosticism starts with the Gnostic myth, present in various of the writings, like the Apocryphon of John, and readily sketched and taught. In this myth, a dark and stormy one to be sure, especially from our wildly different, material, global age perspective, one first sees and names the *Realm of light*. *Lux perpetua, lux eternal, lux, lux, lux*. God is light. In God there is no darkness at all. If we walk in the light, as God is in the light, we have fellowship with one another. The *Realm of light* embraces, or harbors, the *Supreme God*, the God beyond God, if you will. The *Realm of light* also embraces, and harbors, the fullness, the *Pleroma of Aeons*. There is thus both a spatial and a temporal dimension the *Realm of light*. From the realm, some light fell, falling finally to creation, earth, life. To this realm, all of the fallen light shall ultimately return, or be returned. The light fell (the *fall* is cosmic and pre-creation in Gnosticism) due to a mistaken action by *Sophia*, and is returned (in the Christian form of the myth), through Christ.

How did Sophia produce the fall? By consorting with the chief archon of darkness, Yaldabaoth, in an attempt, a blundering attempt to mimic God by creating, Sophia also let escape some light particles. The *fall* is the lack, the deficiency in the *Realm of light* caused by the loss of some portion of light. All creation and non-creation is yearning for the full deck of cards to be reassembled. Christ, the heavenly redeemer, the heavenly savior, comes down to bring the one thing needful for deliverance, which is *gnosis*. Through knowing who and whose they are, the light is empowered to return, as the Savior returns with his elect to a house with many rooms, a house not made with hands, a house eternal in the heavens.

The story of creation the Gnostics understood on the basis of Genesis 1 and 2, though admittedly under their own divergent interpretation. After *Sophia* and *Yaldabaoth* misconstrued creation, *Yaldabaoth* emanated archons, who emanated the creation itself (known also by other terms—chaos, death, afterbirth, abortion, and so on), which brought forth Adam and Eve. From Eve did spring Cain and Abel, and we know how that all came out. From Eve also did spring all the non-gnostics, the worldlings, those trapped and lost forever in Yaldabaothic darkness. From Eve, also, though, did spring the Gnostics, the race of Seth, the Sethians, the children of light. To these few, these proud, these enlightened, the Christ comes, coming to them and coming for them, only. He preaches, teaches and heals. He gathers, identifies, prepares. He takes them all to himself, that where he is, they may be also. And they know the way where he is going. After all the light particles have returned to the *realm of light*, the *Pleroma of Aeons*, the *God* who is the God beyond God, then the Archons and Chaos (heaven and earth) will be destroyed. (It is for this reason chiefly that apocalyptic eschatology is retained in Gnosticism, by the way). Thus, with Pagels, we may quickly summarize four basic theological perspectives embedded in Gnosticism, and symbolized in the myth. "There is an irreconcilable contradiction between the cosmic system of this world, and the absolutely transcendent God... The 'I' of the Gnostic, the spirit, or inner man, is unalterably divine... This spiritual element has however become mingled with two lower elements (body and soul)... Only an emissary from the divine world above can release these bonds."[1]

The Gnostic myth and the Gnostic worldview have coherence and clarity only to the extent that we can see them at work in the actual work of particular persons. One may find that the 'Treatise on the Resurrection,' whose author, clearly a devotee and disciple of Paul, relies on such mythological perspective for his essay to the dubiously gifted student, Rheginos. The earlier mentioned, central document, the Apocryphon of John also relies on this myth and this worldview. These two references will stand for

---

1. Elaine Pagels, "Gnosticism," in *Interpreter's Dictionary of the Bible: Supplementary Volume*, 364–68 (Nashville: Abingdon, 1982) 366.

Gnosticism

the many dozen which one explore in the NHL. We cannot identify their authors, however. By contrast, the names of several Gnostic teachers from antiquity are known, and well known, to us. Marcion, the author of the first Christian Bible (Luke, the Letters of Paul and no Hebrew Scripture), argued that if God is God he cannot be good and if God is good he cannot be God (so, JB). Jesus must then have prayed not to the God of Genesis, but to another God, whose is light and whose name is love. He was excommunicated, along with his ascetic, encratic, devoted followers. Not all of the mythological features identified above are found in Marcion, but the worldview is his. Valentinus supersedes and surpasses Marcion, both in Gnostic identity and in Gnostic imagination. Valentinus walked and talked like the Egyptian he was. He *may* have been the author of Treat.Res. Most of the myth and the heart of the worldview are found in Valentinus. Valentinus had a student named Ptolemaeus, who wrote a lengthy commentary on. . . John 1, and another, Heracleon, who wrote a whole commentary on the Gospel of. . . John. Basilides, like Marcion and Valentinus active in Rome in the mid-second century, was picked up for attack by Irenaeus and Hippolytus. A general question for us may specifically be applied here. Just how much did the patristic writers know about the Gnostics? Did they more than we, or, like we, did they know them through their writings, or through some of their writings? We cannot be sure, but the latter seems more probable, and is certainly more prudent as a basic understanding.

What difference does this make for the 21st century interpreter? It makes a great deal of difference. The variety and complexity of history and theology heretofore described cautions the interpreter at least to ponder whether unity preceded diversity or whether, more probably, diversity preceded unity in earliest Christianity. The mental picture of John 1:9 as a singular possibility, presented within a welter of other, complementary, and competing possibilities, both tugging at and supporting 1:9, is a very different picture from that of a verse itself emanating from the eternal realm of light. Furthermore, the presence and influence of subsequently defeated teachers who rejected the OT (Marcion), championed fiercely the elect (Valentinus) and imaginatively (and entertainingly?) redescribed the heavens (Basilides), all teaching at about the time of the writing John 1:9, and all communicating with power to a certain number of earlier Christians, places 1:9 in a conversational setting, a mode of interactive discourse, rather than simply a *haec dixit dominus* medium. More generally, the dark laughter, the pessimism of the Gnostics with regard to this world, hard as it is for us to understand and hear, helps us escape, perhaps, a part of our own entrapment in the global age. We are hearing a word re-read in the global age that comes out of a decidedly anti-global worldview, supported by a decidedly anti-global myth. The other verses from John, so regularly draped as banners at the Super Bowl and during the World Series (John 1:1, John 3:14, John 8:32), and so familiarly known, are probably the best-known and least understood portions of the New Testament. To disallow the faux-interpretations that abound of these verses is itself a responsibility of today's interpreter.

It should be noted that our appreciation and understanding of Gnosticism has changed subsequent to the publication of the NHL. The picture of Gnosticism provided by the heresiologists has been significantly modified, based on the material now available in the Coptic Gnostic library. There are places where the NHL material is congruent with heresiological writing, notably in the concurrence of the Apochryphon of John and Irenaeus about the Barbelo-Gnostics.[2] This, by the way, shows clearly the antiquity and reliability of some of the NHL, at the least. But the NHL does not confirm the interest in doctrine, attributed by the fathers to Gnostics. Quite the contrary. These documents show little to no interest in doctrinal debate or control. And many of the documents, to this writer's mind perhaps a third, are clearly and easily orthodox, in the later sense of the term. Wisse: "The truly Christian Gnostic works, on the other hand, such as the Gospel of Truth, the Gospel of Thomas, and the Treatise on the Resurrection, lack the typical mythological extravaganza and thus may have gone unnoticed. . . It is likely that these books originated and found their use in a heterodox, Gnosticizing Christian environment which was not seen as a serious threat by the heresiologists."[3] The Gnostics were neither system builders nor systematicians. What they did seem to share, and what draws together the NHL, is an interest in an ascetic ethics.[4]

Where did Gnosticism come from? Harnack, following Irenaeus, thought it came out of Christianity, as Christianity came out of Judaism and into the Greek world ("acute hellenization"). Others have argued that the myth and worldview originated in Persia, or out of the speculations within iconoclastic Judaism, or out of some syncretistic combination of many sources. One strong argument is that Gnosticism, while it did not pre-date Christianity, may have grown up alongside Christianity, in sibling rivalry with it, and in consequence of some of the same experiences (disappointment of apocalyptic hope, dislocation from religious homeland). It behooves the interpreter to monitor very closely what is said and what is

---

2. Frederik Wisse, "The Nag Hammadi Library and the Heresiologists," *Vigilae christianae* 25 (1971) 208.

3. Ibid., 217.

4. Ibid., 222.

Gnosticism

not said about the dating of various documents used in various arguments. Gnosticism alongside, outside, and slightly antecedent to earliest Christianity is the probable answer to a part of the question of origins.

GNOSTICISM AND NEW TESTAMENT

We turn now to some consideration, not of Gnosticism on its own or in general, but rather to Gnosticism and its interrelationship with the New Testament. The influence of Gnosticism on the New Testament has, of course, largely been attributed to the Gospel of John, with attendant interest in the Pauline corpus. The gradual dissemination of and understanding of the materials from the NHL has continued to ferment, partly to further clarification, and partly toward confusion and obfuscation of the NT/Gnostic connection. In fact, the Gospel of Thomas has confirmed the existence, not of Q, but of a document very like Q, and very like the kind of literature assumed, intuited in the sources behind the Synoptics. This is a truly underrated advance in understanding. It is like the moon landing in terms of our desire to land on Mars. Likewise, the multiple sayings and sayings collections have confirmed what earlier scholars intuitively expected in the background of the Synoptics. We are still bogged down in a first, or early second generation of interpretation of the NHL documents, and many of the current assessments of this material are done by those whose fine interests are nonetheless, in contrast to an earlier generation's, not close to the needs arising from New Testament exegesis. Here also, the pendulum has widely swung, from church and seminary professorial influence to religious studies and non-ecclesiological interests.

R. Bultmann and H. Jonas defined the modern study of the New Testament and Gnosticism. Neither of them had, for all of their brilliance and brilliant intuitions, direct access to the NHL. Now we have the NHL, and the material has far from settled the matter. On the other hand, for instance, the closeness of John 1, including our text at hand, John 1:9, and passages from one NHL document, the I-sayings in the Trimorphic Protennoia, proven in the work of G. Macrae, expand and illumine a closeness heretofore muted between John and Gnosticism. Reading the two lists of I-am sayings, Johannine and Gnostic, one after the other, is an impressive exercise for most unbiased hearers.

Our study of *Treat.Res.*, included below, adds further fuel to the argument of proximity between the NT and Gnosis. Other NHL documents allow similar access to related themes. The connection between some passages in the Pauline epistles, and the myth and worldview of Gnosticism, becomes clear or clearer, with regard to the teaching on resurrection. Furthermore, as Wrede showed and as Robinson confirmed, the themes of silence and mystery in Mark are close to those in John and congruent with those prevalent in the Coptic Gnostic documents. The Paraphrase of Shem, consistently and transparently, employs obfuscation in its revelation discourse in a way that exaggerates but focuses similar moves in Mark and John. In all these documents, Coptic and canonical, the point of resurrection and the point of view following (either actually or rhetorically) resurrection becomes the interpretative fulcrum. Though seldom identified by commentators, this would be the main point of the Emmaus road account. With regard to mystery, to silence, to parable, to resurrection, the line from Mark through John, then, may best be drawn out further into Christian Gnosticism, which alone, in full measure, continued these emphases.

The literary character of the Gnostic movement further heightens our awareness of diversity, obscurity and mystery in Gnosticism. The church fathers, perhaps having many of the same documents we now possess, and, ironically, perhaps sharing the same levels of ignorance of further aspects of Gnosticism which challenge us, may have thought too highly of the Gnostics capacity for communal life. They may rather have related largely in literary form. Their insight and imagination roamed freely, without worry or regard for doctrinal fences.

As Wisse and others have cautioned us, then, we should not expect that the references in later NT documents to heretics should conjure up competing churches with highly developed doctrine. Rather, the concern is simpler, more simply with roving teachers who prey on unsuspecting women and others, and who claim secret, mysterious, insight and knowledge. The Gnostic influence on the NT at this point then would be better described as broad but not deep. One key difference between Irenaeus and Timothy, however, is that the apocalyptic key in which the Gnostic music is played has disappeared by the time of the patristic attacks, for obvious reasons. Further understanding of Gnosticism may help us somewhat with the deuteron-Pauline letters, and somewhat less with Paul's letters themselves.

With regard to John, however, the case is different. Gnosticism shares with John, and John with the Gnostics, a kind of freedom. They share a freedom to know and disregard past sacred writings. They share a freedom to know and criticize the content of the Hebrew scripture. They share a freedom to play inherited tunes, like those of the synoptic gospels, with a jazz rhythm quite foreign to the earlier canonical gospels, a mode connecting John strongly to the Gnostic gospels of the NHL. They share a freedom in assessment of creation, this world, the cosmos that is rare, with a few Pauline verses excepted, in the rest of the NT. They share a freedom in imagination, both in cosmic speculation, and in revelation discourse. They share a freedom of interpretation, which, depending on one's own interpretation, either rightly and keenly heralds the marrow of the NT, or wrongly mistakes the same. In any case, they share freedom, its voice, its defense, its community, its calling. Frederik Wisse smartly attuned our ears to freedom of this sort. His argument requires and deserves full citation.

> The problematic relationship between Gnosticism and the gospel of John will come to stand in a new light. The focus should shift away from the unanswerable question whether the author did borrow, or could have borrowed, a dualistic vocabulary, the redeemer myth, certain literary forms and a de-emphasis of the sacraments, future eschatology and ethics from Gnosticism. Not only are these characteristics to be found outside of Gnosticism, but they are not really typical features of the Christian Gnostic writings. The question should be whether John stands in the uncontrolled, speculative tradition of Gnostic literature and whether it shares in some way the gnostic's pessimistic worldview and elitist self understanding. I think the answer is affirmative.
>
> The author of the fourth gospel obviously did not feel bound by the early traditions about Jesus which are were incorporated in the Synoptic Gospels, and his reinterpretation of Jesus is in many ways as daring as that found in gnostic gospels. The framework of salvation has been refocused in terms of a vulgar, Greek dualism between flesh and spirit or this evil world and the realm of light. One could even apply Harnack's definition of Gnosticism to the Gospel of John and see it as an acute Hellenization of Christianity.
>
> The supposed anti-Gnosticism of the Gospel and the Epistles of John is part of a modern attempt to rescue John from the hands of the gnosticizers. As we see from their writings, Gnostics had little difficulty affirming the incarnation or the virgin birth, though as in the case of the author of the Gospel of John and many others in the early church, the real interest was in the divine presence. It is also meaningless to point out that the identity of the knowledge of God and knowledge of the self is lacking the fourth Gospel. One looks in vain for this modern abstraction in Gnostic writings.
>
> Of course, the Gospel of John is not Gnostic, not because of inherent reasons, but because it received a secure place in emerging orthodoxy. All pre-orthodox, early Christian literature shares to some extent the idiosyncratic and heterodox character of Gnostic literature. There were not yet clear limits within

which these authors had to stay in order to be accepted by a Christian audience. The success of the Gnostic teachers, in spite of the often grotesque nature of their claims is proof of this.[5]

John is a Gnostic gospel. It is still gnostically and emphatically anti-gnostic. It is still a product of Jewish heterodoxy. It is still a two level drama. It is still imbued with the Essene spirit. It is still a vulgar Greek document. Yet, still, John is a gospel located within the Gnostic literature, Gnostic tradition, Gnostic pessimism, and Gnostic enthusiasm. Bultmann, Martyn, Brown, and Ashton do still and truly hold a part of the elephant. It is Wisse, though, who names the grey color of the elephant's hide.

---

5. Wisse, "Nag Hammadi Library," 10.

27

Toward a New View of Eschatology in Gnosticism

A. Introduction

The purpose of this thesis has been to test an assumption involving gnostic eschatology. After describing its use in Johannine scholarship, we examined the assumption in the light of a trend in apocalyptic studies and also in the light of the Nag Hammadi Library. The result of this study suggests that the assumption is unwarranted. Apocalypticism does make use of vertical eschatology; Gnosticism does make use of the horizontal variety. In this regard, both religious expressions from late antiquity appear remarkably congruent with early Christianity.[1] With regard to their imaginative theological reflection on eschatological issues, they are not formally or essentially different. Within apocalyptic studies, as we have shown, an emerging consensus about a new view of eschatology in Apocalypticism is identifiable. A clearer, more accurate picture of eschatology within Apocalypticism takes shape in this trend. Within gnostic studies, on the other hand, no such consensus has developed. No trend is as yet visible. The dearth of writing on the subject precludes any such development. Consequently, it is necessary to provide a sketch of a new view of eschatology in Gnosticism.

---

1. See also Wisse, "The Nature and Purpose of Redactional Changes in Early Christian Texts," in *Gospel Traditions in the Second Century*, edited by W. L Peterson, 39–53 (Notre Dame: University of Notre Dame Press, 1989) 44.

THE COURAGEOUS GOSPEL

We can perceive within Apocalypticism a new portrait of eschatology by reference to the secondary literature. In gnostic studies such a portrait needs still to be painted. Because this dissertation has challenged the traditional view of gnostic eschatology in the course of analyzing the assumption, it may be useful at the end of the thesis to suggest some lines and colors for future use in a corrected portrait of eschatology within Gnosticism. What follows is only an initial sketch. The full portrait lies well beyond the limits of the dissertation. Still, the results presented in the preceding six chapters require a change in our picture of gnostic eschatology. The following materials are offered as necessary, though not by themselves sufficient, ingredients in a new view of the eschatology of Gnosticism.

B. Step One: Retain Accurate Aspects of the Old View

It is not the Manichaean literature alone which abounds with interest in the ascent of the soul through the spheres to its eternal rest, as all light is recollected in the Godhead.[2] Jonas correctly emphasized this element. It remains a crucial concern within Gnosticism.

In the standard gnostic myth, the deity continually re-creates his substance by gathering to himself the particles of light which tragically have become enmeshed in human life. Such re-creation follows the death of the believer. This is classic vertical eschatology. It remains fundamental to an understanding of gnostic eschatology. Jonas eloquently expounds this point.[3]

We can step even a little farther along on this theme. Not only does the "ascent of the soul" command center stage in this drama, but also the other actors take their cues from it. With slight qualification, Jonas's point stands firm: "Thus the history of the world and of man is a continual process of the freeing of light, and the arrangements of the universe, like all events of history, are considered from this point of view."[4] The qualification involves Jonas's implication, here and elsewhere, that the completion of this process is incidental to the process itself.

The six tractates we have analyzed here have offered no cause to erase this part of the traditional view of gnostic eschatology. *Treat. Res.* and *Gos. Phil.* Clearly exemplify such a vertical eschatological concern, while the other tractates also contain vertical eschatology in

---

2. Hans Jakob Polotsky, *Collected Papers* (Jerusalem: Magness, 1971) 11.

3. Hans Jonas, *The Gnostic Religion: The Message of the Alien God and the Beginnings of Christianity* (Boston: Beacon, 1963) 45.

4. Ibid., 233.

Toward a New View of Eschatology in Gnosticism

differing degrees. From the traditional view of gnostic eschatology we may safely retain the central importance of vertical eschatology. Gnostic writings respond to this question formulated in the Apocalypse of John: "And I said to the savior, 'Lord, will all the souls then be brought safely to the pure light?'" (N.H.C. II, 1, 25:17).

C. Step Two: Remove Inaccurate Aspects of the Old View

Some aspects of the traditional view need to be removed from discussion. We may begin with the issue of realized eschatology. Our study of the six Nag Hammadi documents offers no clear support for this kind of eschatological teaching. One does discover suggestions of anticipation of eschatological glory, and even an occasional enthusiastic exclamation of resurrection "now." Nevertheless, these references do not seem very radical or eccentric when they are read in context, and when they are compared to early Christian documents such as the letters of Paul. Paul also spoke of dying and rising in anticipation of eternity (Rom 6:8), without denying an horizontal eschatological expectation (Rom 8:18). In another way, moreover, our study strongly questions the usefulness of the concept of realized eschatology. If time had somehow stood still for the Gnostic, there might be some *prima facie* reason to investigate the concept of realized eschatology. A complete disinterest in time, in the progression of history, of such radical proportion might produce this kind of enthusiasm, as occurred in the nineteenth century utopian communities.[5] But the bulk of our new data on Gnosticism, and particularly the documents analyzed here, indicates to the contrary that the Gnostics had considerable interest in time and history, albeit for their own reasons related to the gnostic vision. The Nag Hammadi documents studied show a keen interest in the movement of history. The gnostic attention to history makes suspect a highly realistic version of "now" eschatology. Consequently, the use made of the concept of realized eschatology by many New Testament scholars finds little or no support in gnostic literature from Nag Hammadi.

Our study also raises a question about another major element in the traditional view of gnostic eschatology. Church historians have tended to describe gnostic eschatology as non-apocalyptic eschatology. Some discover the origin of Gnosticism in the disappointment of apocalyptic hope. This aspect of the traditional view also needs modification. No easy division can be created between gnostic eschatology and apocalyptic hope. We rather recognize within Gnosticism

---

5. J. P. Noyes, *A Godly Heritage* (Toronto: Clark, 1958).

the active and purposeful presence of apocalyptic eschatology. The specific uses of apocalyptic material need further description, and we turn now to this project. In sum, however, a new view of eschatology in Gnosticism will be constructed in tension with the traditional view. The important place of the "ascent of the soul" is not in question; gnostic eschatology cannot, however, be equated with realized or non-apocalyptic eschatology.

D. Step Three: Identify Gnostic Questions
Answered by Apocalyptic Eschatology

It is no longer possible to describe gnostic eschatology as non-apocalyptic. Also, it is no longer possible to give only passing reference to apocalyptic material in gnostic texts. In light of the six Nag Hammadi tractates studied in this dissertation, horizontal eschatology deserves a place of prominence.[6]

As shown earlier, gnostic documents are replete with apocalyptic imagery and eschatology. The apocalyptic material tends to complement or fill out the gnostic eschatological hope. The gnostic writers eschew strictly systematic precision in their combination of vertical and horizontal eschatology. They are not systematic theologians. Their musings are more theoretic than philosophical. Their writings correlate questions that might have troubles the gnostic believer with answers that were available from the apocalyptic tradition. The Gnostics had no scruples about using this material; it was not anathema to them. In fact, they needed the insights provided by Apocalypticism in order to articulate important features of their own expectation. We assert, quite surprisingly in view of past scholarship, that gnostic eschatology needed the presence of apocalyptic ingredients. Answers to serious gnostic religious questions were given in terms of Apocalypticism. Without the apocalyptic material, the very dreams central to the traditional gnostic myth would be jeopardized. Scholarship has thus far not appreciated this. Gnostics could not avoid ongoing dialogue with apocalyptic themes, any more than the early church could dispense with 1 Thessalonians, Mark 13, or the Revelation of St. John. Apocalyptic eschatology is not peripheral to Gnosticism, but necessary in ways peculiar to the gnostic hope. A preliminary sketch of the necessary functions provided by the apocalyptic material within Gnosticism would include, at a minimum, four roles described below. The functions involve religious themes that were truly significant within gnostic speculation. At this point we are handling the kernel, not the husk, of a religious hope. Gnostic speculation relied on

---

6. Kurt Rudolph, *Gnosis: The Nature and History of Gnosticism* (New York: Harper & Row, 1983) 194.

Toward a New View of Eschatology in Gnosticism

apocalyptic eschatology to answer questions about death, judgment, heaven, and hell. In this, the functions of Apocalypticism ran parallel to their uses in early Christianity.

1. Question: "Is the expected ascent into the light permanent?"

    Response: "Apocalyptic eschatology assures the reader of gnostic writings that the light which enlightens every Gnostic will be permanently protected from darkness, throughout the destruction of matter at the end of time. The ascent of the soul can bring true freedom only if no further outbreak of chaos, no further creative activity by the demiurge, lurks in the future. Final destruction is a commonplace in Apocalypticism (cf. Rev 22:8). Jonas alludes to the importance of such a final destruction, although without offering deliberate investigation of its meaning for the Gnostic.[7] Darkness will be shut up finally in the dwelling that was established for it. Darkness will be bound up forever, unable again to assert itself against the Light. *Paraphrase of Shem* amply illustrates this function of apocalyptic eschatology within Gnosticism. The apocalyptic eschatology in *Paraphrase of Shem* could not be more realistic or historical. *Paraphrase of Shem* makes ample use of stock apocalyptic imagery in order to underscore the assured deliverance of Light from Darkness, or Nature: "Then Nature will have a final opportunity. And the stars will cease from the sky... and in the last day the forms of Nature will be destroyed" (Nag Hammadi Codex [NHC] VII, 1 *Paraphrase of Shem* 12:18). The Gnostic maintains an ongoing, individualistic, religious interest in time and history, which culminates in a classic form of apocalyptic hope. His own real deliverance dependes upon the destruction of the created order. Without this horizontal hope, his escape ascent is in jeopardy. Outside the scope of the tractates studied here, another example is offered in the ending of *1 Apocalypse of James* (NHC V, 3, 36:15). The dissolution and destruction of nature, wherein the stars fall from the sky and nature reaches completion, means a great deal within the context of the pessimistic worldview of Gnsoticism. A gnostic existential concern about the light and the dark receives an apocalyptic response.

2. Question: "Will the wicked come to judgment?"

    Response: Although an earlier understanding of Gnosticism may have excluded a concern for ethics in this life, the Nag Hammadi Library

---

7. Jonas, *Gnostic Religion*, 235.

gives plentiful evidence of gnostic ethical interest.[8] A logical consequence of this arises then in the form of a hope of judgment. Will justice be done? Will judgment be meted out to the impure and the ignorant? The Gnostic was not above a religious interest in this issue. Apocalyptic eschatology assures the Gnostic that judgment will come at the end of time. Our six tractates abundantly illustrate this. This is of vital religious importance if the Gnostic is to maintain an ascetic or encratic lifestyle and self-discipline, and expectation of righteous judgment is required. Apocalyptic eschatology, presented in the clothing of Biblical apocalyptic imagery, answers this question about the judgment of the wicked: "When he has completed the established time of the kingdom of the earth, then the purging of souls will come since wickedness is greater than you." (NHC VI, 4 *Concept of our Great Power* 42:25).

3. Question: "Will the recollection of Light finally be completed?"

Response: Apocalyptic eschatology assures the Gnostic that at some point in time the final goal of the process of salvation will be achieved. The individual soul's resurrection, ascension, or rest depends in part for its fulfillment on this cosmic completion. A soul entirely at rest requires a cosmos entirely at rest. Ironically, the gnostic system in one sense may rest more heavily on final eschatology than does orthodoxy. Lacking the Gnostic's radical pessimism about history and nature, the more moderate ancient, Christian or pagan, could afford more easily to neglect or to de-emphasize teaching about the end of time. Not so for the Gnostic. Heavenly hope in its fullest, most secure sense necessitates a culmination of tragic history and the disappearance of corrupt nature. Apocalyptic eschatology is more important at this point for the Gnostic than for the Orthodox. Frequently in Gnosticism emphasis falls upon the final, total ingathering of Light. *Book of Thomas the Contender* contains this expectation: "Whenever all the elect abandon bestiality, then this light will withdraw up to its essence, and its essence will welcome it once it is a good servant" (NHC II, 7, 139:30). *On the Origin of the World* offers a nearly identical hope: "In the consummation of your works, all of the deficiency which appeared in the truth will be dissolved" (NHC II, 5, 103:15). Gnostic protology requires apocalyptic eschatology. In sum, apocalyptic, horizontal provides the guarantee that the hopes expressed in vertical eschatology

---

8. Alexander Böhlig and Frederik Wisse, "Die Sextus-Sprüche und das Problem der Gnostischen Ethik," in *Zum Hellenismus in den Schriften von Nag Hammadi*, edited by Alexander Böhlig and Frederik Wisse, 55–86 (Wiesbaden: Harrassowitz, 1975).

Toward a New View of Eschatology in Gnosticism

will be finally completed, and that all the imprisoned light will be eternally freed.

4. Question: "Will not only judgment but also punishment await the Darkness?"

   Response: The punishment of the wicked is a fundamental feature of Apocalypticism. Both Biblical and apocryphal apocalypses contain much discussion of punishment at the end of time. In Gnosticism, apocalyptic eschatology assures the gnostic believer that desire for vengeance directed at an ignorant, flesh-loving humanity is not to be disappointed. The dissolution of history, the world, and time itself provide the occasion for revenge upon the denizens of darkness. Numerous illustrations of this penchant for revenge are found in the six tractates here studied. Thundering throughout the gnostic literature there resounds a vengeful litany of fear and loathing which is simply astounding for the modern interpreter. The prospect of punishment for the reprobate is meat and drink for the Gnostic. Apocalyptic eschatology alone can assure the Gnostic that, in time, appropriate vengeful punishment will be administered to the reprobate. In order to slake a violent thirst for revenge, the Gnostic drinks deeply from the cup of final eschatology.

The character of gnostic horizontal eschatology is best displayed in the various memorable passages themselves.[9] When she will not find anything else to burn she will destroy herself" (NHC VI, 4 *Concept of our Great Power* 40:15).

With this sentence we conclude our suggestions for modifications in a new view of eschatology in Gnosticism. The Gnostics made eclectic and practical use, as we have seen, of apocalyptic eschatology. In retrospect, it is difficult to understand how or why consistency in mythology and doctrine was expected with regard to eschatology. This may well be the least likely place for consistency in religious literature. Church doctrinal struggles did not produce eschatological diversity as much as they were produced by it. The tensions in Paul's apocalyptic perspective are, in this reading, less the result of ecclesiastical debate and more the source of such debate. The literature of early Christianity might better be understood in view of the history it creates than in terms of the history it reflects.

---

9. NHC II, 7 *Book of Thomas the Contender* 142:10; NHC VI, 4 *Concept of our Great Power* 40:15; NHC VII, 2 *Second Treatise of the Great Seth* 38:30.

28

Hill's Thesis

IN JOHANNINE STUDIES IT is often assumed that apocalyptic eschatology offended the Gnostic and that vertical eschatology was uncharacteristic of the Apocalypticist. The thesis demonstrates that this assumption is unwarranted. First, the assumption is identified and described as it functions in Johannine studies. Second, the assumption is compared to the the trend in current apocalyptic studies. Third, the assumption is compared to evidence from recently discovered Gnostic tractates. The thesis concludes that this assumption, widely present in scholarship devoted to the Fourth Gospel, is unwarranted in light of contemporary apocalyptic studies, and in light of new evidence from Gnostic documents. Consequently, a new understanding of eschatology in Gnosticism, parallel to the new trend in Apocalypticism, is needed. Further, the assumption can no longer function as it has in Johannine scholarship.

29

An Overview of Hill's Thesis

THE SCOPE OF THE THESIS

In order to expound this thesis with a modicum of precision and brevity, limitations in the three main areas of study have necessarily been made. Three large areas of scholarship come under scrutiny and are observed in their interplay. Their interplay at *one small point*, an assumption about Apocalypticism and Gnosticism in Johannine studies, is the focus. Here the intention is three-fold. We intend to display the presence and function of the assumption in Johannine studies. We also intend to explore the assumption's background in Apocalypticism. We further intend to examine the assumption in the light of six Nag Hammadi tractates. We then summarize our conclusions and offer additional information in the appendices.

Consequently, the treatment here of Apocalypticism, Gnosticism, and Johannine studies can be designed according to the specific study of the assumption in question. We do not need to present a new and complete history of Johannine studies, nor a new review of all that now composes the study of Apocalypticism, nor a novel summation of gnostic scholarship. A judgment about Biblical studies lies behind this strategy. We are at a point, it might be argued, at which one may refer to other scholars in Biblical studies (e.g., R. Kysar on John, P. Hanson on Apocalypticism, Rudolph on Gnosticism), and then make some *use* of their findings, with critical handling of them, as is the purpose of such surveys in the first place. This thesis suggests both in its form and in its content that we have arrived at a time wherein certain limits and warnings, and so also some alterations, need to be added to the collective wisdom of our discipline. The hope is modest. We hope to see the assumption *frequently used* and widely present in Johannine studies. We also hope to describe a *trend* in apocalyptic studies. We additionally hope to highlight, improve, and export *a more accurate portrait* of Apocalypticism within Gnosticism. In order to challenge the assumption as it is found to be used in Johannine studies, we offer an examination and critique of the understanding of the relationship between Apocalypticism and Gnosticism at the point of contact with the Fourth Gospel.

JOHANNINE STUDIES

The thesis proposes a method of identifying the presence of the assumption through the discovery of the functions of the assumption in Johannine studies. The assumption to be identified in this sub-section is the following: "Apocalypticism involves final eschatology and moves along a horizontal, temporal axis; Gnosticism involves personal eschatology and moves upon a vertical, spatial axis." This hypothetical contrast between Apocalypticism and Gnosticism operates, this thesis argues, in at least five distinct ways within Johannine scholarship. With the help of major examples and instances, and with the aim of apt, brief description ever present, the thesis intends to demonstrate the presence and function of the assumption at the basic level of use by current interpreters. It is very important to note that this use is uncritical, and therefore undefended. It is *assumed* that apocalyptic eschatology offended the Gnostic. This is not argued, nor proven, nor disproven. One major contribution of this thesis, quite apart from its argument's success or failure, lies in raising the issue to a conscious level. The authors assume; the thesis raises the stakes. We examine an assumed contrast, an hypothesis. Simply to unearth the problem and sharply to raise the question is of primary value for scholarship.

The five functions here depicted are presented under two categorical subheadings. Three are related to the question of the so-called ecclesiastical redactor; two are functions more broadly related to the issues of Johannine scholarship, Apocalypticism and Gnosticism.

APOCALYPTICISM

In Part Three we examine and critique the background of the assumption in Apocalypticism. The categories of definitions and descriptions of

An Overview of Hill's Thesis

Apocalypticism which dominated scholarship over the past one hundred years (so ably summarized by P. Vielhauer) receive new attention and basic critical scrutiny in the work of Koch. At this date, relying on these and other prominent writers, it is possible to chart the emergence of a trend in apocalyptic studies which helps to analyze the validity of the assumption. Here the trend is referred to as the 'emergence of vertical eschatology' in Apocalypticism. If new discoveries predominate in changes within gnostic scholarship, here it is rather new appreciation of old material which occasions a re-evaluation. What R. Charles viewed as the rubble of religions in late antiquity, P. Hanson and others uphold as buried treasure. Consequently, given new interest and new appreciation, and so a different kind of attention to the material, the emergence of a enw and different emphasis in scholarship becomes possible. In order to plot the coordinates of this trend it is not necessary to summarize, in the manner described above, a completely or exhaustively thorough compendium of apocalyptic texts and critics. In order to chart, to describe, the emergence of vertical eschatology within current understandings of Apocalypticism, a three-fold argument is required. To begin, an historical foundation for further work arises out of study of the key figures in earlier scholarship (J. Weiss, A. Schweitzer, Charles, Bultmann, M. Werner, Vielhauer, Koch). Although these past scholars, and others not reviewed, worked and wrote from quite different vantage points, most shared a view of Apocalypticism that highlighted horizontal eschatology as the central idea and the motivating power with Apocalypticism. Then, from this historical foundation, we move toward a closer look at the corssroads of this kind of scholarship, found at the intersection of the work of Koch and Vielhauer. Here the major questions of definition and description receive careful, new argumentation. Interpreters must still choose, in exegesis, at some point, between the views of Koch and Vielhauer, and the results are predictable. Finally, stretching out from this crossroads, and as a primary result of the questions entertained by Koch, the trend of the emergence of vertical eschatology is traced at seven different levels of scholarship.

GNOSTICISM

In Part Four we test the foreground of the assumption in Gnosticism. It is within Gnosticism that the most significant findings of this dissertation can be brought to light. Our understanding of Gnosticism must now refer directly, primarily, and freshly to the new discoveries encased in the Nag Hammadi Codices. Any suppositions about the character of limits of gnostic teaching, its range of interests and its limits of gnostic teaching, its range of interests of tolerance, now must receive new evaluation on the basis of exposure to new material. We perceive no trend similar to that charted in the section on Apocalypticism. Insufficient work has been done to date to warrant such a claim. Rather, here in the foreground of the assumption, its foundation shakes and rattles when accosted by new material. Just how tolerant or intolerant of horizontal eschatology were the Gnostics?

Comparatively little pertinent scholarship needs review at the outset (M. peel, H. Attridge, Rudolph, G. MacRae). Quickly we enter into examination of the primary material. Six tractates from Nag Hammadi are inspected. Their selection is not intended as a comprehensive exemplification of the Nag Hammadi data; nor, however, did the six come simply from random selection as titles drawn, as it were, out of a top hat. As a group they will represent the range of material in the Nag Hammadi Library. It is difficult to be very definite regarding matters of introduction. The six treatises exhibit a variety of characeristics. They come from a diverse range of dates (100–300 C.E.), genres (apocalypse-catechism), theological positions (non-Christian, mythological Gnostic, Christian Gnostic), and possible intentions on the parts of their authors (mystical speculation-edification of believers). They do exhibit interest in eschatology. And they provide, with regard to quality of exposition, a mixture of eloquence and vulgarity.

EXPECTED CONCLUSIONS

We expect that the conclusions, and so the positive contributions to original knowledge, of this thesis will include the following:

1. The assumption is widely present in literature devoted to the Fourth Gospel
2. The assumption is invalid with regard to Apocalypticism as currently described.
3. The assumption is invalid with regard to Gnosticism as exemplified in recently discovered Nag Hammadi Library.
4. The assumption needs modification or rejection.
5. The exegetical need in Johannine interpretation for the hypothesized presence of the hand of an ecclesiastical redactor, which rests heavily on the assumption, is greatly lessened; thus, the importance of the hypothetical redactor decreases.
6. New directions for study at the border between Apocalypticism and Gnosticism may be discovered to include: a general blurring of the

An Overview of Hill's Thesis

formerly distinct and useful line of separation, in the history of religions, between the two world-views; another look at the problem of definition of terms; renewed concern for the manner in which these ancient esoteric mysterious texts are properly to be read.

DEFINING OUR TERMS

Great variety, and so confusion, attends the vocabulary of debate in this area. One crucial effect of this study that takes place at the borderline between Apocalypticism and Gnosticism may be that the growing consensus with regard to definitions in the first area may lead to clarity in the second area. A parallel three-tier division of terminological labor might help gnostic studies (i.e., gnostic revelatory discourse, Gnosis, Gnosticism as parallels to Hanson's Apocalypse, apocalyptic, Apocalypticism).[1] Many authors have addressed the issue of definition.

Two dangers consistently threaten the scholar. On one hand, overly narrow, concise definition of terms tends to conclude discussion before it begins, even as such narrowness ill corresponds to the diversity of ancient religion and literature. On the other hand, overly broad, minimal definition of terms tends to create nets through which all fish can swim. Scholarship has not reached a point of consensus about the meanings of many terms related to Apocalypticism and Gnosticism (including these two).

In this thesis, a middle road is followed. Here we suggest and identify the core references of the terms used (resting heavily on other scholars). These are working definitions. They are meant to encourage debate, not conclude it. Thus, we provide a beginning but not an ending for the meanings of these terms. Three sets of terms require attention.

Easiest to describe is the apocalyptic set. This thesis accepts and affirms Hanson's three-fold distinction and definition. If "Apocalypse" refers to a particular literary genre and "apocalyptic" means a kind of eschatology, then "Apocalypticism" is the religious perspective related to these two. Somewhat more difficult are the parallel words from Gnosticism. Here "Gnosticism" means the religious perspective contained in gnostic literature. Some consensus presently exists regarding what conattempts to use the commnstitutes gnostic texts: the Nag Hammadi Library, in particular, can be used as a way to measure the scope of gnostic literature. Most troublesome, perhaps, are the words related to eschatology. Here we may need to be more definitive in order to communicate clearly. "Horizontal eschatology"

---

1. P. Hanson, "Apocalypticism," *The Interpreter's Dictionary of the Bible* Supplementary Volume, edited by K. Crim, 28–34 (Nashville: Abingdon, 1982).

means expectations related to the end of time. "Vertical eschatology" means personal immortality, the ascent of the soul, or a radical anticipation of this known as "realized eschatology."

In all three sets of terms this thesis this thesis attempts to use the commonly accepted meanings for words, to the extent that they exist. Where no consensus obtains, we have tried to avoid the word (e.g., Gnosis). Part of the wonderful frustration of work in this area is exacerbated by this thesis. In one respect, we intend here to further weaken our common grasp of terms. The assumption here examined was, at least, ne solid line of demarcation. Without it, the picture becomes even murkier.

30

The Treatise on the Resurrection (NHC I, 4)

INTRODUCTION: THE NATURE OF THE TRACTATE

THE TREATISE ON THE Resurrection (*Treat. Res.*)[1] has received much attention not only because it was one of the first of the Nag Hammadi tractates to be published,[2] but especially because it appears to represent the view, combated by the author of the Pastoral Epistles: *anastasin ede gegonenai*, "the resurrection has already occurred" (2 Tim 2:18). Of the six tractates here discussed, *Treat. Res.* Has provoked the most discussion and hence the largest bibliography.[3] The earlier attention to *Treat. Res.* is a mixed blessing for our thesis. On one hand, the study of the tractate has cleared away many difficulties in the text and translation, difficulties which to some degree still remain in the other Nag Hammadi documents.

---

1. Citations from the tractate follow the manuscript pagination, lines, and translations (except where otherwise noted) found in M. Peel, "The Treatise on the Resurrection," *Nag Hammadi Studies*, vols. 22 and 23, *The Coptic Gnostic Library, Nag Hammadi Codex 1 (The Jung Codex)*, edited by H. Attrdige (Leiden: Brill, 1985); "Introduction, Text and Translation," vol. 1, 123–57; "Notes," vol. 2, 137–215.

2. M. Malinine, *De Resurrectione (Epistula ad Rheginum): Codex Jung* (Zurich: Rascher, 1963) 43–50. Peel, "The Treatise on the Resurrection," *Nag Hammadi Codex I*, vol. 1; see also the list of texts and translations on pp. 123–25. Of these, the most significant is that of B. Layton, *The Gnostic Treatise on Resurrection from Nag Hammadi*, edited by G. MacRae and H. Cox, Harvard Dissertations in Religion 12 (Missoula, MT: Scholars, 1979).

3. See n7 below.

On the other hand, the interpretation of *Treat. Res.* has tended to follow the lead of the first interpreters by accepting their basic judgments on the eschatology of the tractate. Our study will re-examine this issue by asking, "What precisely does the author teach about eschatology and what views does he avoid?"

We have reason to expect that *Treat. Res.* will address the issue of eschatology. The title of this brief "letter" identifies its main them as the question of *anastasis*, "the ressurection." The author begins his instruction by warning against doubt and misunderstanding on the issue (44:1). His essay approaches the issue the issue from the side of faith (44:8). While allowing for difficulties in regard to such a mysterious matter, the author of *Treat. Res.* yet expects to make clear a number of points of doctrine which will actually and personally edify his reader (44:5). The intent of the epistle is pastoral.

The treatise has been used as evidence that Gnosticism includes an understanding of realized eschatology, akin to the thought of the adversary mention in 2 Tim. 2:18.[4] Just how this interpretation accords with the tractate's actual teaching is a major part of the question before us.

We do not know when, where, or by whom *Treat. Res.* was written. A standard suggestion is that the writing comes from the late second century, and was produced by a Christian Valentinian Gnostic.[5] No internal or external evidence, however, can be summoned to prove this. Even the question of the Valentinian character of the tractate cannot be answered with certainty, Valentinian influence is at best superficial sine the mythological speculation which is characteristic of Valentinianism is not evidenced here. Furthermore, the language and focus of *Treat. Res.* are closer to the Johannine and especially Pauline writings than any other.

Regarding the composition of the tractate, it should be noted that this treatise is in the form of a letter, and is written as a response to a friendly inquiry about he nature of resurrection. The response does not become an excuse to philosophize, but instead provides a pastoral intention to strengthen faith. There is no obvious polemical intent visible in *Treat. Res.*

Although the Valentinian character of this Christian document is not obvious, nevertheless its general gnostic demeanor cannot be denied. The vocabulary alone would suggest this. We find in *Treat. Res.* such terms as "pleroma," "know," "the all," "truth," and "this element," which are common

---

4. Layton, *The Gnostic Treatise on Resurrection*. This is Layton's thesis throughout this important study.

5. See, for instance, B. Layton, *The Gnostic Scriptures* (New York: Doubleday, 1987) 316.

The Treatise on the Resurrection (NHC I, 4)

in gnostic writings. Furthermore, the general doctrinal interests of the whole treatise bespeak Gnosticism, though many of these same themes and concerns are also found in non-gnostic Christianity. *Treat. Res.* exemplifies the gnostic interest in pre-existence, in the Platonic separation of illusion and reality, and in the general devaluation of the created order. On the other hand, it is difficult, even after conceding the gnostic character of the tractate, to call it heretical. When one considers the careful Christological thinking evident in the treatise (44:24–33), its reliance on the Scripture (45:24–26), its homiletical call to faith (46:5–9), its dual attack on doubt and ignorance (44:1–12), and its surprisingly orthodox soteriology (44:30–41), the suggestion of heresy seems inappropriate and anachronistic. As we shall see, the specific teaching on the resurrection supports this judgment.

THE MAIN THEMES

An assessment of the main teachings in *Treat. Res.* proceeds best when unencumbered by an overlay of previous study of the tractate. *Treat. Res.* serves as its own best introduction. In this treatise, we receive an ancient response to a perennial question about death. Although the argument of the tractate is neither smooth nor highly organized, the main point is clear. One is to approach death in faith. Repeatedly, the author advances this point (44:1–12, 46:2–6, 48:31–34). His teaching on the resurrection carries the author into four related clusters of thoughts.

The author first considers the Resurrected Son. His order of argumentation thus follows that of St. Paul (1 Cor. 15, 1 Thess. 1). References to Christ appear often in the tractate (43:35, 44:20, 45:15, 48:10, 49:8, 50:1). However, it is at the very outset of the letter to Rheginus that the Savior's nature and work are directly discussed This teaching can be described as thoroughly Biblical and even orthodox Christological speculation, couched in Platonic or Middle-Platonic terms. The Apostle to the Gentiles is referred to by way of summary and conclusion for this first theme (45:25).

Immediately on the heels of this reference to Paul, a second line of argument emerges. Believers are to share in a resurrection like that of Christ. Philosophy cannot contain this truth. Nevertheless, reliance on resurrection befits the wise man. The structure of the universe, the nature of the mind, the history of divine election, and the perduring quality of the person are given as incentives for the wise man to trust the resurrection. *Treat. Res.* argues: The resurrection is ours. We must think and live as those who accept it.

THE COURAGEOUS GOSPEL

The author moves on less abruptly to the next theme. Here he advances the doctrine of the resurrection itself. Concisely rendered, his view is that the resurrection is so real that compared to it, the world is unreal. Resurrection as ultimate reality thus assures the believer. Resurrection brings such assurance by revealing the hidden. This same resurrection creates the new and the good, and qualifies all life. It is what one receives in exchange for the conditions of this world. Resurrection in this theosophical essay is portrayed as thoroughly trustworthy. One can trust the resurrection when facing death. The tractate concludes with an exhortation to practice the faith in resurrection in terms of daily life. Christ makes his resurrection our own in order to give us confidence to face death. Therefore, we are to practice this hope. *Treat. Res.* is thus every inch an eschatological essay.

PREVIOUS RESEARCH[6]

Unlike many of the Nag Hammadi documents, this treatise has already a substantial amount of secondary literature devoted to it.[7] The first extensive

---

6. D. Scholer, *Nag Hammadi Bibliography 1948-1969*, Nag Hammadi Studies 1 (Leiden: Brill, 1971); and as supplemented annually by Bibliographia Gnostica in *Novum Testamentum* beginning in 1971.

7. Several translations and editions of *Trat. Res.* are now available:

Michel Malinine and Henri-Charles Puech, *De resurrectione (Epistula ad Rheginum)*: *Codex Jung* (Zürich: Rascher, 1963) 43–50; F. Bazán, "Sobre la Resurrectión (Epistola a Reginos): Traducción, Introducción, y Commentario," *Revista Biblica* 38 (1976) 147–78; R. haardt, "'Die Abhandlung über die Auferstehung' des Codex Jung aus der Bibliothek gnosticher koptischer Schriften von Nag Hammadi: Bemerkungen zu ausgewählten Motiven, Tell I: Der Text," *Kairos* 11 (1969) 1–5; M. Krause, "Die Abhandlung über die Auferstehung," *Die Gnosis*, vol. 2, edited by W. Forester, 85–163 (Zurich: Artemis, 1971); B. Layton, *The Gnostic Treatise on Resurrection from Nag Hammadi* (Atlanta: Scholars, 1979); L. Martin, "The Epistle to Rheginos: Translation, Commentary, and Analysis" (PhD diss., Claremont, 1971); M. Peel, *The Epistle to Rheginos: A Valentinian Letter on the Resurrection: Introduction, Translation, Analysis and Exposition* (Philadelphia: Westminster, 1969); For this dissertation, the latest work of Peel is most significant: "Treatise on the Resurrection: Introduction, Text, Translation, and Notes," *Nag Hammaid Codex I*.

A number of important articles on *Treat. Res.* have also been published: H. Gaffron, "Eine gnostische Apologie des Auferstenhungsglaubens: Bemerkungen zur Epistula ad Rheginum,'" *Die Zeit Jesu*: *Festschrift für Heinrich Schlier*, edited by G. Bornkamm and K. Rahner, 218–27 (Fribourg: Herder, 1970); B. Layton, "Vision and Revision: A Gnostic View of Resurrection," *Colloque international sur les texts de Nag Hammadi*, 190–217 (Québec: Laval, 1981); L. Martin, "The Anti-Philosophical Polemic and Gnostic Soteriology in 'The Treatise on the Resurrection' (C. G. I,3)," *Numen: International Review for the History of Religions* 20 (1973) 20–37.

J. Ménard, "L'Épitre á Rhéginos et la Resurrection," *Proceedings of the XII International Congress of the International Association for the History of Religions, Stockholm,*

The Treatise on the Resurrection (NHC I, 4)

study of *Treat. Res.* was made by Peel.⁸ A second equally significant study came somewhat later from Layton.⁹ These two authors present distinct interpretations of the tractate. Layton emphasizes the vulgar Platonic or Middle-Platonic characteristics of the treatise. Peel, on the other hand, emphasizes the Biblical, particularly Pauline, aspects of the treatise. A combination of the two readings would seem appropriate for future interpretations of the tractate. Our study, however, goes beyond the scope of previous research, since no previous scholarship adequately addresses the issue of horizontal eschatology in the tractate. In fact, the extensive bibliography on this document is not of great help with regard to the principal concern of our thesis, the role of final eschatology in Gnosticism.

Non-eschatological Studies

With Peel and Layton, a number of other authors have explored *Treat. Res.*[10] Generally these writers have further developed lines of argument and points of view introduced by Layton and Peel. For example, the possibly anti-philosophical character of *Treat. Res.* has been studied,[11] as has the doctrine of the resurrection within *Treat. Res.*[12] Other studies have investigated the form of the tractate,[13] its place in the history of religions,[14] and its relationship to other tractates from Nag Hammadi.[15] No full study has been made solely of the Biblical background of *Treat. Res.*, or of its relationship to Patristic theology. There is need of such studies, since it is not yet clear how we

---

Sweden, August 16–22, 1970, *Numen: International Review for the History of Religions*, 189–99 (Leiden: Brill, 1975); M. Peel, "Gnostic Eschatology and the New Testament."; H. Schenke, "Auferstehungsglaube und Gnosis," *Zeitschrift für die Neutestamentliche Wissenschaft* 59 (1968) 123–26; J. Zandee, "De opstanding in de brief aan Rheinos en in het evangelie van Philippus," *Nederlands Theologisch Tijdschrift* 16 (1962) 361–77.

    8. Peel, *Epistle*.

    9. Layton, *Gnostic Treatise*.

    10. See n7 above.

    11. Martin, "The Anti-Philosophical Polemic and Gnostic soteriology in 'The Treatise on the Resurrection,'" 37. "Monistic ontology is the metaphysical presupposition of the author of C. G. I,3 for a 'realized' soteriological possibility, the spiritual resurrection (45:39–46:2), which Rheginos already has (49:9–36)."

    12. J. Ménard, "La Notion de 'Résurrection' dans 'L'Épître á Rhéginos,'" *Essays on the Nag Hammadi Texts in Honor of Pahor Labib*, edited by M. Krause, 110–24 (Leiden: Brill, 1975).

    13. K. Schäfer, "Eisagoge," *Reallexikon für Antike und Christentum* 4 (Stuttgart: Hiensemann, 1959) 862–904.

    14. Schenke, "Auferstehungsgaube und Gnosis."

    15. Zandee, "De opstanding."

are to assess the relationship of *Treat. Res.* to orthodox Christianity. Because of its presence in the Nag Hammadi collection, scholarship has tended to begin with the assumption that *Treat. Res.* stands outside the orthodox stream. Reassessment of the tractate over time may change this judgment. For example, if the treatise shows intolerance of horizontal eschatology, as this thesis intends to demonstrate, this would support its proximity to theological currents within the great church. One other general study of the tractate needs mention to complete an overview of the history of study of this important document.[16]

Many of these earlier studies depend heavily on the seminal work of Layton and Peel. We now turn to a brief review of their respective positions, attending particularly to their understanding of the tractate's eschatology.

Layton

Layton's interpretation of the eschatology of *Treat. Res.* can be readily summarized.[17] In Layton's judgment, *Treat. Res.* reflects an essentially Platonic understanding of the last things, which precludes any meaningful place for horizontal, apocalyptic eschatology. The apocalyptic ideas of the end of the age, the culmination of history, the final judgment, the destruction of evil, and the resurrection of the just at the end of time are absent here, according to Layton. In fact, they must be absent because their presence would directly contradict the principle teaching within the tractate. "Resurrection" thus becomes the lone remaining vital aspect of apocalyptic eschatology, and this receives a new, non-apocalyptic definition.

The treatise itself, however, provides no evidence that a non-apocalyptic cast of mind lies behind the writing. The purpose of the treatise, as Layton correctly emphasizes, is strictly limited to a basic review of a few essential points concerning the resurrection.[18] Furthermore, this teaching is delivered to a student about whom the teacher consistently assumes the worst, and in a form that is rough or vulgar. It is unlikely then that this kind of occasional, brief, reflective essay would be intended to exclude or reject the complex ideas associated with apocalyptic eschatology. Such a project lies well beyond the purpose of the treatise, and is in no way suggested by

---

16. Kurt Rudolph, *Gnosis: The Nature and History of Gnosticism* (San Francisco: Harper and Row, 1983).

17. Layton, *Gnostic Treatise*.

18. Ibid., 122. Layton provides a helpful discussion of the *aporia* which conclude the Treatise.

The Treatise on the Resurrection (NHC I, 4)

the author's argument. Rather, he addresses what he claims is the proper, real meaning of "resurrection."

In Layton's view, *Treat. Res.* provides a clear example of gnostic vertical eschatology. The believer expects the ascent of his soul at the point of death and prepares for this during his earthly life.[19] His resurrection is not then, as in Paul, something which involves the whole person, body and soul, but something closer to the Platonic dualism which expects immortality only for the mind. The precondition for this escape, this resurrection or ascent into the unchangeable, is bodily death.

Notably, Layton does not entirely rely on this view, which is his own primary reading of the tractate. Rather, his interpretation highlights the earthly *anticipation* of this ascent. This anticipation is, in Layton's unfolding argument, the author's real point. Resurrection can be anticipated in this life, and this very anticipation is the real, proper understanding of resurrection. This is realized eschatology. It is important to underscore the significance which Layton attaches to one verse in *Treat. Res.*: "This si the resurrection of the spirit which 'swallows' resurrection of the soul along with resurrection of the flesh" (45:39–46:3). Layton interprets this verse as a reference to a proleptic resurrection, an anticipation of the heavenly life in earthly experience. He thus offers an interpretation of *Treat. Res.* which depicts its eschatology. "By an act of faith the 'nous' can direct its thought totally away from the body and totally towards the truth. This amounts to total separation from the body already. Physical death is thereupon no more than the physical expression of what will already have happened. Thus questions about bodily resurrection or ascent of the soul after death become irrelevant."[20]

Peel

Layton's interpretation is to some degree a reaction to Peel's earlier work.[21] Peel's later writing in turn responds to Layton's work. Peel's most recent summary of his own position identifies three important interpretative features regarding resurrection in the tractate. *Treat. Res.* presents resurrection first as a matter of faith, second as concerning the whole person, and third as essentially and completely operative in the present.[22] "One already

---

19. Ibid., 3–5.
20. Ibid., 127.
21. Peel, *The Epistle to Rheginos*.
22. M. Peel, "The Treatise on the Resurrection (I,4)," *The Nag Hammadi Library in English*, rev. ed., edited by J. Robinson (San Fracisco: Harper & Row, 1988) 52–54.

has the resurrection in the present."²³ This current assessment echoes others Peel has offered. He has long seen the tractate as significant teaching in regard to individual eschatology. In Peel's judgment, *Treat. Res.* represents a blend of Platonic and Pauline teaching. An overly Platonic interpretation of the tractate does harm to our understanding of its teaching, as does an overly Pauline interpretation.²⁴ The instrument of distinction with which Peel separates Platonic and Christian eschatology is the "new body." Platonism excludes a resurrection body, while Christianity requires it.²⁵

Peel rounds off his interpretation of *Treat. Res.* with comparisons between this gnostic tractate and its second century milieu: "Our author's thinking has been influenced by Platonic thought. Even so, this Platonism is radically altered by a gnostically inspired cosmic dualism and by a spiritually conceived, Christian-inspired idea of resurrection that clearly owes something to the apostle Paul."²⁶ One appreciates this adept attempt to cover all bases, and to broaden the possible background for *Treat. Res.* An even broader background for *Treat. Res.* would emerge with additional insight into and emphasis on the place of horizontal eschatology in the treatise. Both Layton and Peel fully agree that this tractate's eschatology is to be placed on the vertical axis. On this view, personal, individual, vertical eschatology is the concern of the author of *Treat. Res.* It is our argument that this conclusion needs modification.

Rudolph

A final word is needed regarding the work of Rudolph on this tractate.²⁷ Some of the direction of his analysis at this point converges with our thesis. Rudolph offers a balanced review of the teachings of *Treat. Res.*, which gracefully acknowledges the flexibility of gnostic thought. In contrast to Layton, Rudolph assesses the central importance of the post-mortem fate of the believer for the writer of *Treat. Res.* Resurrection occurs after death. Rudolph gives no attention to the so-called realized eschatology of the tractate, other than to show that the tractate teaches that the resurrection is anticipated in the lives of the enlightened faithful. We note that this echoes St. Paul (Rom. 6). Still, the proper condition of the resurrection lies beyond the realm of this world or age.

23. Ibid., 52.
24. Peel, "The Treatise on the Resurrection," *Nag Hammadi Codex I*, vol. 1, 134.
25. Ibid., 135.
26. Ibid., 137.
27. Rudulph, *Gnosis*, 191–93.

The Treatise on the Resurrection (NHC I, 4)

Rudolph may not be as accurate in his description of the universal and horizontal eschatological aspects of *Treat. Res.* The tractate simply does not fully address the issues of apocalyptic eschatology. It cannot and should not be read as an argument from silence against Apocalypticism. The tractate's thought itself gives a place to final eschatological themes. Even a predominantly vertical eschatological description of resurrection, and its anticipation as it can be experienced on this earth, does not necessarily stand in tension with speculation about the end of all things.

In sum, our critique of earlier studies focuses on their shared emphasis on vertical eschatology in *Treat. Res.* As we shall see, important passages in the treatise confound this view. These interpreters have emphasized the vertical dimension, but the horizontal is present, too. A related issue is that of realized eschatology. Peel seems most reliable at this point. All earlier views will require some modification in light of a fresh study of the text itself. *Treat. Res.* has seemed to provide the strongest kind of evidence in the past for the traditional view of gnostic eschatology. If this interpretation does not hold, we shall have forceful motivation to reassess and modify also the interpretation of other documents. *Treat. Res.* is the keystone in the arch of the traditional view of gnostic eschatology. The analysis to which we now turn removes this keystone.

ANALYSIS

Horizontal Eschatology

Ancient speculation about the end of the age included, along with other related and minor concerns, a clear interest in the general resurrection of the dead at the end of time, and an equally lively interest in the final consummation and destruction of the created order. These two ever-present apocalyptic concerns tended to support each other, and to make sense out of one another. As in the Revelation to John, so in apocalyptic eschatology speculation about the final resurrection often went hand in hand with speculation about the final consummation.[28]

Treat. Res. provides no full account of either of these loci of apocalyptic speculation. Its brevity and its intention to present the certainty and meaning of resurrection preclude such a full account. Along the way, however,

---

28. John Wesley, *Explanatory Notes Upon the New Testament* (New York: Eaton and Maine, 1903). Commenting on the Revelation Wesley writes, "Christ when on earth foretold what would come to pass in a short time, adding a brief description of the last things. Here he foretells the intermediate things, so that both put together constitute one complete chain of prophecy" (652).

Treat. Res. drops hints of interest in horizontal eschatology. Allusions to apocalyptic eschatology may be more largely present in the tractate than has been allowed in the past. In fact, several passages provide tantalizing partial evidence of apocalyptic eschatology (44:35–38; 47:27–29; 48:24–26; 49:2–5). One of these is particularly alluring (47:27–29). None is compellingly clear on the matter.

Other passages, however, are remarkably clear. *Treat. Res.*, contrary to much past interpretation, includes unmistakable references to the general resurrection of the dead and to the consummation at the end of the age. These transparent occurrences of apocalyptic eschatology in *Treat. Res.* can be readily displayed.

The General Resurrection

Treat. Res. commends to faith a belief in the raising of all the dead together at the end of time. As in the New Testament, this teaching stands in some tension with a more vertical eschatological program. When the text of *Treat. Res.* is approached afresh, one easily sees the endorsement of faith in the general resurrection.

A case in point is found at 46:5–8: "For it is the claim of faith my son and not that of argument. The dead shall arise!" There are no serious textual problems in this verse about the dead who shall arise. Peel notes the scribal emendation of the second at 46:7.[29] Layton argues and adds a question about the voice of the verb or gerund, noting that there is no way to distinguish the active from the middle-passive.[30] Problems with this verse, however, arise in interpretation. *Treat. Res.* appears to affirm the basic apocalyptic hope for the resurrection of, precisely, the dead (the general resurrection). It is exactly this ancient religious hope for the resurrection of the dead which is thought to have been rejected by Gnostics.[31] A simple, literal reading of 46:5 in its larger context, within the minor polemic against sophistry and philosophy, would appear to affirm a hope similar to what may be an early New Testament pre-Pauline fragment (1 Thess 1:9–10).[32] This is in fact the proper reading of the verse. The dead will rise. Faith places this truth before the reader. The reference is to the general resurrection on the last day. A collective hope, rather than an individualized or spiritualized rendering of

---

29. Peel, "The Treatise on the Resurrection," *Nag Hammadi Codex I*, vol. 2, 169.

30. Layton, *The Gnostic Treatise on Resurrection*, 100.

31. See chs. 14 and 15 above.

32. On this passage and related issues see the article of H. Koester, "From the Kerygma Gospel to the Written Gospels," *New Testament Studies* 35 (1984) 361–81.

The Treatise on the Resurrection (NHC I, 4)

apocalyptic eschatology, is present here. Moreover those being raised are not merely mortal but mortified. They are raised *after* they die. The gnostic tractate *Treat Res.* suddenly appears to have an apocalyptic underside.

Hermeneutical contortions arise when this literal reading is abandoned. Layton, in particular, must resort to a most indirect approach to this verse.[33] He suggests that here the author "makes maximum concessions to traditional modes of speaking."[34] More likely, though, the author of *Treat. Res.* is, as elsewhere, saying directly what he things. The dead will arise, and this raising is a future event. This future event is the apocalyptic hope of the general resurrection of the dead at the end of time. Layton surmises that the "diction is deceptive."[35] The diction is deceptive only if a prior understanding of the limits of gnostic eschatology are imported into the verse (46:5).

Peel takes a more moderate position.[36] He suggests that the "full" resurrection comes after death, but not the resurrection itself. His interpretation is that the dead will arise fully, while others will simply arise. Again, hermeneutical contortions are needed when the plain reading of the text is abandoned.

The literal reading of *Treat. Res.* 46:5 is far less upsetting to the tractate as a whole than it is to various interpretations of the tractate. The literal reading fits quite as well as 1 Cor. 15 fits with the rest of 1 Corinthians. With early Christianity, *Treat. Res.* retains a clear affirmation of the mystery of the final resurrection. We have evidence of horizontal eschatology.

Exactly what the author has in mind, however, with regard to the final resurrection remains clouded until a bit later in the tractate. At 48:4–6 we find a crucial piece of evidence on this very point: "(The resurrection) is the eternal revelation of those who have risen." A review of the major interpreters at this point would suggest that their overall conception of the treatise tends to fill in this grammatical void. If, that is, one reads the tractate as a discussion of the resurrection which has already occurred, then this verse can become supporting evidence for that theory. If one uses a less uniform interpretation, the verse is more easily left in some obscurity. Interpretation in the past has focused on the subsequent verses, which include the reference to the transfiguration. In short, no current exegesis of the verse has proven to be entirely satisfactory.

An alternative reading of 48:5 might proceed in the opposite direction. If the verse is read in the light of what precedes rather than what follows,

---

33. Layton, *The Gnostic Treatise on Resurrection*, 67.
34. Ibid., 68.
35. Ibid., 68.
36. Peel, "The Treatise on the Resurrection," *Nag Hammadi Codex I*, vol. 2, 171.

some progress might be made. The prior pericope entertains the question whether one is saved immediately at death (47:35). *Treat. Res.* answers its own question in the affirmative (47:38). Immediately at death the believer, the living member, is saved. Now, however, another problem appears. If one is saved immediately, what then is the resurrection? (48:3–4). In other words, what is the final resurrection? *Treat. Res.* answers, "It is the eternal revelation of those who have risen." To avoid the suggestion that the final resurrection is superfluous, the author appends 48:5 to his presentation. His meaning is apparent. The final resurrection is far from superfluous! It *is* the resurrection! It is a kind of public viewing, at the last trumpet, of all who have been saved.

Attention to apocalyptic eschatology in the course of a discussion that otherwise focuses on vertical eschatology is very similar to Paul's apocalyptic theology. The reliance on a dialectical ambivalence between immediate postmortem salvation and ultimate cosmic resurrection harkens back to the Apostle to the Gentiles, whose own complex teaching on this subject created, among other things, the Thessalonian correspondence (1 Thess. 4:13–18). *Treat. Res.* 48:5 answers a logical question about final resurrection. This also is clear evidence of horizontal eschatology in Gnosticism.

The End of the Age

Apocalypticism often combined a hope of the general resurrection with an expectation of final cosmic destruction, the omega point in history. A similar combination is present in *Treat. Res.* The tractate places alongside its apocalyptic understanding of resurrection an apocalyptic picture of the end of the age. The world in *Treat. Res.* is described as perishing, coming to an end. A case in point is 45:16–17: "For he (the Savior) put aside the world which is perishing." No textual difficulties arise in these verses. They contain a clear reference to a dying cosmos. Included here is an understanding of history which depicts the world as hastening to an end. As often happens in this document, the language seems to be borrowed from the Pauline letters. The framework of the passage is apocalyptic. Peel is certainly correct that at this point the author exhibits no interest in particular historical events.[37] However, the description of the world as perishing may say a great deal about the author's understanding of cosmology, providence and eschatology. Peel aptly outlines the references to "world" and related concepts in *Treat. Res.*[38]

---

37. Ibid., 160.

38. Ibid. We not the contrast to the concept of world in Middle Platonism: "The world here is eternal and indestructible, as there is nothing outside it which can affect

The Treatise on the Resurrection (NHC I, 4)

He accurately highlights the similarity to Johannine terms and the primarily evil character of the world in *Treat. Res.* The allusion to a "perishing" world puts *Treat. Res.* well beyond the range of Middle Platonism on which Layton relies for his interpretation. For the Middle Platonists the world itself was thought to be eternal.[39] For others, such as Philo, the world was not eternal, but could be expected to last forever anyway, on the basis of divine providence.[40] Neither the religious nor the pagan Platonists gave active attention to this apocalyptic eschatological them. *Treat. Res.*, however, in harmony with Paul, with Enoch, and with several gnostic tractates, postulates not only a changing world, but a dying world. This si further evidence of horizontal eschatology at work in *Treat. Res.*

Vertical Eschatology

Treat. Res. provides a great deal of evidence that Gnosticism also involves personal eschatology and moves along a vertical, spatial axis. Earlier interpreters have accurately attended to the vertical eschatology of this tractate.

---

it." John M. Dillon, *The Middle Platonists, 80 B.C. to A.D. 220* (Ithaca, NY: Cornell University Press, 1977) 83.

39. Dillon, *Middle Platonists*, 157–58. *Treat. Res.* has been carefully mined for its Platonic ore. At a number of points, Dillon's careful history of Middle Platonism provides helpful background and important information pertinent to the study of Apocalypticism and Gnosticism. His description of the "dominant themes" of Middle Platonism is particularly useful. Dillon does not treat the subject of eschatology. He does, however, indicate the overriding significance, in Middle Platonism, of various themes which took on more radical tones in Gnosticism and Apocalypticism. Dillon helpfully divides his discussion into the areas of ethics, physics, and logic. These philosophical concerns correspond to religious concerns about eh soul's relations with others, with creation, and with its own highest principle.

In general, Dillon's review of Middle Platonism, published in the late 1970s, weakens the arguments connecting *Treat. Res.* with this philosophical school. This is also broadly true for the kind of acosmic pessimism of *Treat. Res.* The gnostic enthusiastic pessimism of this tractate does not correspond at all with the physics generally employed by the philosophers Dillon describes. There are still of course many parallels, but not the telling ones that would connect our tractate with the broad Middle Platonic mood. Middle Platonism, to take one crucial example, revered Nature. *Treat. Res.* calls Nature "death."

Summarizing the thought of one Middle Platonist, Dillon writes, "The ultimate good of man is life in accordance with human nature, developed to its full perfection, and supplied with all its needs" (ibid., 158). *Treat Res.* envisions another kind of good, ultimately one opposed to this world.

The gnostic eschatology of *Treat. Res.* should rather be located within the sphere of emerging Christian orthodoxy.

40. Ibid.

In fact, it is difficult to imagine clearer references to the standard gnostic hope for the ascent of the soul than the ones present in this tractate. Here we present three striking examples of vertical eschatology in *Treat. Res.*

1. In *Treat. Res.* the knowing believer, embraced throughout his life by the beams of the Savior's presence, is at death drawn on to heaven, with no impediment (flesh, doctrine, past, future). So stipulates 45:36–46:1: "We are drawn on to heaven by him, like beams by the sun. This is the spiritual resurrection." Immortality (45:20) follows instantly on death. This argument and imagery are found also in the Gospel of John. In John 12:32, we also read of Christ drawing others to himself. The Greek verb seems to have a stronger meaning than the verb of *Treat. Res.*, connoting something like "dragging." The two verses, however, are substantially similar. In John 6:44 we also encounter "drawing." Here the Fourth Gospel distinguishes between the ongoing drawing of the Father and the raising up at the last day. *Treat. Res.* also makes this combination of vertical drawing and horizontal end-speculation, though only the drawing is presented in 45:35. Both John and *Treat. Res.* combine apocalyptic and gnostic elements in their eschatological teaching. What is striking here is the further sharing of the drawing imagery. In 45:35 the author is speaking of immortality at the point of physical death.[41] He thus presents a part of his fuller teaching on the resurrection by highlighting a classic statement of vertical eschatology. Whether this imagery is to be taken literally or figuratively[42] may remain an open question. The repeated reference to the filling up of the Pleroma (44:30, 46:35) may tell slightly in favor of the literal reading. Peel counters this with a grammatical argument that seems strained.[43] In any case, this part of the teaching on resurrection is, first, a clear use of vertical eschatology, and, second, only a secondary aspect of the total doctrine on resurrection in the treatise.

2. Another example of the importance of the ascent of the soul in *Treat. Res.* is found at 47:6–8: "Why will you not receive flesh when you ascend into aeon?" A minor textual issue arises in the translation of this verse. Is the verb to be translated "take"[44] or "receive"?[45] Layton's argument is caught up with a larger interpretative scheme on his part, namely that an "imaginary interlocutor" here receives response. It

---

41. Peel, "The Treatise on the Resurrection," *Nag Hammadi Codex I*, vol. 2, 165.
42. Ibid.
43. Ibid.
44. So Layton, *The Gnostic Treatise on Resurrection*, 77.
45. So Peel, "The Treatise on the Resurrection," *Nag Hammadi Codex I*, vol. 2, 179.

The Treatise on the Resurrection (NHC I, 4)

is difficult to see how Layton's translation can prevail. The argument about the flesh, before and after death, is well presented by Peel.[46] The similarities to Pauline arguments on this are evident (1 Cor. 15, Phil. 3). In the Gospel of John we also find discussion of flesh and spiritual realities, though not in the sense of post-mortem speculation presented here (John 6:63). A similar reference to the resurrection flesh is also found in the Gospel of Philip (68:34–35): "But this is true flesh." This verse cannot be reconstructed with certainty, but it is clear that the reference to the difference between true and false flesh. The reference may, however, have only to do with Christ himself (see 68:26–30).

Peel has ably summarized parallel references to the ascent of the soul into the "Aeon."[47] We have here a transparent use of vertical eschatology.

3. The vertical eschatology in *Treat. Res.* stands out as the central eschatological theme of the tractate (see above). A number of other verses might be explored (44:24–38, 45:14–17, 45:23–29, 47:2–9, 47:19–25, 47:31–37). They simply add further evidence of the presence and centrality of vertical eschatology in *Treat. Res.* To provide exegesis of these passages would be redundant. There can be no doubt that *Treat. Res.* repeatedly refers to the ascent of the soul at the time of death.

Realized Eschatology

Treat. Res. provides evidence of horizontal and of vertical eschatology. It remains to consider the exegetical evidence in the tractate of so=called "realized" eschatology. We have seen that Layton's monograph renders *Teat. Res.* a thoroughgoing presentation of realized eschatology. Peel advances a modification of this extreme, if consistent, reading: "*Treat. Res.* presents a mostly realized eschatology. The Pauline 'eschatological reservation' has dissolved, with resurrection of all the faithful at the end of time being replaced with individually experienced resurrection in the Now. Not future hope, but present knowledge is emphasized."[48] Helpfully, Peel lists the examples of this realized eschatology, which he finds in the tractate (49:16, 44:27–29, 45:14–15, 45:25–26, 47:26–29). Of these five references only one, the first, is a truly strong candidate, while the other four ride along on its coattails. To an exegetical analysis of these passages we now turn.

---

46. Ibid., 178.
47. Ibid., 180.
48. Peel, "The Treatise on the Resurrection," *Nag Hammadi Codex I*, vol. 1, 141–42.

THE COURAGEOUS GOSPEL

1. 49:15-16, "And already you have the resurrection."

Of the five verses we discuss here, this one lays the only serious claim to realized eschatology. The others, as we shall see, are considerably off the mark. In 49:16, though, it does seem that the author of *Treat. Res.* expounds a variant of the doctrine combated in 2 Tim. 2:18. "You now have the resurrection" (49:16). Virtually every commentator has extrapolated from this verse to connect *Treat. Res.* with the history of heresiology regarding realized eschatology. Is this interpretation warranted?

The text itself offers no particular difficulties. We are left to consider the proper interpretation of what Peel has called the "over-realized" eschatology of this pericope.[49] A fundamental decision for any interpretation occurs with the selection of the proper context for a verse or passage. Other commentators, fascinated by the verses themselves, have not paid much attention to their context in the argument of *Treat. Res.* Granted that the tractate's argument is not always easy to follow, we believe it does break down into four manageable foci. This verse occurs in the last section, the one involving an exhortation to "practice." Just prior to 49:16, the author of *Treat. Res.* has finished his formal teaching on the resurrection itself with a densely phrased description of "symbols and images" of the resurrection (49:5). These in turn are meatn to illuminate the meaning of resurrection itself, concisely summarized in the terms revelation, transformation, and transition (48:34-36). Suddenly the author turns his back on doctrine and begins a concluding exhortation. The reader is prepared for paraenesis by the 76wste ("therefore") of a 49:9. Thinking and living are now a matter of explicit exegetical mandate: no conformity, flee divisions and fetters (49:15). Furthermore, as the pericope concludes, each one is to practice in many different ways, to avoid error and receive deliverance from the God of this world (49:30).

In this context, the over-realized eschatology occurs. The context is purely paraenetic, and utterly non-systematic. The author exhorts his student to a life worthy of the resurrection. The lengthy discussions in the literature of the heresiological antecedents and eschatological significance of 49:16 miss the author's paraenetic purpose. Rightly paraphrased, his argument is: "Eschew conformity with flesh and its death, die to this world and live the resurrection, for in this way the resurrection is already yours (revelation, transformation, transition.)" The letter to the Hebrews in the New

---

49. Peel, "The Treatise on the Resurrection," 206. But see also F. Wisse, "The 'Opponents' in the New Testament in Light of the Nag Hammadi Writings," in *Colloque international sur les textes de Nag Hammadi (Québec, 22-25 août 1978)*, edited by B. Barc, BCNHE 1, 99-120 (Québec: Les Presses de l'Université Laval, 1981) 110-12.

The Treatise on the Resurrection (NHC I, 4)

Testament carries much the same message, and so also exhorts its reader to the certainty of faith.

In sum, this important passage must be interpreted in its context. The context is ethical exhortation. The purpose of the eschatological material within 49:16 is to justify and intensify the paraenesis. There is, however, no suggestion that "the resurrection has already occurred." 49:16 is not an example of realized eschatology, at least in this classical sense. The resurrection is very much yet to come.

2. It is possible to summarize briefly the analysis of the other four passages listed by Peel and also used by others as evidence of realized eschatology in *Treat. Res.*

   a. 44:27–29: This verse offers no evidence at all of realized eschatology. It simply reports that Christ has conquered death.

   b. 45:14–15: This verse provides another Christological statement, reporting that the Savior has overcome death. Death still occurs, we learn in the verse itself, as a part of a perishing world (45:17).

   c. 45:24–25: This is a quotation from the Apostle Paul (Rom. 8:17).

   d. 47:27–29: "The salvation we have received extends from the beginning of all things until the end of all things." Here the Coptic is obscure. Peel provides a review of the discussion.[50] Perhaps wisely, he declines to suggest a solution. Again, the reference to salvation received echoes Paul. An anticipation of eschatological glory and reference to a saved "All" completes the meaning of this verse. It is difficult to find a clear reference here to realized eschatology. If anything, one might read into this verse some reference to the "end" of time and history. This verse then would be further evidence of *horizontal* eschatology in the tractate.

In summary, we find little if any evidence of realized eschatology in the tractate. Previous scholarship has tended to suppose an expression of "now" eschatology within *Treat. Res.* and then to read particular passages in light of this interpretative framework. If one begins with the decision that *Treat. Res.* teaches realized eschatology, then one can shade the readings of certain verses in that direction.

A neutral reading of the same verses produces a different result. We find no statement that the resurrection has already occurred, or has been realized. We find no doctrine that makes of the eschaton a present or past event. We find anticipations of the resurrection, so so clear that, influenced by them, one "already has the resurrection." Paul, John, and the author of

---

50. Peel, "The Treatise on the Resurrection," 185.

Hebrews and others say the same. In *Treat. Res.* the "eschatological reservation" is at least as strong as that in Romans. We have no evidence in *Treat. Res.* of realized eschatology in the full sense of the term.

DISCUSSION

The Eschatology of *Treat. Res.*

The author of *Treat. Res.* rejects the judgment that the resurrection is illusory, implausible, or insignificant. The resurrection, on the contrary, is both the chief support of faith and also faith's fondest object. His clumsy student, the author hopes, will continue in the resurrection faith.

The few paragraphs of *Treat. Res.* contain no full doctrine of eschatology. This tractate particularly responds to an actual or conjectural question. The resurrection question receives here both a general response and then related discussion of corollary points. Bearing in mind these limitations, we may attempt a characterization of the eschatology of *Treat. Res.*

Treat. Res. presents a traditional hope, familiar both to Gnosticism and to Christianity, for the ascent of the soul. This vertical eschatology dominates the tractate. The believer is to await deliverance from this world, and inclusion in the fullness of light beyond this world. He has a sure hope of immortality. His thought will not perish. This hope is a consequence of the "rest" which the knowledgeable believer already has. Resurrection is a personal hope of an ascent into the Eternal. Neither death, nor the flesh, nor the world, nor nature, nor the speculations of the philosopher stand in the way of this hope. *Treat. Res.*, as shown above, abounds in evidence of personal, vertical eschatology (44:25, 45:15, 25, 30, 35; 47:5, 20).

Attending this generally vertical eschatology stand particular related teachings. One is the expectation of salvation immediately at death. The salvation of the individual is part of the restoration of the All. Furthermore, this spiritual resurrection includes, in a way not fully described, other meanings of the resurrection ("psychic," "fleshly"). Because the faith in the resurrection raises particular questions, the author of *Treat. Res.* addresses a few of these specific concerns.

Although overshadowed by this vertical eschatology, horizontal eschatological themes also make their contribution to *Treat. Res.* The apocalyptic eschatology of the New Testament and other writings is muted but still present here. Final eschatology, the resurrection of the dead and related issues, is not rejected by the author of *Treat. Res.* The author shows a negative attitude toward philosophy. He also flatly rejects those who deny the resurrection.

The Treatise on the Resurrection (NHC I, 4)

Such sensitivity and rejection are not directed at apocalyptic eschatology. Horizontal eschatology is present and active in *Treat. Res.* (45:14–17; 46:5–8; 48:4–6). We find here, as is evident in other ancient eschatological writings, that vertical and horizontal eschatology are not mutually exclusive. They rather tend to be mutually enriching, interdependent, and interrelated.

The eschatology of *Treat. Res.* has an ethical consequence. The knowing disciple who hears and believes must also practice. In this practice, this benign neglect of the world and nature ("but I call it Death!"), one anticipates the resurrection. One already has the resurrection if one has a sure hope for it and leads a resurrected life. Although this has been called "realized eschatology" it might better be called radical ethics. No doctrine of the last things is at stake here. No rejection of traditional eschatology occurs here. Rather, the tractate's conclusion connects piety with the hope of glory.

In summary, the eschatology of *Treat. Res.* focuses on personal, vertical eschatology. This vision of the ascent of the soul overshadows but does not eliminate an understanding, present in the tractate, of apocalyptic eschatology. Vertical and horizontal eschatology are combined in the concluding paraenetic exhortation. *Treat. Res.* thus informs its reader with regard to a logical progression of eschatological questions:

Q: What eschatological reality is already present?

A: An anticipation of the resurrection is now present.

Q: What happens at the individual's death?

A: The individual is saved immediately and waits in a naked state for the final resurrection of the dead.

Q: When does the believer receive his spiritual flesh?

A: At the resurrection, at the end of time.

Q: What happens at the end of time?

A: The dead are raised and disclosed as those who have arisen. (Presumably also the final judgment will occur at this time, though this is not specifically mentioned.) The world will dissolve. The restoration of the elect will be complete.

This is the eschatological timetable of *Treat. Res.* One notices that while the gnostic character of this teaching is clear, it is also easily within range of early orthodox Christianity.

The Role of Final Eschatology

No intolerance of final, horizontal, apocalyptic eschatology is evident in *Treat. Res.* Horizontal eschatology is not only present in the tractate, but also functions in significant ways in combination with the vertical eschatology.

Apocalyptic eschatology plays an important role in *Treat. Res.* While the absence of overt rejection of final eschatology is sufficient proof for the argument of this dissertation, the additional operation of this theme within *Treat. Res.* is highly illuminating for the interpretation of the tractate and so warrants attention. We find three primary functions of the apocalyptic eschatology in *Treat. Res.* collected under the themes of restoration, destruction, and completion.

In the first place, apocalyptic eschatology in *Treat. Res.* articulates the hope for final restoration of the All (45:9-17; 46:5-8; 48:38—49:8). According to these passages, the dead will rise at the end of time. This raising will disclose the number of the elect and restore the light to its full and imperishable eternity. This is strictly a matter of and for faith. Such restoration is certainly not present "now." At the end of time, as a consequence of the Savior's defeat of death, the pleroma will be restored. Further, this hope for restoration is essentially a corporate hope, one that contrasts with and balances the generally personal eschatology of the tractate. It is, eventually, the All that will be saved. *We* will celebrate and await a salvation from end to end (47:27-29). An imperishable aeon awaits the elect (45:14-17). *We* are predestined to this from the beginning of time (46:25-29). Apocalyptic eschatology is used in *Treat. Res.* to present a final hope of restoration. We thus disagree, at all three points, with the summary judgment of Peel on this score: "Thus, in contrast to Pauline views of the resurrection (1 Cor 15; 1 Thess 4), our author severs the event from the history of salvation, eliminates from it end-time speculation, and individualizes that experience."[51] Rather, we argue, our author *corroborates* Pauline views, *maintains* the connection of the restoration with history, and *resists* a total individualization of the experience.

A second function of the apocalyptic eschatology relates to destruction at the end of time. This is a standard apocalyptic theme. This dying world is bound for destruction (45:15). *Treat. Res.* clearly refers to a sense of time and history which sees the world as hastening to its end. As so often in this document, the language is borrowed from the Pauline letters. The radical pessimism regarding the created order, expressed here, is shared by Apocalypticism and Gnosticism. The final conflagration receives mention at a number of points in the tractate (45:9, 18; 48:23). The law of Nature, also called Death, has only temporary dominion. The ultimate demise of this Power is an essential part of this eschatological treatise. The last trumpet is not at all a matter of indifference in *Treat. Res.* In fact, destruction is a necessary corollary to restoration and completion. Apocalypticism provides the language and thought for this part of the tractate.

---

51. Ibid., 142.

The Treatise on the Resurrection (NHC I, 4)

Thirdly, apocalyptic eschatology provides the material for the ultimate vision of the treatise. The resurrection is ultimately a disclosure of the saved, much like Matt 25:31–46 or 2 Thess 2:1. The resurrection of the dead at the end of time is a public viewing of the sheep and the goats. The vision is of an assembly on the plain of judgment. The resurrection is fundamentally "a disclosure of those who have arisen" (48:5). The believer wants to be sure that what the Savior began, he also will complete (44:34). The final destiny of the All is a matter of highest importance in *Treat. Res.* (44:30; 46:28). Apocalypticism provides the material for the hope of completion in the tractate.

In sum, the presence of apocalyptic eschatology in *Treat. Res.* is clear, contradicting a part of the assumption here tested. Gnosticism, as exemplified by *Treat. Res.*, has a surprisingly fertile apocalyptic imagination. Apocalypticism is not a luxury but a necessity in this tractate. Without it, the important themes of restoration, destruction, and completion would disappear from *Treat. Res.*

CONCLUSION

Our study highlights the horizontal eschatology in this gnostic tractate. One consequence of this approach is that, after the above analysis, *Treat. Res.* looks surprisingly orthodox. Gone is the interpolation of a resurrection that has already occurred. Crippled is the preoccupation with anticipated eschatology. Qualified is the emphasis on personal eschatology. At a minimum, the burden of proof would now seem to be on those who would read *Treat. Res.* in a heretical light. Interpreters who have tried to read the tractate in a Valentinian, heretical, suspicious way will now need justification for that point of departure.

Peel has to date produced the most judicious study of *Treat. Res.* He of all the commentators moves *Treat. Res.* the closest to emerging orthodoxy. He does not, however, go far enough. Our study suggests that *Treat. Res.* is very close to Paul and to the Fourth Gospel. The notable presence of apocalyptic eschatology in the tractate makes the earlier suspicious readings of *Treat. Res.* themselves suspect. The eschatological teaching, summarized above, is typical of New Testament and early catholic thought. "From the beginning there has been a twofold emphasis in the Christian doctrine of the last things. While stressing the reality and completeness of present salvation, it has pointed believers to certain great eschatological events located in the future."[52]

---

52. J. N. D. Kelly, *Early Christian Doctrines* (New York: Harper, 1959) 459.

THE COURAGEOUS GOSPEL

PART FOUR

31

A Brief History of Christian Theology

DAWN

Jesus is Crucified and Risen. His Gospel is preached by Paul. The Synoptic Gospels are written to preach the same Gospel, with the aid of His story, teachings, deeds. Other letters are written to apply the Gospel to the growth of the church.

MORNING

In response to the small Bible (Luke and the Letters of Paul) of Marcion, a Roman Gnostic, the Christian Bible (sixty-six books) is assembled. John translates the preaching of the Gospel into the idiom of neo-platonic, gnostic thought.

LATE MORNING

Augustine of Hippo, converted from Manicheaism (an eastern Gnosticism), develops a full theological system, relying largely on Paul, in conflict with the British Monk Pelagius. Both Reformers and Counter Reformers rely later on him.

THE COURAGEOUS GOSPEL

NOON

Thomas Aquinas in the 12th century constructs a medieval theological system, blending the basics of Aristotelian philosophy with the Scripture and tradition of the church.

AFTERNOON

The medieval synthesis begins to unravel under the influence of the early renaissance and pre-reformation.

LATE AFTERNOON

The great reformers of Germany (Luther), France (Calvin) and England (H8 and later Wesley) shatter the Roman medieval synthesis on the basis of faith alone, Scripture alone, and a return to Augustine and Paul.

EVENING

Post-Enlightenment modern theology reaches its zenith in the 19th\mid 20th century work of liberals (Schleiermacher), neo-orthodox thinkers (Barth) and culminates in the last full systematic theology to date (Tillich).

DUSK

Post-modern Christian theology, skeptical of universal systems, and indebted to particular, autobiographical witnesses, accentuates the varieties of religious experience and theological perspective (Black: Cone; Latino: Guttierez; Asian: Koyama; Feminist: Ruether; Canadian: Hall, other).

32

The Gospel of John

Final Examination

BOSTON UNIVERSITY SCHOOL OF THEOLOGY
AUTUMN 2007

CHOOSE TWO OF THE following essay questions, and write as thorough and cogent answers as you can:

1. The conceptual background to the Fourth Gospel has puzzled scholars for many years. Review the possible solutions to this problem, and then offer your own point of view.

2. The eschatological teaching found in the Gospel of John differs to a significant degree from that found in the rest of the New Testament. On the basis of primary and secondary reading from this term, provide your own analysis of Johannine eschatology.

3. J. L. Martyn's analysis of John 9 opened a new chapter in studies of John. Hill has based some of his commentary on Martyn's work, and our class has deliberated about Martyn's theory. How does Martyn understand the history and theology of John, from the vantage point of John 9, and what is your considered view of this thesis?

4. One of the great NT scholars of our time, E. Kasemann, described the Christ of the Fourth Gospel as "God striding upon the earth." Do you agree? Include careful reference to titles, terms, texts, and tensions found in the Gospel as you develop your response.

33

The Gospel of John
Midterm Examination
BOSTON UNIVERSITY SCHOOL OF THEOLOGY
AUTUMN 2007

A. *True or False?*

1. There are seven signs, or miracles described in the first 12 chapters of the fourth gospel.

2. Robert Fortna of Vassar did the most extensive and lasting work in developing a contemporary understanding of John's "signs source."

3. The so-called prologue to the fourth gospel is really an ancient Christian hymn, taken over by the gospel writer and used for the author's own purpose.

4. One of the few Synoptic miracles which appears in John is the miraculous feeding of the five thousand with two fish and five barley loaves.

5. The account of Jesus' protection of the woman taken in adultery, John 8, is often thought to be a later addition to the text.

6. Jesus' teachings, or discourses, are often thought to be based on a source which John used, known as the "sayings source."

The Gospel of John

7. The account of the healing of the blind man, in John 9, reveals a rich history of religious conflict between Jews and Christians in the early Christian era.
8. The visit to Jerusalem in John 2 is only one of three such visits recorded in the fourth gospel.
9. The relationship between the author's material and the editor or ecclesiastical redactor's material in the fourth gospel is crucial to our understanding of John.
10. The fourth Gospel was written in the third century of the common era.

B. Please list ten of the major differences that John displays in comparison to the so-called Synoptic Gospels.

1.
2.
3.
4.
5.
6.
7.
8.
9.
10.

C. Choose three of the following terms and describe their importance in the fourth Gospel: light, life, truth, knowledge, darkness, grace, freedom, cross.

1.
2.
3.

D. List six of the titles ascribed to Jesus in the fourth Gospel, and briefly comment on their significance.

1.
2.
3.

4.

5.

6.

E. Identify and Describe three central aspects of John Ashton's commentary on the fourth Gospel.

F. Argue for or against this assertion: "As in life, so in the history of the Gospel of John, the creative tension between writers and editors plays a powerful formative role."

34

The Gospel of John
Quiz #0
BOSTON UNIVERSITY SCHOOL OF THEOLOGY
AUTUMN 2007

1. Please locate in John the account of the Last Supper, including the traditions of Paul (1 Cor 15) and Mark (14).
2. Find verses (apart from Chapter 21) in which Simon Peter is celebrated as hero, first friend, and rock.
3. Situate the first of Jesus' parables, that of the Sower, as it appears in John.
4. Where is the usual one visit of Jesus to Jerusalem on the Passover found in John?
5. Pick out two or three of the more well known Parables of Jesus that John shares with the Synoptics.
6. Find the agony of the cross as it is depicted in the utterances of Jesus from the cross (eg, "my God, my God. . ."; "Father forgive them. . .")
7. As the gospels usually do, John has placed the cleansing of the temple early in 'holy week' as an explanation for the death of Jesus. Where is this regular feature of the gospel found?

8. The Gospels describe the birth of Jesus in various ways, a mixture usually of human and wondrous occurrence. This is also true of John, is it not?

9. Paul (I Thess 4)and Mark (9, 13) expect the end of time, soon and very soon. Please identify very similar, traditional expectations in John.

10. In the Gospels, Jesus teaches (Matt 5, Luke 6). Please find the parallels to these teachings in John, especially in the long discourses, 14–17.

35

The Gospel of John
Quiz #1
BOSTON UNIVERSITY SCHOOL OF THEOLOGY
AUTUMN 2007

A. True or False?

1. The Old Testament consists of the Law, the Prophets, and the Writings.
2. The New Testament consists of the Gospels, the Letters, and the Apocalyptic Writings.
3. Genesis, Exodus, and Leviticus are Books of Law.
4. Matthew, Mark and Galatians are Gospels.
5. The most important resource for the study of the New Testament is the Old Testament.

B. Essay

Provide an overview, a "bird's eye view," of the Bible, with as much detail as possible. Make reference to the three parts of the old and new testaments.

36

The Gospel of John
Quiz #2

BOSTON UNIVERSITY SCHOOL OF THEOLOGY
AUTUMN 2007

A. Short Answer

1. List six major differences between John and the Synoptic Gospels.
2. What two similarities are there between John and the Synoptics?
3. The central description of Christ in John is the Son or the Son of Man: what layers of meanings lie in these titles?
4. At several point in John Jesus says "I am. . ." Name three things He says he is:

B. Essay: In three paragraphs comment critically on this statement:

"The religious experience of the Christian community is thus the first basis on which the Evangelist formulated the thought of the Gospel. The second is the opposition the church faced from the synagogue."

C. Reading Ashton:

In two or three sentences please identify what Ashton means by the following phrases:

1. The Two Riddles
2. Diachronic and Synchronic

3. The Johannine Community
4. The First Edition

37

The Gospel of John
Ashton Content: Quiz #3
BOSTON UNIVERSITY SCHOOL OF THEOLOGY
AUTUMN, 2007

1. What are the two fundamental issues that Ashton addresses (as do we in this course) with regard to the Gospel of John?

2. Ashton uses the phrase "odium theologicum." What does this mean, and what does he mean by it with regard to John's history?

3. Ashton draws his argument about a two-level drama, and about the expulsion from the synagogue, from J. L. Martyn's earlier work. What chapters and verses from the Gospel do they rely upon for this argument?

4. Who were "the Jews" in John, according to Ashton?

5. Bultmann found the 'powerful tradition' behind the Jesus of the Fourth Gospel in Gnosticism. Ashton recognizes the need to replace this with another, equally strong theory regarding the background for Johannine Christology. What is his proposal?

6. What is a pesher interpretation, and how does Ashton think John compares to such?

7. What does Ashton say about John's theology of the cross?

8. According to Ashton, was the gospel genre of central importance for John? Please explain and comment.
9. Are there a few synoptic-like features in the Gospel of John, according to Ashton? Explain and comment.
10. Ashton argues that the gospel may have begun life as a series of homilies, later compiled or stitched together. Do you agree or disagree?

38

The Gospel of John
Ashton Content: Quiz #4
BOSTON UNIVERSITY SCHOOL OF THEOLOGY
AUTUMN 2007

SHORT ANSWER

1. R. Bultmann laid out the two great riddles of the Gospel long ago. What were they?
2. What myth stands behind John, according to Bultmann?
3. Who (according to Ashton) were Bultmann's two most influential scholarly successors?
4. What serious weakness most undermines Bultmann's interpretation, according to Ashton?
5. What is the difference between synchronic and diachronic approaches to the Gospel?
6. Define *aporia*.
7. What was the *Birkat ha-Minim*?
8. What chapters in John does Ashton exclude from the first edition of the Gospel?

9. What textual evidence do we have that Chapter 21 was a later addition to the Gospel?
10. Ashton eliminates two "bogies," and celebrates their "disappearance" from scholarship. One is the hypothesis of an "ecclesiastical redactor." The other?

SHORT ESSAY (3-5 PARAGRAPHS)

Ashton interviews a first time reader of John named Debbie. What are the strengths and weaknesses, to your mind, of this interview?

39

The Gospel of John
Quiz #5
> BOSTON UNIVERSITY SCHOOL OF THEOLOGY
> AUTUMN 2007

ESSAY ONE

THE GOSPEL OF JOHN presents a distinctive portrait of Jesus the Christ. Given your reading of the Gospel, and secondary literature thus far, how would you characterize this portrait?

ESSAY TWO

The Fourth Gospel, following its majestic prologue, divides neatly into two parts—signs and sayings. Identify, analyze and criticize the seven signs in the first part of the Gospel

40

The Gospel of John
Quiz #6: Content of the Gospel
AUTUMN 2007 BOSTON UNIVERSITY

1. The religious teacher with whom Jesus spoke at night in John 3 is named:
2. The location of the wedding during which this gospel reports the first of Jesus' signs is:
3. The designation for the leading disciple within the Johannine community and memory is:
4. The number of Passovers mentioned in the Fourth Gospel is:
5. Jesus meets a woman from a certain region during a conversation near a well. That region is:
6. The unusual name given to the Spirit, in this Gospel, is:
7. Peter is outrun to the resurrection tomb by whom?
8. In what chapter does the 'word became flesh and dwelt among us' appear?
9. Philip is from what city?
10. How long did it take for the temple to be built?
11. Aenon and Salim are locations for what activity by whom?

12. Bethzatha is Hebrew for what?
13. Give another name for the Sea of Galilee.
14. In what chapter does Jesus say, "all who came before me are thieves and robbers?"
15. What does Siloam mean?
16. What is the commandment given in the Farewell Discourse?
17. Who was Joseph of Arimethea?
18. Jesus' last word on the cross was what?
19. Who was Clopas?
20. Didymus means...?
21. Where are the three uses of *aposynagogos*?
22. The last disciple mentioned in the Gospel is whom?
23. Where does Jesus say "the poor you have always with you?"
24. In what chapter do we hear, "I and the Father are one?"
25. Two fish and five loaves or five fish and two loaves?

41

Finale
The Gospel of John for Today
ASBURY FIRST UNITED METHODIST CHURCH
OCTOBER 1996

INTRODUCTION (10/2/96)

- Opening comments on the Fourth Gospel and its difference from the synoptics, with issues of introduction (date, author, place, other)
- Brief overview of the Scripture
- OT: Law, Prophets, Writings
- NT: Gospels, Letters, Apocalyptic Writings
- Survey of the 21 chapters in John, their content and order
- The Process of Canonization
- Life in Community in John: Life in Community at Asbury, viewing of 1996 stewardship video
- Various points of discussion

THE COURAGEOUS GOSPEL

JOHN 1-3 (10/9/96)

- Questions from reading: surprise, fact, judgment
- Some notable Johannine differences
    1. Beginning
    2. Sources: Signs and Discourse
    3. Passovers (3)
    4. Temple cleansing early, not late
    5. Role of Peter
    6. Absence of Last Supper
    7. Passion differences
    8. Vocabulary
    9. Person of Christ
    10. Crucifixion\Glorification
    11. Teaching about the end of time
- The "community" of the beloved disciple and the historical background of the gospel
- John 1, some lights along the path
    1. Prologue 1-18
    2. Word 1
    3. Light 9
    4. Know 18
    5. Titles 20 ff
    6. Baptism 32
    7. Spirit (note for next week)
- John 2, some lights along the path
    1. Hour 4 (hour coming and now is)
    2. Belief 22 (always point of signs)
    3. Testimony 24
    4. Hidden Messiah 24
    5. Other

Finale

- John 3, some lights along the path
- Other discussion

John 3–6: Highlights

- Introduction, Conversation, Questions, Disputations: Your reading of the text counts! Surprises, Questions, Opinions? Including past questions: 1. "Born from Above" and 2. "History of Canon."
- Cinquaine and Spirit: Review
- DRAMA! John and the theory of the 2 level drama
  1. History of Scholarship
  2. John 9 in parts
  3. Points of emphasis from J.L. Martyn, *History and Theology in the Fourth Gospel.*
  4. The meaning for today.
  5. Discussion

Verse References

- John 7
  7:11. The Jews—cold, officious reference
  7:27. ??
  7:40. The Prophet
  7:41. Galilee
- John 10
  10:16 Probably a reference to the apostolic churches in Near East
  10:18 A curious comparison of Jesus1 power and "Father's" power
  10:21 Ends a scene that began with 9:1
  10:22 Dedication: Hannukah—Review of Jewish feast days (main 6). The consecration of the temple becomes, somehow, the consecration of Jesus. Major issue in faith—nature of God.
- From OT, God is the God of both risings and fallings, victories and defeats. Genesis 50: God can bring good out of evil.
- We do best when we "theologize first, moralize second"

THE COURAGEOUS GOSPEL

- God's grace works through human sinfulness.
- In OT, main image of people of God is of a pilgrim folk—itinerant, on the move. Abraham (Gen 15) promised progeny and land, fulfilled by Solomon in 1 Kings 18.
- Troubles abound. Satans in the Bible are more often human than not ("adversaries"). From 1 Kings 11 through 2 Kings 25, its all downhill, with just a few bumps. Then, after 2 Kings, total defeat—Jehoiachim sees his sons killed, and then has his eyes taken out, and then the story ends.
- So, with the people of Israel and the apostolic church, we live "in the gap" between God's promises and their apparent lack of fulfillment.
- All the great hymns in the Bible emphasize both risings and fallings.
- The prophets say 4 things:
  1. It is not God who let us down.
  2. It is we who let God down, (through polytheism, idolatry, breaking the third commandment)
  3. If, in exile, the people take the prophets' words to heart, then God's joy is to restore. We cannot box God in.
  4. God had sent the prophets early and often (16 case histories. All came before the fall of Israel in 587, and all predicted it and all thought theologically about it.
- God can reach through death and destruction to new life. God is the God of death as well as of life.

  10:38 Example of "high" Christology

  10:42 Appears to some to be a conclusion
- Travel
- interlude: a visitor's story
- tell a move story around the table
- John 11

  11:17 Instead of cleansing of temple, as immediate cause of Jesus demise, John has put in the scene of Lazarus 11:24–25 Contrast. Older belief—resurrection on the last day—dead arise from their graves. Other belief—No advantage to being alive on the last day. Either way, in light of Jesus' life, death has no force. Walking in God's friendship becomes very important, and this life becomes very important, because God's life is already here. This is the place we encounter God's spirit. So: 1. Death is a terrible tragedy, for we have no idea of life without the body, and 2. Death has no absolute power over us.

11:50 Unconscious prophecy. Caiaphas thinks politically, John takes it salvifically. Caiaphas principle deeply rooted. A bureaucracy interested in the total good will almost always get rid of the individual to save the group (e.g. recent Olympics story.)

- John 12

    12:1 Lazarus raised (11), last sign, most impressive, signals Jesus' coming crucifixion

    12:13 Palm trees. Evidence for Palm trees in ancient Jerusalem? Palm fronds used in Maccabaean era to celebrate the liberation of Jerusalem

    12:19 The world. Does this mean that John sees gentiles following Jesus during his earthly ministry?

    12:23 The hour has come. Glorified (crucified). Through his death he bears fruit. Death becomes a part of the victory.

    12:29 "The Lord our God is one" is never breached, but the relationship between Jesus and God is very delicately expressed. Here, thunder.

    12:31 Typical reference to "this world," and its prince.

    12:35 Light (good time to look at key John words)

- Light: moral\spiritual force, presence. The divine spark within the human sphere.

- Love: philia, eros, agape/ affection, desire, selfgiving. Verb in Johannine literature used 71 times, noun 30 times (more often a verb than a noun!) See John 15:13. 1 John 4:7-13

- Truth: understanding, enlightenment, the Spirit of truth —counselor, advocate;

- Knowledge: recognition, understanding, unity with God\eternal life

- Word: eternal principle of order in the universe (Heraclitus), mind of God controlling, guiding, directing all things (Stoics), Philo used the word 1200 times (1st century). John alone personifies the logos. Hebrew: dabar which can mean word but also thing, affair, event, action-word and deed. In John, Jesus' deeds are his words and words are his deeds. Biblical wisdom literature uses word\logos to mean personified wisdom. Proverbs 8:22–23.

- John 13: Great Division here in John

    13:1 Second section (not signs but "glory" very different). Style of great last testaments. Patriarchs. Moses. Last will and testament. Speaking to those outside through believers. Reference to all Christians. Suspension between heaven and earth—melange of heaven and earth.

    13:8 Feet washing. Why no eucharist here? Resistance to ritualization? Interesting example of the way traditions affect each other.

- Most of the writers of the Bible are having to explain defeat or shame. Such is only possible in monotheism—one God of both death and life. Explanations of the uses of adversity.

- We live in a post-modern era: which means emphasis on the limits of human achievement and emphasis on community.

- All literature is made up of previous literature: Quotations; Weaving of ideas; Paraphrases.; Allusions to events and persons; Structure and echoes.

- Valedictory

- Interlude—tell story of valedictory heard

- John 14

    14:6. Way, Truth, Life ? Way\Goal not separated (Barrett)

    14:10. Ditheism

    14:12. Going to: gnostic vision

    14:16. Advocate

    14:20. Mysticism (No, says Bultmann)

    14:22. Not of the world

    14:28. Going\coming—gnostic again

- Almost all teaching in fourth gospel is transfered to the last night. Why?

- John 15

    15:1. "I am"

    15:2. Abide

    15:10. Union

    15:11. Joy and happiness

Finale

15:13. See NRSV reading

15:14. "Friends" theme

15:16. Doctrine of election

15:17. Love-one-another

15:19. Out of the world

15:22. Sin\judgment

15:25. Their law

15:27. Advocate

Darkness: night, cold, evil

Nicodemus: absence of love, refusal to believe, sin\evil as the adversary.

Glory: *doxa*—to seem, honor, majesty, brightness of godliness, wisdom, reputation, praise, honor, human glory and the glory that comes from God, light, life, visible manifestation of God in OT—nature, eye\ear, miraculous signs, absolute divinity.

- John 16

    16:2. *Aposynagogos*

    16:7. Advocate

    16:9. Sin\righteousness

    16:16. Presence\absence

    16:21. Pain\joy

    16:28. Gnostic

    16:29. Inside\outside

    16:32. is coming\now is

Synagogue=world; jews=world; Jesus=spirit. 2 level forecast of suffering. Role of the Paraclete.

- John 17

    17:1. Glory

    17:3. Know\knowledge, again gnostic

    17:5. Faith

    17:9. Again, not of this world

    17:12. Destiny

    17:20. Importance of preaching

    17:21. That the world may believe!?!

    17:25. So much Father language

    17:26. Did not know

THE COURAGEOUS GOSPEL

Four central confusions in this chapter: eternal life, world, presence\absence, name. Three central themes: glory, holiness, unity.

- John 18
    - 18:9. Fulfill
    - 18:10. Malchus
    - 18:17. Peter's Denial
    - 18:18. Charcoal
    - 18:28. Cleanliness
    - 18:31. Not permitted\Roman authority
    - 18:36. My kingdom not from? or of? (crucial choice in translation)

Three themes: arrest, trial and denunciation, condemnation

www.ingramcontent.com/pod-product-compliance
Lightning Source LLC
Chambersburg PA
CBHW051105230426
43667CB00013B/2446